Appalachia Revisited

Appalachia Revisited

New Perspectives on Place, Tradition, and Progress

EDITED BY

WILLIAM SCHUMANN

AND

REBECCA ADKINS FLETCHER

UNIVERSITY PRESS OF KENTUCKY

Scholarly publisher for the Commonwealth,
serving Bellarmine University, Berea College, Centre College of Kentucky,
Eastern Kentucky University, The Filson Historical Society, Georgetown College,
Kentucky Historical Society, Kentucky State University, Morehead State
University, Murray State University, Northern Kentucky University, Transylvania
University, University of Kentucky, University of Louisville, and Western
Kentucky University.

Editorial and Sales Offices: The University Press of Kentucky
663 South Limestone Street, Lexington, Kentucky 40508-4008
www.kentuckypress.com

Library of Congress Cataloging-in-Publication Data

Names: Schumann, William R., editor. | Fletcher, Rebecca Adkins, editor.
Title: Appalachia revisited : new perspectives on place, tradition, and progress /
    edited by William Schumann and Rebecca Adkins Fletcher.
Description: Lexington, Kentucky : University Press of Kentucky, [2016] | Series:
    Place matters: new directions in Appalachian studies | Includes index.
Identifiers: LCCN 2016018539| ISBN 9780813166971 (hardcover : alk. paper) |
    ISBN 9780813166995 (pdf) | ISBN 9780813166988 (epub)
Subjects: LCSH: Appalachian Region—History. | Appalachian Region—Social
    conditions. | Appalachian Region—Economic conditions. | Appalachian
    Region—Environmental conditions.
Classification: LCC F106 .A5775 2016 | DDC 974—dc23 LC record available at
    https://lccn.loc.gov/2016018539

ISBN 978-0-8131-7441-9 (pbk. : alk. paper)

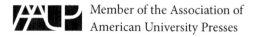

Contents

Introduction

Place and Place-Making in Appalachia

William Schumann

News from the Appalachian Mountains of the United States rarely garners national media attention, yet the region was in the national spotlight on several occasions during the first weeks of 2014. In the first case, journalists and a few politicians noted that 2014 was the fiftieth anniversary of the War on Poverty, a project that began during the presidential administration of Lyndon B. Johnson to assist areas of widespread socioeconomic deprivation that had been "rediscovered" in the postwar America of the 1960s. A previous presidential campaign visit by John F. Kennedy had marked Appalachia as an epicenter of the conflict. Reporters returned to the region in 2014 to assess the impact of the "war" and declare it unfinished. In the second instance, national coverage focused—very briefly—on a coal-related chemical spill into West Virginia's Elk River, which left hundreds of thousands of people without access to safe water. The polluting corporation (America First) announced bankruptcy as reporters raised questions about a link between the spill and underregulation of the coal industry. However, the media's attention soon shifted. In a final case, cable news and the popular media discussed the death of a Pentecostal preacher from eastern Kentucky who died from being bitten while handling venomous snakes. The preacher had been featured on a reality television series about snake handlers, but commentators focused on the "dangers" of traditional beliefs instead of recognizing the place of the deceased in the modern entertainment industry (the same place from which his critics spoke). If it was unusual for the region to be nationally recognized so often in a short span of time, it is also true that these cases drew attention for quite characteristic reasons.

Whether defined by the intensity of poverty, the dominance of energy interests, or the persistence of unorthodox lifestyles, each of these Appalachian stories operated on the principle of marking regional difference from a larger, more cosmopolitan United States. In fact, Appalachia has been defined by its distance from mainstream ideals and the practices of American modernity since the nineteenth century. It is not that reporters discovered new truths about the region's essential qualities; these representations were remarkably thin, dated, and based on simplistic reductions of politics, economics, and culture in Appalachia. The reality is, first, that Appalachia has never been fully reflected in the mirror of America's popular imagination, and second, it has always been characterized by cultural diversities and global interconnections that challenge easy categorizations of regional identity. Exploring these dynamics, *Appalachia Revisited* examines "Appalachia" as a by-product of human-environmental relations in specific locales *and* as an outcome of creating knowledge about the region over time. Thus, this book is about Appalachian *place* and Appalachian *place-making* in the twenty-first century. We examine "place" as a human construct involving diverse human practices within changing environmental and historical circumstances. We analyze "place-making" as the production of popular and academic knowledge that establishes Appalachia as a distinctive cultural, economic, and ecological region.

The contributors to this volume offer a wide range of perspectives on the relationship between Appalachian places and place-making in Appalachia. Representing the humanities and social sciences, including academic and applied work, chapters address issues of regional health, environment, race, ethnicity, gender, economic development and tourism, linguistic and cyber identities, energy policies, prisons, activism and organizing, educational engagement, farming, and politics. These topics intersect at different points in case studies representing Appalachian Alabama, Kentucky, New York, North Carolina, Ohio, Pennsylvania, Tennessee, Virginia, and West Virginia. They trace an "Appalachian map" made up of dialectical speech networks, artistic performances, institutional relations, ecological communities, political and consumer practices, and virtual representations.

In order to examine the relationship between regional knowledge and how that knowledge is produced, the chapter authors were asked to actively discuss how they apply one of three tools of academic research to their

Appalachian work: theory, method, or context. Chapters focused on *theory* outline key concepts of analysis that enable particular interpretations of Appalachia-specific data. Chapters focused on *method* explain the rationale for and application of a particular research or policy strategy for regional data collection and analysis. Chapters focused on *context* set Appalachia in a comparative framework to consider regional issues from national, global, meta-ecological, and/or cross-cultural perspectives. All chapters are united around a commitment to engaging a wide range of readers about regional studies of Appalachia, including undergraduate and graduate students, scholars, and professionals. To facilitate student learning, each chapter is accompanied by a classroom lesson plan that is featured in the book's appendix.

The Problem of Defining Appalachia

Appalachia's boundaries can be defined in numerous ways, and these ways reflect the research objectives, worldviews, and/or power positions of the individuals, groups, and institutions making claims about what constitutes the region. Some academic writers limit "Appalachia" to the coalfield areas of eastern Kentucky, northeastern Tennessee, southwestern Virginia, and West Virginia, and others expand the borders up from Alabama's northern foothills northward into the mountains of Vermont, New Hampshire, and beyond.[1]

Geologists and natural scientists typically operate from a map that recognizes the extension of eastern North America's largest mountain chain from Alabama into Canada, or the predominance of unique biogeographic features, including distinctive plant species, microhabitats, and wildlife communities. The most commonly referenced "Appalachia" is the Appalachian Regional Commission's (ARC) federal map, which includes all of West Virginia plus sections of Alabama, Georgia, Kentucky, Maryland, Mississippi, New York, North Carolina, Ohio, Pennsylvania, South Carolina, Tennessee, and Virginia (see map i.1). Over 25 million people are dispersed across 205,000 square miles on this map. The ARC's Appalachia has a rural population rate that is twice that of the United States average, though 64 percent of residents actually live in metropolitan centers of various sizes.[2]

Each map of Appalachia can be said to reveal the objectives of the mapmaker. While useful to planners and academics, for example, the ARC's map marks an advanced stage of political consolidation in the eastern mountains of the United States. A brief historical review of regional "mapmak-

Source: Appalachian Regional Commission

Map i.1. Appalachian Regional Commission map of Appalachia

ing" illustrates this point. The earliest human adaptations to Appalachia's mountain environs were foraging and horticultural subsistence strategies by indigenous peoples about ten thousand years ago. By the time of European contact, hundreds of Native languages, cultural beliefs, environmental adaptations, residence patterns, and social orders were broadly dispersed across the region. Appalachia's rich ecological zones and cultures were first encapsulated within European political concepts of cartographic boundaries by Old World explorers and colonizers. The term *Apalchen*—later changed to *Appalachian*—was first used by Spanish explorers and mapmakers in the first half of the sixteenth century. Eventually, regional maps delineated territorial divisions between Native nations and competing colonial powers, divisions influenced by expressly economic processes of surveying, trade, and land speculation. Appalachia's eastern slopes marked the limits of British colonial authority at the time of American independence. The founding of the United States and subsequent population pressures incorporated Appalachia into America's westward expansion in the ensuing decades as well as surrounded Native peoples within reservation territories.[3] Appalachia was thereafter an internal topographical boundary within the United States and a region under state and federal control that surrounded the Cherokee within the Qualla Boundary of western North Carolina. The American Civil War redefined the borders of Appalachia again with the creation of West Virginia in 1863. In the twentieth century, the Appalachian Regional Development Act of 1965, which resulted in the creation of the ARC, recognized the region as a special territory of federal intervention in ten American states. Indicative of the politicking behind this modern map, the US Congress initially debated whether to include sections of Arkansas and Massachusetts as part of the ARC's Appalachian territories.[4] The ARC's map eventually included thirteen states, which was a sure way to broaden potential congressional support for regional policies. In short, borders sometimes change even when geology and geography do not, illustrating how the meanings of places are constructed by humans as much as they are determined by topography or climate. The three cases of national media coverage of Appalachia discussed above exemplify the power relations inherent in naming the places, regions, and peoples that are encapsulated into maps.

The coverage of the War on Poverty in the first news story rightfully revisited central Appalachia's concentrated poverty yet overlooked many of the structural conditions—limited economic diversification, chronically underfunded services, and pro-industry politics—that contribute to the reproduction of these conditions. Yet this model of natural resource-driven capitalism has dominated the regional economy since the nineteenth century. Different areas of Appalachia historically developed around the exploitation of timber, coal, oil, and/or natural gas supplies, but did so within a common pattern of absentee landownership. Employment in extractive industries has expanded and contracted at different times and for various reasons, but a general lack of economic diversification has contributed to high levels of socioeconomic deprivation relative to the United States as a whole.[5] In the present, Appalachia's poverty rate between 2008 and 2012 was 16.6 percent, compared to the national average of 14.9 percent, which is a vast improvement from the mid-twentieth century, but Appalachian Kentucky

(25.1 percent), Mississippi (23.3 percent), Virginia (18.6 percent), North Carolina (17.9 percent), and Tennessee (17.8 percent) remained well above the regional and national averages.[6] The global economic recession of the early twenty-first century has increased regional rates of poverty and food insecurity; social services and supports associated with poverty eradication are also underdeveloped in much of the region; welfare dependency is reinforced by the region's low range of support services and job opportunities; and Appalachia's educational attainment gap relative to the rest of the United States has widened under the weight of nationwide teaching and testing bureaucracies.[7] Research also shows that any war on poverty must also be a war waged against poor health. Many communities face higher than average and increasing rates of drug use, cancer, heart disease, depression, obesity, and diabetes. Of particular concern is a growing epidemic of OxyContin abuse, which is undermining the social networks that have traditionally sustained many rural Appalachian communities.[8] Many of these problems are comparable to conditions in mining-intensive regions globally, which indicates a cross-cultural correlation between the intensity of poverty-related problems and the stark exploitation of natural resources.[9] The War on Poverty has had important positive impacts, but it has also been waged in the context of addressing regional deprivation without significantly challenging the contributions of extractive mono-industries to the problem.

The second news story focused on the devastating impacts of a chemical spill in West Virginia without addressing a larger pattern of energy resource extraction that regularly endangers mountain communities and ecosystems. The underregulation of coal-processing chemicals near West Virginia's state capital was a mere adjunct of an unadulterated process of environmental damage related to mountaintop removal. Mountaintop removal mining (MTR)—the top-down removal of mountains by large machinery and explosives to get at buried coal seams—is already at an advanced stage of development in central Appalachia, having emerged in the 1970s as a labor cost-saving means of harvesting coal. Reshaping thousands of square miles of mountain topography, MTR practices of valley fill, blasting, and chemical use threaten the ecological renewability of wildlife habitats and human communities.[10] There exists a close relationship between policy makers, regulators, and the coal industry. The coal industry provides millions of dollars in annual political campaign contributions to promote a regulatory framework that is supportive of MTR.[11] In similar fashion in northern Appalachia, the more recent development of hydraulic fracturing (or "fracking") technologies—the pumping of high-pressure chemical/water solutions into shale rock formations to force natural gas to the surface—is reminiscent of coal extraction.

Like coal mining, fracking is promoted as a cure for the ills of Appalachian deprivation. Billions of investment dollars have flowed into shale-rich areas of Pennsylvania and Ohio in recent years, and natural gas energy prices have dropped in the United States. (The cheap price of natural gas has also strained the monolithic economies of Appalachia's coal-producing area.) Gas development in the massive Marcellus shale field has lured investment and brought some jobs into depopulating areas of the region but has also raised concerns about water contamination, safe chemical storage, and geologic stability in the shale fields. Whereas MTR threatens freshwater supplies (and the habitats' water supports) through valley fill, the sheer volume of water required in the fracking industry menaces the availability of clean water as a public resource. In 2012 alone, reports indicate that 4.5 *billion* gallons of water were used in US-based fracking efforts; current industry growth rates predict that number will increase to 260 billion gallons by 2060.[12] And as with coal in central Appalachia, the fracking industry in Pennsylvania has divided public opinion by extensively drilling in the Allegheny National Forest and on state forest lands, maintaining secrecy about the chemicals used in the process, and avoiding any statewide drilling taxes with the aid of industry-first politicians.[13] In both cases, it can be argued that the legacies of Appalachia's energy industries have been as much about chemical spills, coal slurry accidents, and well and stream contaminations as they are about the promises of jobs and economic stability. The Elk River chemical spill of January 2014 provided an important opportunity to bring national attention to a global-regional issue, but the brief and decontextualized nature of the coverage was a reminder of how the scope of the questions one asks about Appalachia shapes the range of answers one receives.

The third news story, about regional religious practices, offers a vital illustration of how culture—or, more accurately in this case, cultural representations—can define the boundaries of "Appalachia." Foremost, the media's focus on the "cultural backwardness" of mountain people collapsed the region's diversity into a white, anti-cosmopolitan singularity. As mentioned above, the contradictions between this representational strategy and the deceased's participation in the modern reality television industry is obvious. Less recognized in popular and media cultures (in particular) is that rural-white-male signifiers of regional difference are commonly invoked at the expense of regional diversity.[14] At the time of writing (2015), about 84 percent of Appalachia's inhabitants were white, 9 percent were African American, 4 percent were Latina/o, and 3 percent were Native American. These numbers reveal less diversity than in the United States as a whole, but the region's cultural diversity is unevenly distributed, with Appalachian Kentucky, New York, Ohio, Virginia, and West Virginia composed of 90-plus percent white populations. More important, these cultural distributions are neither enduring nor constant. In addition to the forced removal of indigenous peoples in the eighteenth and nineteenth centuries, Appalachian history is characterized by several migrations by people of color and different ethnic groups into and out of the region. These population demographics remain in flux today. Latina/o in-migration into southern Appalachia is responsible for nearly half of all of the region's population growth since 1990, which contrasts with greater levels of white out-migration and lower cultural diversity in the North.[15] These immigrant communities are entering depopulated areas of Appalachia and revitalizing communities with new forms of human and social capital.[16] In contrast, the media's overrepresentation of rural, white class politics reproduces regional stereotypes of cultural homogeneity. Regional stereotypes sometimes bear some relation to reality: for example, high concentrations of white voters from Appalachia's "rural, highly evangelical, southern places with low socioeconomic status" were notable for opposing Barack Obama's 2008 election in numbers that set the region at the low end of national support for an African American presidential candidate.[17] In other instances, however, Appalachia's cultural politics have not conformed to popular notions of rural conservatism. The region can boast of a long history of inclusive progressive politics, such as the Highlander Education and Research Center in New Market, Tennessee, Kentuckians for the Commonwealth, and several environmental movements organized around overcoming racial, class, and gender barriers to participation.

In sum, these recent examples of media coverage suggest the importance of taking a different approach to answering the question "What is Appalachia?" Appalachia is a region made up of embedded cultural traditions, only some of which are amplified, distorted, and circulated in the popular media. It is also a region of cross-cultural, political, economic, and environmental interconnections that transcend specific locales. Appalachian places are often mixtures of political conservatism and progressive activism, persistent poverty and enormous socioeconomic potential, and immense natural beauty amid unnatural ecological waste. Yet Appalachia is also the product of place-making strategies to map the region's distinctiveness. Given this dynamic, it is vital to focus on both localized constructions of Appalachian places and broader place-making strategies of representing Appalachia.

Place as a Construct

The concept of "place" has become an important theoretical tool of research across several academic disciplines and beyond Appalachian scholarship.[18] *Place* offers a way of thinking about how time (that is, change) and physical space (that is, the built and natural environments) intersect and take on meaning through human interactions. More than the sum of human adaptations and environmental changes within a set of geographic coordinates, *place is relational:* place is a reflection of social relations of past and ongoing action; place is an indicator of relations of power between individuals and groups. The meaning(s) of place reflect(s) the negotiations of actors representing diverse interests and operating at multiple levels of authority and influence. Thus, *place-making* is a process of selectively cultivating some narratives of belonging while erasing other meanings from public discourse.[19] Appalachian place-making is often dominated by powerful economic and political actors, such as energy companies and elected officials, who define resource exploitation as a way of ensuring regional economic development and the national security of the United States. Other definitions derive from local experiences that enable resistance to dominant, exploitive narratives and encourage democratic solutions to pressing problems.[20] In short, humans construct, contest, and reinforce the meanings of place through processes as diverse as everyday conversation, acts of public history/memory, academic writing, and the regulatory, juridical, and legislative operations of governments. Yet all place-making in Appalachia operates on the principle of *marking difference* between one reading of human-environmental relations and all others. Many factors can be marshaled to outline place-based difference in/of Appalachia at regional or local levels. Economic class and geography/topography are common designators of Appalachian difference, yet Appalachia's boundaries are also encoded through race, ethnicity, gender, age, sexuality, and disability, among other factors.

Geographer David Harvey is a leading figure in academic discussions about place, power, and meaning. While there are many other perspectives that merit consideration, Harvey utilizes the useful principles of *political economy* to analyze how the politics of place are necessarily local and yet still related to global patterns of change. Political economy describes how human patterns of economic production, distribution, and consumption—from the macro level of global industrial transformations down to the micro level of social relations within workplaces and communities—can be understood in reference to the decision-making structures, divisions of labor, and resource uses within and between societies. Harvey's use of political economy is also relevant because it is a common theoretical backdrop of historical and social scientific writing in Appalachian studies. Harvey argues that places contribute to the formation of cultural identities that reflect complex processes of globalization down to the minute details of daily life.[21] These processes are fundamentally unequal with regard to access to the resources, authority, and social status that influence the transformation of places over time. In this view, which overlaps with theories of power posed by philosopher-historian Michel Foucault, any place-based political economy is ultimately rooted in the *production of knowledge* about individuals and places.[22] In Appalachia, for example, powerful institutions have historically influenced the life opportunities of impoverished communities by defining them as incapable of understanding and acting on the causes of their poverty; these same cultures of institutional expertise have masked the role of outside forces in the reproduction of Appalachian inequality. Foucault and Harvey share the view that power relations are never exhaustive or immune to resistance, yet the net effect is that the human and natural resources of many Appalachian places contribute to a global system of concentrated wealth accumulation occurring outside the region.

Stephen L. Fisher and Barbara Ellen Smith's edited volume, *Transforming Places: Lessons from Appalachia,* captures the breadth of this problem in Appalachia and points to commonalities with other global regions exposed to *neoliberal* capitalism. "Neoliberalism" values resource privatization, government deregulation, and the dismantling of the welfare functions of the state as a means to market-driven economic growth. Fisher and Smith set the tone of their volume in their introduction by reflecting on the decline in associational cultures under neoliberalism and the potential role of "place" to contribute to "new forms of progressive organizing" that can challenge neoliberalism's "reactionary political impulses."[23] The ensuing chapters present a wide range of opposition strategies and lessons learned from grassroots organizing against globalization. Individual essays tie questions of place to issues of Appalachian cultural identity, gender politics, food politics, unionization, coalfield organizing, the arts, development projects, and local political engagement. While duly noting the risk of place-based politics to reinforce reactionary inequalities, a position shared with Harvey, the volume manages to explore the structural conditions through which Appalachian communities can engage in inclusive forms of social organizing in defense against exploitation. Douglas Reichert Powell echoes this sentiment in *Critical Regionalism: Connecting Politics and Culture in the American Landscape* in arguing for "developing critical strategies capable of recognizing conflict and struggle in forms unique to specific landscapes and creating tactics for intervention and action specific to those landscapes."[24] Like Harvey, Powell views place as a socially constructed, changing network of human-environmental interactions operating in very local geographic, economic, and cultural contexts; in turn, regions are the distinct but overlapping inter-relations of places as conceptualized through wider institutional and histori-cal processes. Most important to Powell's work is the recognition of how the material relations of political economy intersect with cultural processes of rhetorical framing in projects of *place-making*.

A crucial point Harvey contributes to the discussion about place-making is that academic research does not simply uncover hidden geographic knowledge but actively contributes to the constructed meaning of places.[25] Through interactions with/in places, researchers make decisions about what constitutes a *relevant* research question, a process that informs the scope of *possible* methods for answering the question, and this in turn narrows the potential range of *valid* answers to the question. Place is not a neutral field where research occurs; it is a contributing factor in defining "legitimate" research.[26] This is not to argue that there is no "real" Appalachia to be stud-ied but to recognize that our understanding of Appalachia is directly shaped by how we go about asking, "What is the Appalachian region?" As editors we do not intend to privilege one approach to place-making Appalachia as more accurate or authoritative but rather to elicit a strategy for denatural-izing our assumptions about Appalachia as a pre-bound region in order to observe historical continuities of inequality as well as changing human-environmental interactions. By opening up Appalachian research to parallel discussions about theories, methods, or comparative contexts that inform the research process, we hope to indicate the value of regional studies as an important, multidisciplinary standpoint for observing how extra-local pro-cesses are transformed over time by human behaviors within Appalachia's built and natural environments.

Remapping Scholarship: Beyond Place-Making Appalachia as a Colony

One way to illustrate the significance of academic place-making in the construction of Appalachia is to examine the place-making strategies of earlier generations of Appalachian scholarship. I have chosen the edited volume *Colonialism in Modern America: The Appalachian Case* as a case study because it reflects the history of Appalachian studies in many ways. Published by the (now-defunct) Appalachian Consortium Press in 1978 and edited by Helen Matthews Lewis, Linda Johnson, and Donald Askins, this text represents a critical assessment of the Appalachian region over thirty-five years before the publication of the present volume. My goal is not to canonize *Colonialism* as fully summarizing Appalachian scholarship during this or any era but to read the text as indicating how Appalachian scholarship was and continues to be shaped by the conventions of Western academic scholarship operating within specific historical moments of knowledge production. In the case of *Colonialism,* the text can be situated as representative of a wider community of Marxist critique in the 1970s and 1980s as well as part of a smaller related movement to interpret impoverished Western regions as internal "colonies" within a global system of Western capitalist exploitation. Not unlike Harvey's critical geography, the political economy of *Colonialism* is focused on the power relations of production, distribution, and consumption that establish Appalachia as a place of difference from/within the United States.

The editors describe the structure of colonial power in the text's introduction: colonialism entails the forced acquisition of human and natural resources, the establishment of top-down institutional controls over society, and the reproduction of hierarchy through cultural and political means. This approach is clearly influenced by Marxist theory, which posits that the political structure and cultural beliefs of any society reflect the organization of ownership of the economic means of production within that society. Power is derived from inequalities in the control of the material process of production, beginning with the concentrated ownership of private property and the diminished role of women in economic and public affairs.[27] Under capitalism, government activity centers on securing unlimited economic growth and the accumulation of capital for a small number of people. Colonialism, or the forced administration and control of "places" beyond the political boundaries of the home country, becomes an extension of this logic on a global scale. While Marx does not directly address the Appalachian case in his writings on colonialism, he does describe American colonization as the "creation of a finance aristocracy . . . and the granting of immense tracts of public land to speculative companies for the exploration of railways, mines, etc. In short, it has brought a very rapid centralization of capital."[28] The contributors to *Colonialism* can be read as providing glimpses into the consequences of American capital concentration that Marx warned against, albeit in an Appalachia of the late twentieth century.

In particular, *Colonialism* chronicles the socioeconomic and cultural impacts of concentrated landownership on Appalachian places: inflows of finance capital and outflows of coal and timber, complex class divisions and high rates of internal poverty, industrial acceleration and decline, regressive government underregulation, anemic corporate taxation, lack of public services, expansion of privatization, and the commercialization of natural resources. Individual chapters contrast the power of corporate and civic interests to shape public policies and public opinions of Appalachia. John Gaventa articulates the rise of coal camps as illustrative of property theft by speculators, local governments, and others supportive of absentee coal owners. He argues that external ideologies of "progress" under colonialism mask "what is *not* done, *not* allowed, that prevents possibilities for new industry, developments, [and] futures by and for the Appalachian people."[29] Folk musician and activist Si Kahn critiques the US Forest Service's concentration of untaxed land that denies communities "public services, including education and health care."[30] Helen Lewis describes the development of community class divisions of Appalachian missionary work that viewed the region's established social structures "of family and church as problems to be resolved."[31] In another chapter, consumer advocate Ralph Nader pens an open letter to a British mining company in Appalachia to demand corporate responsibility and civic participation in economic decision making. Ron Eller reviews the historical appropriation of the region's human and natural resources to argue that "mountain people have . . . rarely appeared as conscious actors on the stage of American history."[32] Across several chapters, authors attack the government for enabling exploitive corporate interests, such as the Tennessee Valley Authority's reliance on MTR coal or the ARC's economic development strategy (that is, road building), to facilitate coal extraction. Some connect underfunded and poor performing Appalachian schools to pro-industry government policies. Others observe the dissolution of cultural traditions and institutions under industrial modernization.

In total, one is left with a picture of complex, systemic class-based control operating across a range of social, economic, and political fields and at different scales of power.

Most notable about *Colonialism* is a steady commitment to addressing Appalachia's class politics in an analytical rhetoric of place, which establishes "insiders" and "outsiders" as the ultimate reference points of Appalachian difference. The boundaries of regional difference are plotted by other naming strategies throughout the text, such as "mountain youth," "mountain people," and "the old culture," yet it is the insider/outsider dynamic that informs the text's critical method of *place-making by contrast.* Thus, many chapters give meaning to regional class experience in reference to cultural beliefs and behaviors that define life on the "inside" of Appalachia. Some trace regional boundaries through conflicts between a subsistence-based, pre-capitalist Appalachia and a resource-hungry, industrializing America. Others describe the strains of an egalitarian farming ideal in opposition to a cultural invasion by second-home land developers. One analysis of regional education asserts that "many of Appalachia's problems result from the fact that its leaders are middle class and formally educated," a view that distinctly implies that "true" Appalachian places are fundamentally impoverished, undereducated, and isolated.[33] Another critique focused against "super highways directed toward benefitting the outside visitor" strongly suggests that mountain culture can only survive in a cultural-infrastructural vacuum.[34] Some authors identify Appalachian communities of the 1970s as "indigenous," which reinforces a longer history of Native American erasure.[35] These approaches collectively outline a paradox of Appalachian research in the 1970s: the Appalachian "insider" marks the region's nonsimultaneity with modernity by virtue of recognizing modernity's impact on Appalachian subjects and places. The apparent tension between describing an Appalachia apart from American modernity and Appalachia as part of American modernity reflects the historical context of the era's research ethos.

Foremost, the contributors to *Colonialism* were responding not only to the impacts of external capital on Appalachian life in the 1970s but also to previous generations of writers who delineated regional difference in the stark terms of Appalachia's geographic and historic *isolation.* Notions of the isolated mountaineer/mountain date back to the late nineteenth century, when the United States was in the midst of major geographic and demographic changes via westward expansion and mass immigration. Soon Appalachia was elevated in popular writing (such as traveler accounts) as

America's final wild frontier and an undiluted repository of colonial American folk culture. The president of Berea College at the turn of the twentieth century summed up this attitude with the phrase "our contemporary ancestors" to describe Kentucky's mountain communities. The statement, although intended as a celebration of mountain culture, reduced the identity of the region to white, western European, and frozen in time. In a parallel instance in *Colonialism,* a contributor argues that the "profound tragedy [of recreational development] is that the last and most appealing islands of pioneer Elizabethan culture in the world have become victims of that most infectious of American diseases, so-called 'progress.'"[36] Collectively, the text's contributors indicate a challenge to both recognize Appalachian places as globally connected *and* recuperate the popularized isolation thesis to the point of using it to define a unique mountain culture to preserve. Absent, however, is a critical reading of the role of twentieth-century institutions to presuppose regional isolation through projects to document, protect, and market *specific* traditions as distinct and comprehensive of both regional and early American history.[37]

A second discourse of regional isolation justified resource-intensive modernization during the same period. In this second map, Appalachia was defined as a place of underdevelopment compared to the United States as a whole. Economic studies indicated gaps between Appalachia and the United States in the statistical language of government and academic surveys. Modernization studies often found mountain traditions to reproduce regional poverty, a notion that has been reinforced in popular culture from early newspaper cartoons through to recent reality television shows. Many observers by the mid-twentieth century deemed local inaction an expression of "fatalism," or the acceptance of difficult living conditions as beyond the control of an individual or community. Isolation mapped Appalachia not only as a space of economic antimodernity, in other words, but as a cultural space distinguished by an inability to modernize. Against a taken-for-granted backdrop of "hillbilly" inferiority, planners and developers argued that regional poverty would be best addressed by the external agents of modernization. Indicative of the linear thinking about progress in America, Appalachian communities were seen as too far behind the rest of the country to "catch up" to the material conditions of middle-class America without help.

Scholars and regional residents began to turn this argument on its head by the 1960s. A growing body of literature decried the excessive impacts of the coal industry on the reproduction of regional poverty.[38] By the 1970s, scholars and activists formed an Appalachian studies community broadly committed to researching the region's history, folk arts, literature, culture, politics, and economy. *Colonialism* indicates the early crystallization of Appalachian studies as a place-based critique of capital grounded in the material analysis of exploited resource communities. One account from the text succinctly echoes this sentiment: "What on the surface appear to be quaint people whose character can be explained away by the isolation and independence may . . . be more accurately described as the historical reaction of the people to colonialism."[39] While this strategy effectively articulates issues of regional exploitation, the "insider Appalachia" undergirding the text is ultimately created by narrowing the meanings of Appalachian place under capitalism.

Essentially, Appalachian insiders are defined as a unified distinctive class occupying a place of externally controlled resources. The experiences of Native American and African American communities (to name two) are generally omitted.[40] White communities, in turn, are discussed almost exclusively in reference to the experiences of male workers, which implicitly marks Appalachia's patriarchal public sphere as regional culture writ large. The text further narrows the borders of "Appalachia" down to case studies from a handful of Appalachian states. These moves have the cumulative effect of locating "insider Appalachia" within limiting discourses of class (impoverished), race (white), ethnicity (western European), gender (heteronormative male), religious belief (Christian), artistic creation (folk), education (poor), and geography (North Carolina to West Virginia). In fairness, there are instances when the editors and individual authors acknowledge other perspectives, and the final section of the text is dedicated to questioning the limits of the colonial thesis for understanding Appalachia. *Colonialism* also features prescient analyses that have held up over time, including pointed comments on the growing problems of MTR and prescription drug abuse in the coalfields. It also advances important discussions about developing an Appalachian studies curriculum to foster a regional consciousness of exploitation. Yet the focus on working-class, white, male heteronormativity ultimately dislocates Appalachia's women, people of color, middle-class families, educated residents, and all Others as neither inside nor outside of Appalachian history.

Both the strengths and weaknesses of this research paradigm can be said to have encouraged significant shifts in Appalachian studies. Foremost, the text anticipates important continuities between Appalachian studies of the

1970s and today. First, *Colonialism* recognizes nonacademics as experts and coparticipants in the production of regional knowledge, including student research teams, folk artists, freelance journalists, religious leaders, and civic activists. Second, it challenges academia's self-imposed distinctions between maintaining an "objective distance" in research and acting as a participant within research settings. Third, it establishes a commitment to political economy as an enduring theoretical framework of Appalachian studies.

The limitations of *Colonialism*'s class-centered framework have also encouraged more nuanced approaches to understanding the intersection of class, identity, and place in Appalachia. Political economy remains a powerful tool for analyzing socioeconomic change and is increasingly global and comparative in focus. New theoretical models have filtered into regional research agendas to emphasize community-based potentials for resistance to capitalist exploitation.[41] Contemporary Appalachian research continues to support activism in scholarship and to invite broad participation in the production of regional knowledge. Though still subject to criticisms, the ARC has emerged as a partner in dialogue with the Appalachian studies community.[42] Most significant, the racial, ethnic, and gendered experiences of Appalachian communities are increasingly woven into the traditional class-based analyses of place in Appalachian studies.[43] Moving in step with wider changes in academic scholarship, regional research has also opened up to consider such topics as sexual diversity and the environmental impacts of resource-intensive capitalism on societies.[44] Collectively, these studies point to the multiple characteristics that distinguish those on Appalachia's "inside," whatever their shared commonalities.[45] For example, Appalachian communities are less likely to be narrated as uniformly egalitarian or valorized against difficult living conditions and outside forces.[46] This flexibility has yielded nuanced discussions about how the "conservative" Appalachian values can be mobilized in opposition to human and natural resource exploitation.[47] Fatalism, once described as the paralyzing source of local indifference to inequality and poverty, has come to be understood as a strategic engagement with difficult life options.[48] These approaches are far from unified, but many reflect the impact of "postmodern" social theory on regional research.

Briefly, postmodernism rejects the generalizing tendencies of earlier approaches to history and culture (such as Marxism's overarching focus on class) to emphasize the heterogeneity of human experience and the necessity of situating that experience (that is, producing knowledge of place) in specific rather than universal contexts. Rebecca Scott neatly summarizes the theoretical and methodological implications of this shift in her compelling account of mountaintop removal in West Virginia: "Identity and subjectivity are less fixed characteristics of persons than a set of cultural projects, practices, and formations; this understanding emphasizes the open-endedness of social structures.... Far from being a rejection of [Marxist] materialism,... it is precisely the emphasis on materiality—of the body, the house, and the neighborhood—that leads to a consideration of the cultural significance of geography, the built environment, and economic production."[49] The contributors to this volume represent a cross-section of contemporary approaches to Appalachia and Appalachian studies suggested by Scott (which is not to say all chapters utilize postmodern theory). Like *Colonialism, Appalachia Revisited* is a representation of the historical conditions of Appalachia and Appalachian scholarship at the moment of the text's production. We do not claim to present a comprehensive survey of contemporary topics, methods, or theories, but we seek to contribute to emergent conversations about the coproductive roles of social and ecological communities, political and economic networks, and researchers in the making of Appalachian places.

About This Volume

The contributors to this volume focus on Appalachian place and place-making in relation to theories, methods, and comparative contexts that help to situate contemporary Appalachia and contemporary Appalachian scholarship in wider conversations. The text is not exhaustive of all of the issues facing Appalachia in the twenty-first century, but it does present a diverse survey of topics, writing styles, research approaches, and conceptual models that demonstrate the heterogeneity of regional scholarship. The individual chapters are clustered around four themes.

The first four chapters are united under the theme of *race, ethnicity, and gender*. Kathryn L. Duvall, Kelly A. Dorgan, and Sadie P. Hutson (chapter 1) explore the methodological challenges of researching women's cancer survivorship through story circles and in-depth interviews among Appalachian women from northeast Tennessee and southwest Virginia. Yunina Barbour-Payne (chapter 2) examines public discourses of race and Appalachian cultural authenticity in social media debates about the Carolina Chocolate Drops' Appalachian identity. Amanda Zeddy (chapter 3) combines archival research and contemporary feminist theory to evaluate how the public speeches of Louise Broyhill, wife of US senator James Broyhill, reflected social relationships, norms, and practices that defined the "acceptable" forms of women's political participation in late-twentieth-century western North Carolina. Anna Rachel Terman (chapter 4) adds to a rich history of research on Appalachian identity by utilizing the theory of intersectionality to examine how race, gender, and sexuality affect sense of belonging among college-educated youth in West Virginia.

The next three chapters are organized around the theme of *language, rhetoric, and literacy.* Kathryn Trauth Taylor (chapter 5) combines rhetorical analysis and critical theories of literacy to question the stereotype that Appalachia is fundamentally white, illiterate, and rural by drawing on observations, interviews, and residents' writings associated with the nonprofit Urban Appalachian Council of Cincinnati. Jessica Blackburn (chapter 6) reviews critical theories of digital literacy and online rhetoric to analyze the tourism websites of two communities in Appalachian New York in order to reflect on strategies for teaching about regional e-rhetorics in Appalachian studies classrooms. Kirk Hazen, Jordan Lovejoy, Jaclyn Daugherty, and Madeline Vandevender (chapter 7) employ quantitative methods to understand changing dialectical patterns of Appalachian speech in West Virginia in the context of key sociolinguistic variables identified by the West Virginia Dialect Project.

The third section features four chapters clustered around the theme of *economy and environment.* Jacqueline Yahn (chapter 8) questions the long-term viability of hydraulic fracturing in Appalachian Ohio and Pennsylvania by comparing energy exploitation strategies in central and northern Appalachia. Kristin Kant-Byers (chapter 9) explores how Appalachian artists are constrained by structural market forces and popular culture in Appalachian Tennessee to explain the social durability of Appalachian stereotypes long challenged by scholars and many regional inhabitants. Melissa Ooten and Jason Sawyer (chapter 10) analyze qualitative and quantitative data about the social and economic benefits of Appalachia's prison system in the broader framework of America's growing prison industrial complex. Anita Puckett (chapter 11) questions how rural locales of Virginia engage with traditional music to construct a viable monetary economy that reproduces core cultural and environmental processes within global, neoliberal contexts. The final section of the book addresses the theme of *engagement* in four chapters. Tim Ezzell (chapter 12) considers the value of mixed-method approaches to producing local knowledge of Appalachian communities in order to avoid the problems of gathering incomplete or skewed data that characterize many regional-level research projects. Diane N. Loeffler and Jim King (chapter 13) discuss the work of the Federation of Appalachian Housing Enterprises, Inc., emphasizing the value of building social capital for the creation of trusting relationships, mutual understanding, and shared action necessary for sustainable development in Appalachian Kentucky communities. Mark Wilson (chapter 14) presents a case study of student-driven research in Appalachian Alabama based on his teaching experience with the Appalachian Regional Commission's Appalachian Teaching Project, which is focused on using local assets for education, economic development, and the further development of a sense of place among residents of rural Alabama. Gabriel A. Piser (chapter 15) brings a long-standing methodology of Appalachian scholarship, participatory research, into conversation with postmodern theories of power and political ecology to argue for the concept of "reciprocity" in economic, ecological, and political scholarship as a means of producing knowledge through encounters and relations among the land and its inhabitants, and not just "about" them.

Across the book, contributors offer a variety of responses to the call to explain their place-making strategies. Methodological chapters present qualitative, quantitative, and institutional approaches to research and policy formation; in this category are those by Duvall, Dorgan, and Hutson; Ezzell; Hazen, Lovejoy, Daugherty, and Vandevender; Kant-Byers; and Wilson. Comparative chapters situate Appalachia in wider contexts of analysis, including Loeffler and King's work and Ooten and Sawyer's. Theoretical chapters present a range of conceptual perspectives: the work of Barbour-Payne, Blackburn, Piser, Puckett, Taylor, Terman, Yahn, and Zeddy. Several chapters overlap these and other topics. Discussions of race and ethnicity in part 1 are supported by the analyses of Ooten and Sawyer, Taylor, and Wilson. Chapters on economics in part 3 are complemented by the work of Ezzell and of Loeffler and King. The thematic focus on engagement in the fourth section is broadened in the chapters by Terman and Puckett. Barbour-Payne and Blackburn share an interest in the role of electronic media in framing regional identities and social action. Chapters by Duvall, Dorgan, and Hutson; Piser; Terman; and Zeddy provide mutually reinforcing insights into feminist research methods and theories. Blackburn; Ezzell; Hazen, Lovejoy, Daugherty, and Vandevender; Puckett; and Wilson offer different perspectives on university engagement and student learning within Appalachian communities. Issues of regional identities and stereotypes are addressed by Barbour-Payne; Blackburn; Kant-Byers; Hazen, Lovejoy, Daugherty, and Vandevender; Taylor; and Terman. Coeditor Rebecca Adkins Fletcher concludes the volume by exploring these and additional connections across individual chapters and book sections. Framing her discussion in the context of her own ethnographic work in Appalachia, she links Appalachia to transnational and cross-cultural continuities with global experiences of change in the twenty-first century.

Notes

1. As examples, see Al Fritsch and Paul Gallimore, *Healing Appalachia: Sustainable Living through Appropriate Technology* (Lexington: University Press of Kentucky, 2007); and Sara M. Gregg, *Managing the Mountains: Land Use Planning, the New Deal, and the Creation of a Federal Landscape in Appalachia* (New Haven, CT: Yale University Press, 2012).

2. Kelvin M. Pollard and Kathleen Jacobsen, *The Appalachian Region: A Data Overview from the 2007–2011 American Community Survey* (Washington, DC: Population Reference Bureau, 2013), 13, http://www.arc.gov/assets/research_reports/PRB-DataOverviewReport2007–2011.pdf (accessed November 18, 2013).

3. Richard B. Drake, "The Coming of the Europeans," in *A History of Appalachia* (Lexington: University Press of Kentucky, 2001), 25–39.

4. Gordon Taliaferro Saddler, *The Appalachian Regional Commission: Selected Aspects of Institutions and Processes and Their Relationship to Natural and Human Resources Development* (Ann Arbor, MI: University Microfilms International, 1970), 241–61.

5. Ryan Whisart, "Coal River's Last Mountain: King Coal's Après moi le deluge Reign," *Organization & Environment* 24, no. 4 (2012): 470–85; J. Bradford Jensen and Amy K. Glasmeier, "Restructuring Appalachian Manufacturing in 1963–1992: The Role of Branch Plants," *Growth and Change* 32 (2001): 251–82.

6. Pollard and Jacobsen, *The Appalachian Region*.

7. Johnathan S. Gore, Kristina R. Wilburn, Jodi Treadway, and Victoria Plaut, "Regional Collectivism in Appalachia and Academic Attitudes," *Cross-Cultural Research* 45, no. 4 (2011): 376–98; Daniel T. Lichter and David L. Brown, "Rural America in an Urban Society: Changing Spatial and Social Boundaries," *Annual Review of Sociology* 37 (2011): 565–92; Shelley K. Irving, "State Welfare Rules, TANF Exits, and Geographic Context: Does Place Matter?" *Rural Sociology* 73, no. 4 (2008): 605–30.

8. Linda M. Burton, Daniel T. Lichter, Regina S. Baker, and John M. Eason, "Inequality, Family Processes, and Health the 'New' Rural America," *American Behavioral Scientist* 57, no. 8 (2013): 1128–51; Nancy E. Schoenberg, Jennifer Hatcher, and Mark B. Dignan, "Appalachian Women's Perceptions of Their Community's Health Threats,"

Journal of Rural Health 24, no. 1 (2008): 75–83; Adam B. Jones, April M. Young, Carrie B. Oser, Carl G. Leukefeld, and Jennifer R. Havens, "OxyContin as Currency: OxyContin Use and Increased Social Capital among Rural Appalachian Drug Users," *Social Science Medicine* 74, no. 10 (2012): 1602–9.

9. For global comparisons of mining communities, see Anthony Bebbington, Leonith Hinojosa, Denise Humphreys Bebbington, Maria Luisa Burneo, and Ximena Warnaars, "Contention and Ambiguity: Mining and the Possibilities of Development," *Development and Change* 39, no. 6 (2008): 887–914. See also comparisons of coal mining in central Appalachia's child poverty rates with rates in the Mississippi Delta, many tribal reservations, and the Texas borderland, which are addressed in Katherine J. Curtis, Paul R. Voss, and David D. Long, "Spatial Variation in Poverty-generating Processes: Child Poverty in the United States," *Social Science Research* 41, no. 1 (2011): 146–59. The health impacts of mining further reveal "a statistically significant elevation of mortality rates in the Appalachian region as compared to the rest of the country," according to Diana Kaneva, "Let's Face Facts, These Mountains Won't Grow Back: Reducing the Environmental Impact of Mountaintop Removal Coal Mining in Appalachia," *Environmental Law and Policy Review* 35 (2011): 931–71.

10. Kelly Austin and Brett Clark, "Tearing Down Mountains: Using Spatial and Metabolic Analysis to Investigate the Socio-ecological Contradictions of Coal Extraction in Appalachia," *Critical Sociology* 38, no. 3 (2011): 437–57.

11. Kaneva, "Let's Face Facts."

12. Alex Prud'homme, *Hydrofracking: What Everyone Needs to Know* (Oxford: Oxford University Press, 2014), 107.

13. Tom Wilber, *Under the Surface: Fracking, Fortunes, and the Fate of the Marcellus Shale* (Ithaca, NY: Cornell University Press, 2012).

14. Barbara Ellen-Smith, "Degradations of Whiteness," *Journal of Appalachian Studies* 10, nos. 1–2 (2004): 38–57.

15. Kelvin M. Pollard, A *"New Diversity": Race and Ethnicity in the Appalachian Region,* Demographic and Socioeconomic Change in Appalachia (Washington, DC: Population Reference Bureau, 2012), http://www.prb.org/pdf04/anewdiversityappal.pdf (accessed November 18, 2013). For evidence of African American migration to northern Appalachia contrary to the out-migration trend, see Betty L. McCall, "Influx: Black Urban Women's Migration to Rural Pennsylvania," *ANNALS of the American Academy of Political and Social Science* 642 (2012): 200–209.

16. Patrick J. Carr, Daniel T. Lichter, and Maria J. Kefalas, "Can Immigration Save Small-Town America? Hispanic Boomtowns and the Uneasy Path to Renewal," *ANNALS of the American Academy of Political and Social Science* 641, no. 38 (2012): 38–55.

17. Brian K. Arbour and Jeremy M. Teigen, "Barack Obama's 'American' Problem: Unhyphenated Americans in the 2008 Elections," *Social Science Quarterly* 92, no. 3 (2011): 563–87.

18. Examples in anthropology include Akhil Gupta and James Ferguson, eds., *Cul-

ture *Power Place: Explorations in Critical Anthropology* (Durham, NC: Duke University Press, 1997); and Steven Feld and Keith H. Basso, eds., *Senses of Place* (Santa Fe, NM: SARS, 1996). Examples in literary criticism include Roberto M. Dainotto, *Place in Literature: Regions, Cultures, Communities* (Ithaca, NY: Cornell University Press, 2000); and Judith Fetterley and Marjorie Pryse, *Writing out of Place: Regionalism, Women, and American Literary Culture* (Urbana: University of Illinois Press, 2005). Examples from geography include J. Nicholas Entrikin, *The Betweenness of Place: Towards a Geography of Modernity* (Baltimore, MD: Johns Hopkins University Press, 1991); and Wilfred M. McClay and Ted V. McAllister, eds., *Why Place Matters: Geography, Identity, and Civic Life in Modern America* (New York: Encounter Books, 2014). Examples from ecological studies include Tom Lynch, Cheryll Glotfelty, and Karla Armbruster, eds., *The Bioregional Imagination: Literature, Ecology, and Place* (Athens: University of Georgia Press, 2012); and Ursula K. Heise, *Sense of Place and Sense of Planet: The Environmental Imagination of the Global* (Oxford: Oxford University Press, 2008).

19. Margaret E. Farrar, "Nostalgia and the Politics of Place Memory," *Political Research Quarterly* 64, no. 2 (2011): 723–35.

20. Herbert Reid and Betsy Taylor, "Appalachia as a Global Region: Toward Critical Regionalism and Civic Professionalism." *Journal of Appalachian Studies* (2002): 9–32.

21. Harvey states that spatial boundaries play "a key role in the formation of personal and political subjectivities." David Harvey, *Spaces of Capital: Towards a Critical Geography* (New York: Routledge, 2001), 221.

22. See Michel Foucault, "Questions on Geography," in *Power/Knowledge: Selected Interviews and Other Writings, 1972–1977,* ed. Colin Gordon, trans. Colin Gordon, Leo Marshall, John Mepham, and Kate Soper (New York: Pantheon, 1980), 63–77.

23. Stephen L. Fisher and Barbara Ellen Smith, introduction to *Transforming Places: Lessons from Appalachia,* ed. Stephen L. Fisher and Barbara Ellen Smith (Urbana: University of Illinois Press, 2012), 6.

24. Douglas Reichert Powell, *Critical Regionalism: Connecting Politics and Culture in the American Landscape* (Chapel Hill, NC: University of North Carolina Press, 2007), 97.

25. Harvey, *Spaces of Capital,* 217.

26. Jon Anderson, Peter Adey, and Paul Bevan, "Positioning Place: Polylogic Approaches to Research Methodology," *Qualitative Research* 10, no. 5 (2010): 589–604.

27. See Frederick Engels, "The Origin of the Family, Private Property, and the State," in *The Marx-Engels Reader,* 2nd ed., ed. Robert C. Tucker (New York: Norton, 1978), 734–59.

28. Karl Marx, *Capital,* trans. Ben Fowkes (New York: Penguin, 1990), 1:940.

29. John Gaventa, "Property, Coal, and Theft," in *Colonialism in Modern America: The Appalachian Case,* ed. Helen Matthews Lewis, Linda Johnson, and Donald Askins (Boone, NC: Appalachian Consortium, 1978), 152.

30. Si Kahn, "The Forest Service and Appalachia," in Lewis, Johnson, and Askins, *Colonialism,* 98.

31. Helen Lewis, Sue Kobak, and Linda Johnson, "Family, Religion, and Colonialism in Central Appalachia," in Lewis, Johnson, and Askins, *Colonialism,* 129.

32. Ron Eller, "Industrialization and Social Change in Appalachia, 1880-1930," in Lewis, Johnson, and Askins, *Colonialism,* 37.

33. Mike Clark, "Education and Exploitation," in Lewis, Johnson, and Askins, *Colonialism,* 200.

34. Edgar Bingham, "The Impact of Recreational Development on Pioneer Life Styles in Southern Appalachia," in Lewis, Johnson, and Askins, *Colonialism,* 67.

35. Helen Lewis and Edward E. Knipe, "The Colonialism Model: The Appalachian Case," in Lewis, Johnson, and Askins, *Colonialism,* 17; Lewis, Kobak, and Johnson, "Family, Religion, and Colonialism," 135; David Walls, "Internal Colony or Internal Periphery? A Critique of Current Models and an Alternative Formulation," in Lewis, Johnson, and Askins, *Colonialism,* 329.

36. Bingham, "The Impact of Recreational Development on Pioneer Life Styles," 64.

37. See Jane S. Becker, *Selling Tradition: Appalachia and the Construction of American Folk* (Chapel Hill, NC: University of North Carolina Press, 1997); David Whisnant, *All That Is Native and Fine: The Politics of Culture in an American Region* (Chapel Hill, NC: University of North Carolina Press, 1983).

38. One of the enduring texts on this subject is Harry Caudill, *Night Comes to the Cumberlands: A Biography of a Depressed Area* (Ashland, KY: Jesse Stuart Foundation, 1962).

39. Jim Branscome, "Annihilating the Hillbilly," in Lewis, Johnson, and Askins, *Colonialism,* 222.

40. *Colonialism* rarely touches on race and ethnicity, but these discussions were not absent from Appalachian studies in the 1970s and 1980s; nor were the contributors unsupportive of social justice movements. See William H. Turner and Edward J. Cabbell, eds., *Blacks in Appalachia* (Lexington: University Press of Kentucky, 1985).

41. Stephen L. Fisher, ed., *Fighting Back in Appalachia: Traditions of Resistance and Change* (Philadelphia: Temple University Press, 1993); Mary Ann Hinsdale, Helen M. Lewis, and Maxine Waller, *It Comes from the People: Community Development and Local Theology* (Philadelphia: Temple University Press, 1995).

42. ARC strategic planning is increasingly focused on sustainable economic development that is consistent with research in the field. The ARC also organizes an Appalachian Teaching Project conference for student researchers and participates in meetings of the Appalachian Studies Association.

43. Dwight B. Billings and Kathleen M. Blee, *The Road to Poverty: The Making of Wealth and Hardship in Appalachia* (Cambridge: Cambridge University Press, 2000); Leon Fink, *The Maya of Morganton: Work and Community in the Nuevo New South* (Chapel Hill, NC: University of North Carolina Press, 2003); Rebecca Scott, *Removing Mountains: Extracting Nature and Identity in the Appalachian Coalfields* (Minneapolis: University of Minnesota Press, 2010); Julie Ann White, "The Hollow and the Ghetto: Space, Race, and the Politics of Poverty," *Politics & Gender* 3, no. 2 (2007): 271–80.

44. Examples include Mary L. Grey, *Out in the Country: Youth, Media, and Queer Visibility in Rural America* (New York: NYU Press, 2009); Joyce M. Barry, *Standing Our Ground: Women, Environmental Justice, and the Fight to End Mountaintop Removal* (Athens: Ohio University Press, 2012); Shirley Stewart Burns, *Bringing Down the Mountains: The Impact of Mountaintop Removal on Southern West Virginia Communities* (Morgantown: West Virginia University Press, 2007).

45. Kathleen M. Brennan and Christopher A. Cooper, "Rural Mountain Natives, In-migrants, and the Cultural Divide," *Social Science Journal* 45 (2008): 279–95; Ryan A. Brown, Nancy E. Adler, Carol M. Worthman, William E. Copeland, E. Jane Costello, and Adrian Angold, "Cultural and Community Determinants of Subjective Social Status among Cherokee and White Youth," *Ethnicity and Health* 13, no. 4 (2008): 289–303.

46. Two volumes that explore differences between women's and men's participation in public work and community-based activism illustrate this trend: Mary K. Anglin, *Women, Power, and Dissent in the Hills of Carolina* (Urbana: University of Illinois Press, 2002); Shannon Elizabeth Bell, *Our Roots Run Deep as Ironweed: Appalachian Women and the Fight for Environmental Justice* (Urbana: University of Illinois Press, 2013).

47. Shannon Elizabeth Bell and Yvonne A. Braun, "Coal, Identity, and the Gendering of Environmental Justice in Central Appalachia," *Gender and Society* 24 (2010): 794–813; Zachary Henson and Connor Bailey, "CAFOS, Culture and Conflict on Sand Mountain: Framing Rights and Responsibilities in Appalachian Alabama," *Southern Rural Sociology* 24, no. 1 (2009): 153–74; Jordan W. Smith, Roger L. Moore, Dorothy H. Anderson, and Christos Siderelis, "Community Resilience in Southern Appalachia: A Theoretical Framework and Three Case Studies," *Human Ecology* 40 (2012): 341–53.

48. Elaine M. Drew and Nancy E. Schoenberg, "Deconstructing Fatalism: Ethnographic Perspectives on Women's Decision Making about Cancer Prevention and Treatment," *Medical Anthropology Quarterly* 25, no. 2 (2011): 164–82.

49. Scott, *Removing Mountains*, 16–17.

Part 1

Race, Ethnicity, and Gender

1

Revisiting Appalachia, Revisiting Self

Kathryn L. Duvall, Kelly A. Dorgan, and Sadie P. Hutson

From September 2008 through April 2009 we collected stories from women cancer survivors living in southern central Appalachia with the goals of better understanding the intricacies of their lived experiences, and subsequently of appreciating the complexities of our exploration of their experiences. Through a reflexive analysis we confronted, documented, and adjusted to the complexities of investigating cancer in a unique population, including engaging in place-making practices about the region and ourselves as researchers. In this self-reflective piece we explore how this project challenged us individually and as a team, requiring us to revisit Appalachia and revisit self.

This chapter examines methods of reflexive health-care research—that is, qualitative methods—in order to address the embedded role of researchers in the social context(s) of research, specifically the context of working with cancer survivors in East Tennessee and southwest Virginia. Long the norm in social scientific exploration, quantitative-based research methods support the researcher's identity as primarily a data-collecting machine: detached and objective.[1] However, the nature of qualitative research emphasizes the subjective position of researchers as instruments. Qualitative approaches attempt "to understand the meaning or nature of experience of persons with problems" by asking the *why* and *how* of the process in addition to the *what, where,* and *when.*[2] Conversational and observational encounters with participants allow for the exploration of phenomena about which little is known and can be used to obtain intricate details often lost through more objective research methods. We, like many other scholars, believe reflexivity improves the quality of research because we view subjectivity as an opportunity to enhance data; however, not all qualitative research methods or researchers use reflexivity in data collection, citing concerns of self-indulgence or solipsism.[3] Reflexivity examines the close encounters with personal stories that compel the researcher to revisit the *self*.[4] For example, reflexive practices help researchers anticipate, understand, and even embrace the connection among research subject, participants, and themselves; moreover, embracing the connectedness of the research experience potentially impacts researchers in profound ways.[5] It is this very connectedness that contributes to place-making, as the association between researcher and subject serves to help define place in relation to experience. The following layered personal narrative tells an undertold story: that of the researcher's experiences.

Each of us brought unique perspectives to our study of women cancer survivors living in Appalachia. For example, Kathryn, a self-identified Appalachian, was a graduate student in communication at the time of this project. This study united her research interests with her extensive experience working with regional populations from disadvantaged backgrounds. Kelly, then a department of communication faculty member specializing in the intersection of gender, culture, and communication, also identified as Appalachian. Sadie, a women's health nurse practitioner and a college of nursing faculty member, worked in an outpatient cancer center. In this essay, we describe our research process and our reflexive practices, thereby enabling us to better engage the stories of both study participants and researchers. In doing so, we revisit some assumptions about Appalachia and self.

Revisiting Appalachia: Methods and Mindfulness

We focused our research in Appalachia for a number of reasons. First, we all lived here and were connected to the area and the people. Second, because of our educational and research background as well as Sadie's clinical experiences, we recognized Appalachia as a unique population, particularly in matters of health and illness.[6] In this way Appalachia is constructed as a place through the definition of the region's health conditions; troublingly, the population of Appalachia continues to be characterized by numerous health disparities, including cancer.[7] Before undertaking our study, we fully immersed ourselves in the academic literature, attempting to identify factors contributing to the region's documented health and cancer disparities, including population-based causes such as lack of insurance and shortages of health-care providers.[8] Moreover, we noted that several scholars explored how cultural factors may play a role in health and illness in contemporary Appalachia.[9] Armed with this knowledge, we chose a methodological approach that emphasized participants' voices, which enabled us to capture rich and diverse stories of women surviving cancer survivorship in Appalachia.[10]

Considering Our Approach

Our reflexive analysis, undertaken over the whole course of the study, began the moment we conceived of this survivorship project. Our first step was to conduct a bracketing interview of a self-identified breast cancer survivor and fifth-generation Appalachian, thereby raising our understanding of cancer survivorship and addressing biases and assumptions we had about the topic and the population.[11]

Through story circles and in-depth interviews, we collected stories from twenty-nine women cancer survivors living in southern central Appalachia—East Tennessee or southwest Virginia—from September 2008 through April 2009. All participants identified themselves as being situated somewhere along the cancer continuum. As noted in our other works describing the study, the story circle approach yielded twenty-six participants.[12] On the day of the story circle event, we began with a keynote speaker who was an oncology nurse and breast cancer survivor; afterward the participants shared stories of their cancer experiences in two sessions, one in the morning and one in the afternoon.

Our reflexive approach inspired us to reconsider our methods when we realized that three of the women we had recruited for the study, who had explicitly indicated an eagerness to talk about their cancer experiences, were prevented from attending the event because of barriers (work, treatment-related side effects, transportation). To broaden the depth of our survivorship data, we needed to include the stories of those whose voices had not yet been heard.[13] Therefore, Kathryn conducted three in-depth interviews in participants' homes.

Confidence and Credibility: Researcher-Focused Challenges

We engaged in reflexive analysis through study design and data collection to confront legitimate questions about our credibility as researchers and our place within this research. In the planning stages, we spoke openly to each other about our shared concerns regarding our credibility in our own eyes as well as in the eyes of the participants. One obvious threat to our credibility stood out: none of us were cancer survivors. We could gather literature about cancer in Appalachia and draw on our experiences of living in Appalachia, but ultimately we lacked personal, experiential knowledge of cancer. Each of us, however, had experience with cancer: through a family member, work relationships, or both. Kelly's story reflects the struggles we faced throughout the project:

> I knew what it was to be a family member of a survivor, to be placed on "hold" by a disease but have no say in how it was treated or how it would turn out. But I had no idea what it was to be diagnosed, to call loved ones and break the news. I had no idea what it was to try to decide where to put my energies when depleted by chemo. During recruitment, there was one time in particular that I felt like such a fool. I called a woman who had communicated through an oncology nurse her interest in telling her story to us. I explained that the story circle event was going to be like a "retreat," a time to eat good food and share stories with other survivors. She interrupted me and explained she was in treatment and couldn't be too far from her bedpan. I assured her that she would have access to bathrooms nearby—at least nearby from my perspective. But my assurances only forced her to explain in greater detail why rushing to a public restroom wasn't an option. My ignorance of the daily lived experiences of cancer survivors had resulted in me pressing a woman who was already pressed by her disease and the treatments. I thanked her as politely as I could and hung up. What I really wanted to do was apologize profusely for being so ignorant about what *surviving* cancer survivorship actually entailed.

In addition to wrestling with the issue of credibility, we also recognized and reflected on the complexity of our intersecting identities. We were not just researchers but also women, mothers, nurses, students, children, and so on. We were unable to listen to participants' stories impassively and with detachment: their stories evoked questions about our identities and even self-doubt. Sadie, for example, questioned her credibility because of her identity as a healthy mother and a nurse clinician:

I worked in oncology for over ten years, and my mother died from breast cancer when I was thirteen. I knew cancer. I also knew many of the participants because they were my patients or relatives of my patients. I listened so intensely to the women talk about their survivorship journeys that I often forgot I was supposed to be facilitating the group. Then, two things hit me at once: I was only weeks away from having my second child, safe in the fact that I could care for my children without the fear of cancer tearing us apart. Second, the nurse in me became horrified. Participants who were my patients talked about their families and changes in role identity, a topic I had never asked them about. Had I forgotten the importance of holism in my care? How could I have overlooked asking them about these critically important parts of their lives as I focused on their clinical care? Why was I learning this side of the story only now, when I should have known it all along? Had I failed them?

In the discipline of nursing, holistic care is part of professional identity. Although much of the education of advanced practice nurses (APNs) draws from a practical medical model of diagnosis and treatment, the philosophical notion of "patient-centered care" is central to how APNs function. As her story shows, Sadie was challenged to consider whether she truly understood her patients' life situations within their families and communities; in essence, she had to confront whether she had ultimately strayed from the philosophical stance of being a professional nurse.

Kelly also questioned her credibility during the story circles, and she too experienced intersecting identities. Her father had been diagnosed with bladder cancer when she was a young adult, and then years later her father-in-law died of esophageal cancer. Kelly describes her experience facilitating the story circles:

As I walked into the story circle, I fretted: who was I to have a day-long conversation with this group of cancer survivors? I stepped into the room that day, surrounded by a diverse group of complex women, and I knew—just knew—that they would demand of me: "Who are *you* to ask me for my survivorship story?" They never did ask me that question. In fact, they were kind, generous, and brave in their display of emotions. Still, my doubts linger, resurfacing each time I write or talk about this research. Who am I to help convey the voices of survivors?

During the story circle event, in an attempt to connect with the women and explore gender differences in the cancer survivorship experience, Kelly briefly told the story of her father-in-law's cancer diagnosis. There was a catch in her throat and tears in her eyes. Participants passed tissues and began consoling her. Kelly quickly refocused, turning the conversation back to the participants. Later, during the team's reflexive analysis, Kelly questioned whether her disclosure was appropriate, as researchers are "not supposed" to impact the data; however, we all agreed that this is part of the process of place-making in research. We recognized that our connectedness to the research experience impacts us in profound ways, and this connectedness contributes to place-making. Together with our participants we were defining place in relation to experience. Kelly's and Sadie's stories highlight the complexities and challenges researchers experience when conducting research. How do we refrain from becoming emotionally or egotistically involved in the research process?

Painful Encounters, Painful Maneuverings: Participant-Focused Challenges

A downside to conducting research with a population battling chronic illness is health decline and potential death of the participants. During data collection, the participants appeared to experience good mental and physical health. Although these women had battled or were still battling cancer, they appeared healthy, even if that meant lots of makeup and wigs; however, participants reminded us that for older generations in Appalachia, "it's not how it is, but what it looks like." It was easy for us to envision healthy and happy futures for these women, especially with the emphasis on positive-only thinking when it comes to illness, particularly cancer, and appearing healthy.[14]

Our first report of a health decline came less than a year after data collection. One interviewee, an ovarian and breast cancer survivor, notified us that her cancer had metastasized to her brain. We were stunned and saddened. For us, these women would forever be alive, captured in our memories, recordings, and transcripts. We each struggled to reconcile our remembered experiences with the sudden realization that our participants might not live long enough to see their stories published. Not long after we learned of this, a second participant, Janine (pseudonym), died. Kathryn describes her experience with Janine:

> Janine was my first interviewee. At twenty-seven years old, I felt unprepared to interview a woman in her fifties surviving ovarian cancer. Janine discussed her inability to find other ovarian cancer survivors which, upon reflection, seems less about her desire to connect with other survivors and more about her need to know she would survive. She was angry and cried while describing her road to diagnosis. Janine discussed her fears of burdening her sons with her illness and her excitement over her new grandchild. The entire time I could only think about how inadequate I was, as a novice researcher, to ask such personal questions. When the interview was over, I felt connected to her and became a silent cheerleader for her survival. We drove the same roads to work, and I loved the days when I saw her driving home. The news of her death impacted me greatly. Five years later I still miss seeing Janine driving home.

As Kathryn's experience indicates, participants and their stories impact researchers. Participants often share intimate details about their experiences with researchers, details that become part of both individuals' lives.[15] Through this process we became witnesses to the traumatic stories of our participants, which had the potential to lead to secondary trauma for the researcher. Secondary trauma, which impacts individuals working with those that have experienced traumatic life events, leaves researchers prone to experiencing symptoms like chronic fatigue, sadness, detachment, and physical illness.[16] Kathryn now recognizes that many of the poor coping mechanisms and depression-like symptoms she experienced during the research process may have been partly due to secondary trauma.

At the time of this writing, we know of three participants who have died. Each time, we were struck by how brave, determined, engaged, and positive each survivor was, all the things that survivors are "supposed" to be. And we are struck by our own loss, in some respects the loss of innocence: at one point, long ago, we thought it was the research process that mattered—instead, we learn time and again that we are humans investigating other humans. And doing so invites pain and heartbreak—but also inspiration.

Discussion and Conclusion

Investigating women surviving cancer in southern central Appalachia was an experience both awe-inspiring and agonizing, requiring that we constantly revisit our assumptions about Appalachia, regional women, cancer survivors, and our selves. Our constant reflexivity enriched not only the data but our lives as well.

What became evident through this journey is that surviving cancer is messy and complex, and that researching cancer and the region of Appalachia is equally complicated. In asking who is Appalachian and what it means to be Appalachian, we were ourselves involved in Appalachian place-making: as researchers, residents, and women. In research meetings, we studied maps of Appalachia, seeing that, from a geographical perspective, the region appears neatly identified, with four hundred counties in thirteen states.[17] As described in our other publications, though, we quickly realized that defining the region and population was more complicated.[18] Various scholars have also wrestled with this matter, using differing criteria for determining who is "Appalachian."[19] Subsequently, we drew on Williams's seminal work to guide our study, inspired by his description of Appalachia as a geographical and historical place inhabited by different groups.[20] Given the exploratory nature of our cancer survivorship research and the desire to minimize a reductionist approach, we decided to cast a wider net. We recognized that we could not, nor should we, define who is Appalachian; therefore, we focused on gathering the stories of women living and surviving cancer in Appalachia.

Part of our interrogation of our complex subject matter was to interrogate our own assumptions about Appalachia and cancer survivorship, a process that began during the bracketing interview. Our self-examination continued as we faced assumptions outlined in the literature, even those we may have unintentionally absorbed. For example, the topic of cancer fatalism has been used to explain cancer disparities in Appalachia, an explanatory framework that, arguably, has been oversimplified.[21] Almost from the start, we each had to question our own reliance on this framework, challenging ourselves to explore a more complex picture of cancer and cancer disparities in the region.[22]

We acknowledged that Appalachia is a unique population, and we wanted to remain mindful of how our assumptions and our work could further essentialize an already marginalized population.[23] For too long writings like Weller's often-cited *Yesterday's People* have oversimplified a complex region that "holds amazing dichotomies."[24] When engaging in our reflexive practices, we acknowledged and discussed the danger of unintentionally underscoring overgeneralizations about people living in Appalachia.[25] For example, it was easy to support the stereotype that Appalachian women are passive and powerless, even though the two authors who identify as Appalachian do not describe themselves this way. A common theme in many participants' stories was their prioritization of mothering and caregiving roles over their cancer survivor identity. At first we viewed this as more evidence of the repression and self-negation of women within the region. As we discussed these findings and dug deeper into the data, we recognized that we were unintentionally supporting regional stereotypes of women. What we began to uncover was the powerful position these women held within their families before diagnosis. We then argued that prioritizing mothering and caregiving roles was a strategic maneuver to maintain their powerful position within their families.[26] This also gave the voices of women participants, as Appalachians, cancer survivors, and mothers, a space in the remapping of Appalachia in terms of regional gendered stereotypes.

Hunt argues that subjectivity and Self are such a natural part of research that often researchers discover Self through the "detour of the other."[27] We all began this study with naive assumptions about researcher roles and investigating illness. We encountered our selves in multiple ways through this process. For example, we discussed and wrote about how our privileged positions as white, college-educated, middle-class women helped us access certain communities in Appalachia and also influenced our study. We noted that most of our study participants were also white women; persons of color and economically marginalized populations living in Appalachia were largely—and unintentionally—excluded from our cancer studies; obviously, this omission limited our research, yet it is reflective of the sociodemographic makeup of the region.[28]

In addition to reflecting on researcher privilege, we also considered what is "appropriate" when it comes to emotional involvement with the research. Jewkes argues that researchers are trained not to disclose anything about self, including vulnerabilities, anxiety, or confusion, within their research.[29] Even some qualitative scholars encourage researchers to balance objectivity and sensitivity during the research process; however, maintaining that balance can be especially challenging when investigating a sensitive or difficult topic.[30] During data collection, our participants were eager to share with us, reminding us of other studies in which patients, some of them terminally ill, explained that it was easier to talk with interviewers than with family members about their illness.[31] For our part, even though we were not family members, we were undeniably invested in and impacted by the stories. As researchers, we have lived with this data for over half a decade—from data collection to transcription to analysis and finally to publication. Years spent with these stories—including multiple readings of transcripts and reflecting on cancer survivorship stories, all the while visualizing participants' voices and faces—have left us susceptible to secondary trauma, as described above.[32] We often questioned how appropriate these connections and emotions were to our research; however, we argue that these feelings informed our research and motivated us to tell our participants' stories.

We also questioned what makes researchers credible or qualified to investigate a topic about which they have no personal experience. In the planning stages of our research, we spoke openly with one another regarding our concerns about our credibility—from our own point of view and that of our participants. Ultimately, what gave us credibility were the questions we asked about how we could best investigate women's textured experiences. Our training as qualitative researchers led us to reach out to professional researchers from a variety of disciplines, which helped us to question our assumptions.[33] Over the years, we have been humble enough to consult experts in survivorship, feminist scholarship, narrative inquiry, mothering, and the like. Our strategy's success is indicated in the fact that participants appeared to feel we were credible and trustworthy. They did not express concern because we were not cancer survivors. Participants wanted to tell their stories; they let us know after the story circles that they appreciated the opportunity to share survivorship narratives with us and others.

No methodology or theory-based article or book prepared us for the challenges we faced in our research in Appalachia. Reflexivity, both individually and as a team, became part of our place-making practices. It allowed us to revisit and remap our ideas of Appalachia and our ideas about what it means to be researchers, residents, and women in a historically and socially rich region. Acknowledging and working through the complexities of researching with a unique population provided the opportunity for a more credible study. Reflexivity allowed us to turn the problem of subjectivity into an opportunity that led to a more comprehensive understanding of our data. Place-making practices and reflexivity also demanded that we present a fuller story of survivorship among women in Appalachia. As researchers, we, like our participants, have histories, stories, and biases that can create a connection among us, the research subject, and our participants.[34] This connectedness becomes part of place-making, as together we define place in relation to experience. Researchers should not consider the participants' impact on them as shameful or characteristic of weakness. Instead, researchers should be praised for their openness, and more should be done to embrace wider experiences of researching. After all, these experiences are part of the human condition about which qualitative researchers are so passionate.

Notes

This research was grant funded by East Tennessee State University Research and Development Committee.

1. Mari Underwood, Leonn D. Satterthwait, and Helen P. Bartlett, "Reflexivity and Minimization of the Impact of Age-Cohort Differences between Researcher and Research Participants," *Qualitative Health Research* 20, no. 11 (2010): 1585–95.

2. Anselm Strauss and Juliet Corbin, *Basics of Qualitative Research,* 2nd ed. (Thousand Oaks, CA: Sage, 1998), 11.

3. Underwood, Satterthwait, and Bartlett, "Reflexivity and Minimization"; Linda Finlay, "Debating Phenomenological Research Methods," *Phenomenology & Practice* 3, no. 1 (2009): 6–25.

4. DeAnna H. Chester, "Mother, Unmother: A Storied Look at Infertility, Identity, and Transformation," *Qualitative Inquiry* 9, no. 5 (2003): 774–84.

5. Bruce L. Berg and Howard Lune, *Qualitative Research Methods for the Social Sciences,* vol. 5 (Boston: Pearson, 2004); Virginia Dickson-Swift, Erica L. James, Sandra Kippen, and Pranee Liamputtong, "Risk to Researchers in Qualitative Research on Sensitive Topics: Issues and Strategies," *Qualitative Health Research* 18, no. 1 (2008): 133–44.

6. Appalachian Regional Commission, "Moving Appalachia Forward: Appalachian Regional Commission Strategic Plan, 2011–2016," 2010, http://www.arc.gov/images/newsroom/publications/sp/ARCStrategicPlan2011–2016.pdf (accessed August 15, 2013); Susan E. Keefe, introduction to *Appalachian Cultural Competency: A Guide for Medical, Mental Health, and Social Service Professionals,* ed. Susan E. Keefe (Knoxville: University of Tennessee Press, 2005), 1–26; Wendy Welch, "Self Control, Fatalism, and Health in Appalachia," *Journal of Appalachian Studies,* 17, nos. 1-2 (2011): 108–22.

7. Tennessee Comprehensive Cancer Control Coalition, "State of Tennessee Comprehensive Cancer Control Program, 2009–2012," 2009, http://health.state.tn.us/CCCP/TCCC Plan.pdf (accessed August 15, 2013).

8. Irene H. Hall, Robert J. Uhler, Steven S. Coughlin, and Daniel S. Miller, "Breast and Cervical Cancer Screening among Appalachian Women," *Cancer Epidemiology Biomarkers & Prevention* 11, no. 1 (2002): 137–42; Eugene J. Lengerich, Stephen W. Wyatt,

Angel Rubio, Joyce E. Beaulieu, Cathy A. Coyne, Linda Fleisher, Ann J. Ward, and Pamela K. Brown, "The Appalachia Cancer Network: Cancer Control Research among a Rural, Medically Underserved Population," *Journal of Rural Health* 20, no. 2 (2004): 181–87.

9. Bruce Behringer and Koyamangalath Krishnan, "Understanding the Role of Religion in Cancer Care in Appalachia," *Southern Medical Journal* 104, no. 4 (2011): 295–96; Cathy A. Coyne, Cristina Demian-Popescu, and Dana Friend, "Peer Reviewed: Social and Cultural Factors Influencing Health in Southern West Virginia: A Qualitative Study," *Preventing Chronic Disease* 3, no. 4 (2006), http://www.cdc.gov/pcd/issues/2006/oct/06_0030.htm (accessed March 12, 2009).

10. See Kelly A. Dorgan, Kathryn L. Duvall, Sadie P. Hutson, and Amber Kinser, "Mothered, Mothering & Motherizing in Illness Narratives: What Women Cancer Survivors in Southern Central Appalachia Reveal about Mothering-Disruption," *Journal of Appalachian Studies* 19, nos. 1–2 (2013): 59–81.

11. Lea Tufford and Peter Newman, "Bracketing in Qualitative Research," *Qualitative Social Work* 11, no. 1 (2012): 80–96.

12. Dorgan et al., "Mothered, Mothering & Motherizing"; Kelly A. Dorgan, Sadie P. Hutson, Kathryn L. Duvall, Amber E. Kinser, and Joanne Hall, "Connecting Place to Disease and Gender: Cohabitating Morbidities in Narratives of Women Cancer Survivors in Southern Central Appalachia," *Women's Studies in Communication* 37, no. 3 (2014): 292–312.

13. Sarah Nebel Pederson, "To Be Welcome: A Call for Narrative Interviewing Methods in Illness Contexts," *Qualitative Inquiry* 19, no. 6 (2013): 411–18.

14. Dorgan et al., "Connecting Place to Disease and Gender"; Amy Y. Zhang and Laura A. Siminoff, "Silence and Cancer: Why Do Families and Patients Fail to Communicate?" *Health Communication* 15, no. 4 (2003): 415–29.

15. Underwood, Satterthwait, and Bartlett, "Reflexivity and Minimization."

16. Jan Coles and Neerosh Mudaly, "Staying Safe: Strategies for Qualitative Child Abuse Researchers," *Child Abuse Review* 19, no. 1 (2010): 56–69; David Conrad, "Secondary Trauma," 2010, http://secondarytrauma.org/index.htm (accessed July 11, 2014).

17. Appalachian Regional Commission, "Appalachian Region," n.d., http://www.arc.gov/appalachian_region/TheAppalachianRegion.asp (accessed August 15, 2013); John Williams, *Appalachia: A History* (Chapel Hill: University of North Carolina Press, 2002).

18. Dorgan et al., "Mothered, Mothering & Motherizing"; Dorgan et al., "Connecting Place to Disease and Gender."

19. Patricia Hayes, "Home Is Where Their Health Is: Rethinking Perspectives of Informal and Formal Care by Older Rural Appalachian Women Who Live Alone," *Qualitative Health Research* 16, no. 2 (2006): 282–97; Mira L. Katz, Mary Ellen Wewers, Nancy Single, and Electra D. Paskett, "Key Informants' Perspectives Prior to Beginning a Cervical Cancer Study in Ohio Appalachia," *Qualitative Health Research* 17, no. 1 (2007): 131–41; Carol C. Stephens, "Culturally Relevant Preventive Health Care for Southern

Appalachian Women," *Appalachian Cultural Competency: A Guide for Medical, Mental Health, and Social Service Professionals* (2005): 197–217.

20. Williams, *Appalachia*.

21. Renee Shell and Fred Tudiver, "Barriers to Cancer Screening by Rural Appalachian Primary Care Providers," *Journal of Rural Health* 20, no. 4 (2004): 368–73; Welch, "Self Control, Fatalism, and Health in Appalachia."

22. Kelly A. Dorgan, Sadie P. Hutson, Katie L. Duvall, and Gail Gerding, "Culturally Tailored Cancer Communication, Education, and Research: The Highways and Back Roads of Appalachia," *Preventing Chronic Disease* 6, no. 2 (2009), http://www.ncbi.nlm.nih.gov/pmc/articles/PMC2687874/ (accessed May 1, 2009).

23. Richard A. Couto, "Appalachia," in *Sowing Seeds in the Mountains: Community-Based Coalitions for Cancer Prevention and Control*, ed. Richard A. Couto, Nancy K. Simpson, and Gale Harris, No. 94, Appalachia Leadership Initiative on Cancer, Cancer Control Sciences Program (Rockville, MD: National Cancer Institute, 1994), 14–28; Stephens, "Culturally Relevant Preventive Health Care."

24. Jack E. Weller, *Yesterday's People* (Lexington: University Press of Kentucky, 1965); Welch, "Self Control, Fatalism, and Health in Appalachia," 108.

25. Dorgan et al., "Culturally Tailored Cancer Communication, Education, and Research"; Eric Swank, Breanne Fahs, and Holly N. Haywood, "Evaluating Appalachian Distinctiveness for Gender Expectations, Sexual Violence, and Rape Myths," *Journal of Appalachian Studies* 17, nos. 1-2 (2011): 123–43.

26. Dorgan et al., "Mothered, Mothering & Motherizing"; Dorgan et al., "Connecting Place to Disease and Gender."

27. Jennifer C. Hunt, *Psychoanalytic Aspects of Fieldwork* (London: Sage, 1989), 42.

28. Sadie P. Hutson, Kelly A. Dorgan, Amber N. Phillips, and Bruce Behringer, "The Mountains Hold Things In: The Use of Community Research Review Work Groups to Address Cancer Disparities in Appalachia," *Oncology Nursing Forum* 34, no. 6 (2007): 1133–39; Dorgan et al., "Connecting Place to Disease and Gender"; Dorgan et al., "Mothered, Mothering & Motherizing."

29. Yvonne Jewkes, "Autoethnography and Emotion as Intellectual Resources: Doing Prison Research Differently," *Qualitative Inquiry* 18, no. 1 (2012): 63-75.

30. Strauss and Corbin, *Basics of Qualitative Research*.

31. Catherine Exley and Gayle Letherby, "Managing a Disrupted Lifecourse: Issues of Identity and Emotion Work," *Health* 5, no. 1 (2001): 112–32.

32. Conrad, "Secondary Trauma."

33. Joanne M. Hall, "Narrative Methods in a Study of Trauma Recovery," *Qualitative Health Research* 21, no. 1 (2011): 3-13.

34. Berg and Lune, *Qualitative Research Methods*.

2

Carolina Chocolate Drops

Performative Expressions and Reception of Affrilachian Identity

Yunina Barbour-Payne

If you close your eyes and listen to the sounds of the Carolina Chocolate Drops (CCD), the color your ears hear will not be limited to the simple binaries of black and white. Instead, your ears will be filled with a rainbow of Appalachia and its musical identities. If you watch any of the fifty-three YouTube videos of the CCD posted between 2008 and 2012, you may be surprised to see that this group's repertoire is as versatile as its virtual viewership. The band performs and records music as diverse as the old-time music of the string band tradition and 1990s R & B covers like Blu Cantrell's "Hit 'Em Up Style," using instruments ranging from the fiddle to the human beat box. Below any YouTube video of the band, scrolling down the page, you'll find a host of comments from fans and avid supporters. In this community, some commenters may present themselves as more profound musical critics. Others claim an online presence as cultural advocates, that is, individuals who stress personal connections to particular ethnic and regional communities within the virtual sphere, and who are proud to perform their ties to the southern and Appalachian parts of America through YouTube comment streams. There are also virtual wanderers who happen upon the CCD page for the first time, leaving a comment simply bearing witness to the YouTube page and its community of commenters. In moving through these features of the CCD's online presence, clicking from video to video and listening, observing, and reading the comments, it becomes clear that the virtual fan base of the CCD is both national and international. Yet because the members of the CCD are black musicians, the group's recorded and posted presentations of Appalachian and other performance traditions inspire highly contested debates around musical and cultural authenticity.

The Carolina Chocolate Drops provide an important case for understanding virtual receptions of Affrilachian identity, that is, an identity that encompasses multiple ethnic groups within the Appalachian region, particularly people of African descent. The CCD came together in 2005, the result of a gathering of black banjo artists in Boone, North Carolina. The group was mentored by string legend Joe Thompson; their Grammy Award–winning album, *Genuine Negro Jig,* established the musicians as virtuosic performers of the string band tradition. The group acquired increasing popularity between 2005 and 2010. The CCD have been featured in major media outlets such as *USA Today, LA Times,* CMT, CNN, PBS, and NPR, among others. The CCD have performed throughout the United States as well as in Australia and Canada. Since its inception, the group has included African Americans from various parts of Appalachia and other US regions. Its founding members were Rhiannon Giddens, Dom Flemons, and Justin Robinson. Since its inception, the group has undergone some changes in membership, including the addition of Leyla McCalla, Rowan Corbett, Hubby Jenkins, Adam Matta, and Malcolm Parson. Through such shifts, the band offers diverse images of underrepresented black bodies of and in Appalachia on the public stage.

This chapter engages with social theories of performance and race to analyze online public discussions about the status of CCD within musical traditions associated with Appalachia. I offer a case study of the comment threads surrounding one CCD member's body in a particular video performance and the ways in which the comments represent contested definitions of authenticity and images of Affrilachia, which allows for an analysis of intersections among music, diaspora, race, and online activism.[1] Looking at the multiple diasporas, dispersed ethno-national communities from various subaltern populations, that emerge in the online conversations about the CCD, my research examines discourses of Affrilachian images through online discussions about the bodies of the CCD.[2] In this manner, I explore the construction of the body and behavior of the CCD to raise larger questions about race and regional identity in Appalachia. In particular, I ask: How is the image of Affrilachia invoked through the CCD members' bodies? How does the reception of the CCD signify Affrilachian identity and heritage?

What do these significations and representations reveal about Appalachia's active global connectivity through the transcultural circulation of the CCD's musical performances?

Methodology

In this project, I apply digital ethnography, that is, utilizing cyberspace to research sociocultural productions of meaning, to analyze public debates about cultural authenticity, Affrilachian identity, and musical performances. My methods for this project include participant observations of the online YouTube viewing and commenting community. Drawing on my ethnographic observations of fan and critic comments on CCD YouTube videos posted between 2008 and 2012, I seek to understand the racialized and culturally explicit ways in which Affrilachian identity is signified in this virtual community. I approach YouTube as a virtual space in which social geography is constituted and identity meaning created through interactions among commenters. I focus my analysis on the comment thread of one YouTube video in particular, a thread positioned within the context of commenters' receptions of the CCD's lead singers according to racialized and culturally explicit differences. This essay is structured dialogically, using the YouTube commenters' points of view surrounding cultural authenticity to suggest a way of thinking about cultural/ethnic and regional identities as subject to connectivity and cross-cultural conversations enabled through the Internet.

Theoretically Reframing Affrilachian Performance

In performance studies, embodied practices are constituted as "knowledge, emotion and creation."[3] Dwight Conquergood treats embodiment as a theoretical framework that attends to expressions in orality and to symbolic expressions of the body in cultural performance spaces.[4] In support of Conquergood's emphasis on the body as a site of knowing and constructing culture, I look at the ways in which YouTube commenters express their specific receptions of the CCD's bodies in performance. Their discussions of performer Rhiannon Giddens's body ultimately constructs a performative identity of Affrilachia. The term *Affrilachia* was coined by Frank X Walker to signify the presence of African-descended people within the region of Appalachia.[5] The word rhetorically both references and reclaims the racial and cultural diversity within the region, acknowledging a history of invisibility experienced by African Americans in Appalachia. As Giddens embodies Affrilachia, her body transforms into a multifaceted catalyst through which individuals communicate their regional, racial, and national identity connections.

William H. Turner limits the usefulness of Walker's term *Affrilachia* to that of "a recognizable brand," that "carves out a measure of prominence and identity for a group of African Americans in Appalachia."[6] Whether Affrilachia is merely a brand or something more, I apply the term in this chapter to representations on the stage by black musicians. As the CCD is a predominantly African American ensemble, race is a highly contested theme throughout the band's YouTube video posts. The recurring disputes found in the comment sections over what to call (or how to ethnically identify) members of the Carolina Chocolate Drops and their musical performances indicate the difficulty of acknowledging the vitality of Appalachia's black presence in American popular culture. Thus, the group's reception both signifies and transcends regional Appalachian and African American identities.[7]

The historical intersection of folk music and identity within the region of Appalachia necessitates the peremptory black identity activism revealed by contemporary Affrilachian musical conventions. Appalachian folk music is a genre that has been historically categorized by themes of "rugged independence, individualism and traditionalism."[8] The genre has often been featured in studies on cultural survival; many scholars have long recognized the roles of racial diversity and cultural hybridity in the development of Appalachian folk traditions. For example, folk music collector Cecil Sharp highlights the British and Scottish influences on Appalachian music, but neglects to engage the African influences of the region's folk traditions. His work prompts Gold and Revill's assertion that Appalachian music and cultural hybridity "are mediated within an essentialist framework."[9] Though Sharp acknowledges cultural hybridity as an ever-present characteristic of Appalachian folk tradition, his work nevertheless propels notions of Appalachia's racial purity. Others have likewise restricted the racial diversity of the region's folk tradition to its European descendants. Black racial invisibility within the region has been promoted by romantic themes of "cultural, moral and racial purity."[10] This framework is embedded in a folk tradition that demonstrates an anti-black racism that begets Affrilachia through its exclusionary processes.

Moving beyond this essentialist framework, William Archer, Fred Hay, and Cecilia Conway have provided overviews of African American influences on Anglo Appalachian music of the twentieth century. Archer's work looks at Appalachian influences on the American musical form jazz.[11] Hay and Conway argue for the transculturation of African diaspora roots within Appalachian folk music traditions.[12] Hay suggests, "Despite the recent scholarship documenting the African American influence on Anglo-Appalachian music, many are still reluctant to accept the music of African Appalachians as Appalachian music."[13] According to all three of these Affrilachian scholars' works, Affrilachian music is both "traditional and multicultural."[14] I adopt Hay's observation and extend these qualities to Affrilachian musical performance. In this chapter, I take a step beyond celebrating African influence on Appalachian folk to an analysis of the audience communities among Affrilachian performers. Here I address an African American influence that is witnessed not simply in the music tradition but also in the performance of Appalachian folk.

In contrast to the older view of Appalachian folk tradition as an exclusively British and Scottish cultural hybrid, Affrilachian folk performance reconstructs Appalachian folk tradition itself. Affrilachian performance invokes the racial and cultural diversity of the region, embracing Appalachian, indigenous, and African American folk. I treat Affrilachian performance as a tradition most visible in the bodies of performers. The performance style and vocal delivery of Affrilachian performers showcase their regional, ethnic, and national ties. The Carolina Chocolate Drops are racial and cultural performers. By this I mean that as black performers onstage using their bodies in the process of performance, they are linked to African American performance traditions.[15] Those traditions entail a history of cultural expressions associated with virtuosic dance and movement repertoires involving highly syncopated rhythms and vocal tone qualities. In addition to citing black cultural expressions, the CCD also incorporate cultural markers of Appalachia, including the fiddle, the banjo, and old-time and Appalachian country folk music, into their Affrilachian performance repertoires. The fusion of the band's instrument choices and performance traditions results in a distinctly Affrilachian presence on the stage.

Transnational Connectivity

The social connections between people in the twenty-first century are becoming increasingly virtual. With the rise in social networks and major sites such as YouTube, the global stage for performance and sharing is expanding. In a global context, Jan Aart Scholte describes respatialization as "the reconfigurations of social geography with increased trans-planetary con-nections between people."[16] I apply Scholte's concept of respatialization to understand the conversations among CCD YouTube commenters. As a site for social interaction, the YouTube video posts of the Carolina Chocolate Drops provide an opportunity for individuals to conduct global conversa-tions. A new social geography of Appalachian cultural space is therefore constructed through the CCD YouTube comment threads.

As a visible space of participation in which individuals may decide to involve themselves directly or indirectly, the threads both affirm and con-test the given cultural space. Held et al. suggest that social transformation is embodied in spatial organizations of social relations and transactions.[17] I apply their observations to the space of the YouTube commenters feed, which includes participants from the United States, Finland, Spain, Mexico, Amsterdam, Brazil, Canada, Belarus, Denmark, Transylvania, Romania, Scotland, Ireland, and Switzerland. Thus, a global citizenship of the CCD's followers is imagined. Their participation as distinct cultural advocates within the threads enables participants to celebrate and police perceptions of diversity. With these issues in mind, I look to the group's virtual fandom and reception to highlight instances in which these racial, cultural, and transnational significations occur.

The Image of Affrilachia

In the spring of 2013, I surveyed a total of twenty-four YouTube videos of the CCD's performances posted between 2008 and 2012. Of the videos surveyed, I have chosen the most compelling comment posts from one video to talk about transnational conversations prompted by the CCD. In these threads, notions of Affrilachian identity and naming wars occur between represen-tatives of various cultures and countries. Take, for example, a video posted by Joanna Joseph entitled *Carolina Chocolate Drops: Acapella Gaelic Medley by Rihanna PIP*, posted in September 2008. The video appears to have been recorded with a personal camera or phone during a midday performance. Lead singer Rhiannon Giddens sings in Gaelic at a local Pines Bluegrass Festival in Flagstaff, Arizona. Fair-skinned Giddens sits onstage directly in front of a microphone. Her long, curly black hair is pulled back loosely into a ponytail. She is wearing a rustic-looking floral top and blue jeans. The frame of the video shifts between intimate shots of Giddens from her head to chest to wider shots of the full stage that show two darker-skinned male band members, Dom Flemons and Adam Matta, sitting on either side of the lead singer. As the tempo in the music becomes more exciting, Giddens and the other members clap their hands, stomp their feet, and pat their legs in time.

This video was viewed 110,786 times and yielded 116 comments, dated from 2009 to 2013, by May 1, 2013. The comments illuminate the group's signification of Affrilachian identity. For example, themes of cultural hybridity are evoked in YouTube commenter Sailortitan's post: "Always awesome when cultural traditions collide, especially neat to hear a black person singing 'white person' music when it's more common for the opposite to happen. I'd love to see more ethnic variation in the Celtic music scene!"

Sailortitan recognizes the race of singer Rhiannon Giddens as an assumed black identity and compliments her ability to perform an authentic Celtic aesthetic. While Sailortitan's comment seems to embrace the musicians' perceived transcendence of racial barriers in their playing and performance, the comment also alludes to implicit cultural barriers. Sailortitan's statement that the performers are singing "white person" music brings to mind a long history of racial appropriation of musical forms in America. Sailortitan's comment indicates the CCD are perceived to be performing against a hegemonic American musical tradition that has excluded African Americans from music forms privileged and designated as racially white. Within this context of racially marked music traditions, the CCD become black activists through their performance of the medley. Above all, this perception of the CCD's racially progressive song performance affirms this group as Affrilachian through its performance of the music.

Additionally, the activism suggested by Sailortitan's comment connects to a more sophisticated social activism associated with the idea of Affrilachia. As Paul C. Taylor notes, "To conjure the term Affrilachia, is to build and advance the campaign for visibility."[18] Taylor calls for understanding the naming of Affrilachia as an activist reaction against black invisibility within the Appalachia aesthetic. In that context, Sailortitan similarly names the CCD's performance as Affrilachian from a perspective of black subjugation in American music through a Celtic aesthetic. In the CCD's own self-definition, the group has intentionally sought to re-present and reclaim music that has been historically disassociated from African-descended people.[19] When asked about the group's personal vision of its relationship to the future of folk music, Dom Flemons responded that the CCD seek to "create awareness about Black contributions to the old-time music since it's still a lesser known aspect of early American music."[20] While Flemons's remarks clearly present the group's mission, the CCD's intentions are also evidenced in their performances as black musicians continuing to make contributions to traditional folk music. In the video on which Sailortitan reflects, the group members use only their voices and bodies as instruments. In comparison to traditional folk, the group's performance style and content are musically Affrilachian in their radical advocacy of black performers' contribution to folk music. Thus, the commenter's interpretation of the CCD performance as transgressive supports an image of Affrilachia rooted in activism.

In contrast to Sailortitan's celebration of the CCD's performance, other commenters post criticism and refute the claim of racial transgression by the group. In one thread, well over half of the comments preceding this specific discussion focus on Giddens's virtuosic ability to present an authentic performance of the Gaelic songs. One central theme among comments that validate Giddens's performance authenticity is her ethnic ancestry. Conversely, commenters like Grainne O'Malley take offense to the racialized emphasis of some comments and respond in disagreement to Sailortitan's notions of race and music authenticity. Unfortunately (for research purposes), the "racist" comment to which Grainne O'Malley is directly responding is unavailable due to an overwhelming number of "dislikes."[21]

> Grainne O'Malley: I can't believe you Americans are actually saying this woman can't be irish. You're the biggest bunch of thick, racist, backwards foreigners I've ever read. Get a fucking grip on reality and stop speaking for us folks actually in Ireland, we didn't ask you in the first place.
>
> PS: Black Irish in the current Irish census form means Irish of African descent (oh*oops*). If that girl wanted to go and sing some Sean Nós in the Gaeltacht with the locals she'd be made very, very welcome indeed.
>
> nilradem [reply]: My reading of that comment is not that [it is] racist. It is much more likely her Irish ancestors are white, as I have heard her talk about tracing African ancestry back to the slave era. I can't find an interview, but believe one parent is white (with some Irish ancestry) and Native American and one is Black. I may not be exactly right, but am pretty sure her Irish ancestry is white. And until relatively recently, "black Irish" did refer to dark haired, light eyed Irish like my ancestors.

The next part of the thread focuses on comments between nilradem and Europride, a commenter whose comments outraged many commenters and were deleted as a result.

> nilradem [another reply]: One more thing—I was referring to the more recent comments, not to "Europride," as I had not gone back that far. He/she does indeed appear to be a racist. More generally one place I do see racism in this discussion is the reluctance to recognize that many Americans are of mixed race and the desire to label people either white or Black. There is a long history of both intermarriage and forced sex between the races in the US. She *is* Irish, she *is* African American and *is* Native American.

I feature the conversation between Grainne O'Malley and nilradem to draw attention to constructions of race maintained by the commenters. In this comment thread, Grainne O'Malley self-identifies as Irish. Nilradem's ethnic identity is not overtly evident, but it is clear that nilradem speaks within an American context of understanding racial constructs. Both Grainne O' Malley's and nilradem's comments are elicited by their individual perceptions of Giddens's ancestry. Grainne O'Malley begins by criticizing other commenters' perceptions of Giddens's Irish performance authenticity. Grainne O'Malley introduces the history of "black Irish" to assert a possible racial and cultural heritage of the singer. Nilradem's comment removes Giddens from a racial history fixed in binaries of black and white by asserting that Giddens's heritage is multicultural. From this point, as the topic of race is complicated in nilradem's and Grainne O'Malley's contributions to the thread, the YouTube conversation moves from Giddens's ancestry specifically to a dispute about notions of racism in America.

The conversations that arise regarding the singer's race complicate the reception of her cultural performance. Some commenters, like nilradem, attribute Giddens's authentic performance to her familial ties to a Scots-Irish heritage. Here, Grainne O'Malley's explication of "black Irish" reacts against essentialist understandings of Irish cultural representations.[22] Elsewhere, Giddens's cultural performance inspires other commenters' tangents regarding the experiences of various diasporic groups in and outside of the United States. The commenters' supplementary posts validating or denying the singer's musical ability serve to further provoke the topics of music, race, and diaspora in the thread.

Music and Diaspora

The notion of diaspora is a way of locating Giddens's identity in performance. In the conversation between Grainne O'Malley and nilradem, questions regarding Giddens's black ancestry bring up topics of both black and
Irish diaspora identities. As Grainne O'Malley and nilradem debate about
the singer's African American and possibly black Irish ancestry, nuances of
racial cultural heritage and identity become increasingly complex. Nilradem theorizes this complexity in an attempt to settle the dispute over Giddens's black ancestry, referencing a talk the singer gave in which she traced
her ancestry to the "slave era." Nilradem's comments suggest that Giddens
herself embodies an Affrilachian cultural hybridity as a woman of Irish,
African, and Native American descent. Though nilradem tries to reconcile
the heated discussion around Giddens's ancestry by acknowledging multiple
aspects of her ethnic identity, the post spurs additional comments by other
participants regarding race and diaspora.

The following comments encompass topics regarding the cultures of
the Irish and African diasporas. For example, Skrinkle2000 argues for Giddens's cultural authenticity by emphasizing her family heritage of an Irish
diasporic experience.

> Skrinkle2000: She is of Irish-American heritage (not surprisingly,
> with a name like Rhiannon. She also has a daughter named Aiofe).
> There are, of course, also darker skinned people in Ireland as there
> have been for centuries there and in almost all countries who are
> all as native as the lighter skinned people
>
> Europride4Life: haha, she is definitely talented, but she's about
> as Irish as I am African. Well, maybe she is half (mulatto), but please
> don't try to pass off an obviously mixed race African woman as Irish.
> There is no such thing as Negro Irish. The term "Blackmixed" does
> not refer to Negro, but to the Irish with darker hair and typically no
> freckles due to many White Spaniards settling there some centuries
> ago and mixing with White Celtic Irish. Both were White however.
>
> Moustacherodeo: so you must be . . . what, a quarter african?
>
> Mixed race? The entirety of humanity is mixed race! The only
> pure race is probably African. Africa is most likely the spring of all
> humanity!
>
> No such thing as Negro Irish . . . ha ha ha ha ha ha ha ha ha

ha!!!! I am positive there is Negro Irish, and Chilean Irish and . . . Japanese Irish, and Native American Irish, and Russian Irish and Peruvian Irish and on and on as many combinations as there is seed to mix with ovum!

Moustacherodeo: White Irish . . . once again—*ha!* Go back to mid-1800s America and ask any true White American at that time whether they would consider the Irish white and they would spit in your face! The Irish were the dirty foreigners! And no true Yankee would have wanted to mix with their filthy blood! They were the bullet sponges of the Civil War! Get over yourself!

AugustMeteors: I don't believe she's trying to pass herself off as Irish; in interviews she refers to herself as Black. She's an accomplished African American musician who's been to the British Isles and fell in love with some of the music there and learned some of it. By adding it to her repertoire she's paying it a tribute, not masquerading. And look how the audience enjoys it! They're not turning it into something political, they're just having a good time. Why can't we YouTubers do the same?

Jo May: [reply] most blacks in America with long family history here are part irish. especially if both sides of the family are descendants [of] slaves. get a life

AugustMeteors [reply]: Indeed, there's a possibility she has some Irish, in fact I believe she is of mixed heritage. I only observed that she's not trying to pass herself off as Irish in particular. My comment was very supporting of her love of the music and her right to enjoy it and present it, as in [fact I] enjoy Motown music and yet I'm pale as a herring belly . . .

mishsamuels [reply]: Many of us from the African Diaspora have Irish background.

In the above thread, commenters make claims about the lead singer's musical authenticity and identity through personally rigid designations of racial categories. For instance, Skrinkle2000's comment focuses solely on the singer's Irish heritage. Skrinkle2000 emphasizes Giddens's daughter's name, Aiofe, to argue that the singer maintains an Irish cultural knowledge that supports claims of authenticity even as a black performer. Generally, the commenters' responses to Giddens's performance and racially marked body demonstrate strong cultural connections to Appalachia.[23] As disagreements over Giddens's black and Irish ancestry persist in the thread, Affrilachia emerges as a key trope, although perhaps this is not intended by the commenters. The mentions of multiple diasporas challenge essentialist ideas presented by some commenters. The increasingly hostile exchange regarding questions of identity elucidates the highly contested character of Affrilachia within national cultures.

In contrast to Skrinkle2000's emphasis on the cultural authenticity afforded by Giddens's Irish heritage, Europride4Life emphasizes the blackness of Giddens's body. Europride4Life's comments evoke the history of invisibility many blacks experienced within the region by disassociating the singer from both white American and Appalachian heritage.[24] Europride4Life suggests that Giddens is only "passing" as a "mixed" person of "black" descent. In addition to focusing on Giddens's racially mixed black body, Europride4Life makes a distinction between "Negro Irish" and "black Irish." Europride4Life presents a context of blackness in Ireland to suggest the designation black Irish is a reference to the social and class status of an individual rather than race. As a result, Europride4Life's idea of blackness removes the concept from an American understanding of race to a local understanding of identity experience.

While this commenter's racial emphasis seems to displace Giddens from the region of Appalachia, the comments implicitly re-place her at the center of Appalachian heritage. Europride4Life's understanding of black Irish within social class distinctions connects to early understandings of Appalachian whiteness. White racial identity in Appalachia was initially formulated out of an essentially racial logic, within which Appalachians as a community of whites degraded by class expectations could "never be quite white enough."[25] Though initial efforts to distinguish and define white Appalachians involved a distancing from racial dynamics, more contemporary understandings are located within discourses of power, privilege, and race.[26] In the historical process of understanding Appalachians within American culture, the group became racially marked as Other through the effects of classism and racism. More recently, discourses regarding pejorative stereotyping and experiences of Appalachian whites are contextually centered in an ideology of distinctive racism against poor, working-class whites. In essence, Europride4Life's attempt to disassociate the racial history of Giddens's specific racial identity connotes that Giddens does belong to the region by invoking an image of Appalachia's classed history.

In the online YouTube community, the making of Appalachia is still a racial process. In particular, the dispute between Europride4Life, August-Meteors, and Moustacherodeo is primarily over racial meanings and designations. Europride4Life makes it a point to name Giddens's identity as "mulatto," while AugustMeteors refers to Giddens as "African American." Moustacherodeo criticizes the racial purity undertone of Europride4Life's comments. Moustacherodeo's reference to the whitening process of Irish American immigrants, who transitioned from a subordinated status to a more privileged racial position, brings to mind a double otherness in American social history. Roger Cunningham's notion of "double otherness" argues that the region of Appalachia is both an Other of America and an internal Other of America's South.[27] Cunningham explains that double otherness suggests that Appalachian identity is shaped by economic and racial identity politics. Expanding Cunningham's view of Appalachia as Other, Affrilachia also occupies a liminal space of Other, racially, culturally, and nationally. Therefore, the commenters sharing concerns over Giddens's identity place the singer's body within various transformations of racial politics through discourses of otherness.

As a continuation of racialized body politics, Moustacherodeo also identifies Giddens's identity as "mixed race." Moustacherodeo uses Giddens's mixed histories to talk about a number of other potential transcultural identities, such as "Negro Irish, and Chilean Irish and Italian Irish, and Japanese Irish, and Native American Irish," within the Irish diaspora. Moustacherodeo also mentions the class history of Irish immigrants in North America: "Go back to mid-1800s America and ask any true White American at that time whether they would consider the Irish white and they would spit in your face!" Anti-black racism is thus juxtaposed alongside anti-Irish racism; Moustacherodeo alludes to prejudices experienced by people of Irish descent during the early part of the nineteenth century in a discussion of twenty-first-century prejudices against people of African descent. In other words, both Europride4Life and Moustacherodeo introduce local ways of explaining subjugated identity experiences through Giddens's body.

On the other hand, in AugustMeteors's comments, Giddens's black identity is transcended. AugustMeteors challenges Europride4Life's claim that Giddens is only passing as culturally authentic by arguing that the "black" heritage of the singer is a characteristic that should be celebrated. August-Meteors applauds Giddens's performance of international music, praising the singer's expansive repertoire. AugustMeteors calls for YouTubers to celebrate the singer's black presence in global and local spaces. Showcasing a kind of virtual activism inspired by Giddens's talent, AugustMeteors empowers participants to assert Affrilachia into new spaces by painting a picture of Giddens as a talented, culturally authentic black body. Consequently, in the YouTube space, the image of Giddens is temporarily reinvented into the image of Affrilachia.

In short, the major points of contention in this thread are disagreements over vague notions of cultural authenticity. The disregard for the transnational characteristics of diaspora groups whose cultural identities are both black and Irish is a criticism asserted by commenters in prior posts.[28] Commenters recontextualize the two diasporas through the CCD. Using Giddens's history as a point of departure, the commenters allude to the tensions and experiences of both the Irish and black diasporas. As a result, the group's lead singer, as a twenty-first-century musician, is perceived to embody both the local and global character of an Affrilachian (black/Scots-Irish) presence and influence.

The threads I have used in this chapter show how social theory can be applied to address the ways local Appalachian discourses of power and race may enter global forums, such as the YouTube arena. The CCD have become a focal point for local constructions of Appalachia and for global conversations by and beyond Appalachians. I have argued that the CCD, a group of Affrilachian artists and musicians, have created through performance and activism (evidenced in the band's virtual and local presence) and through virtual fandom a specific racial-cultural Appalachian identity. At the same time, the CCD represent Affrilachia as an identity that transcends racial-cultural barriers. As commenters discuss racial identity constructions in personal and local terms, the CCD members' bodies become the site for complicating black identity and diaspora. In light of these conversations, I have shown the ways in which Affrilachia, in its traditional and multicultural sense, emerges as a way of understanding the context and histories in which these performances are located. The performance becomes Affrilachian not simply because the members represent black bodies onstage but also because of what their performances as black bodies inspire.

These performances inspire the disruption of racial discourses of Appalachian whiteness. However, I have also shown ways in which those same discourses are enlivened through cross-cultural associations to outside community experiences entwined with the region's ethnic histories. These discourses reveal parallels in the classed and racialized experiences of black Irish and white Appalachians. The highly contentious nature of the debates offers insight into understanding Appalachia locally and globally. The comments regarding the CCD members' black bodies on the public stage present the group and consequently its viewership as transcending boundaries of Appalachian music and race through performance. Presenting an opportunity for a unique form of social interaction, the videos of the performers allow commenters to individually evoke the ways in which Affrilachian identity is constructed and exceeded. Thus, the group's mode of self-presentation amounts to representations of cultural hybridity, marking it as what performance theorist Richard Schenner would call "not and not not" Affrilachian.[29]

Notes

1. I offer this definition of diasporas as "ethno-national communities" from Kim D. Butler's "three basic features" of diasporas outlined in her "Defining Diaspora, Refining a Discourse," *Diaspora: A Journal of Transnational Studies* 10, no. 2 (2001), 192.

2. Ibid.

3. D. Soyini Madison, *Critical Ethnography: Method, Ethics, and Performance* (Thousand Oaks, CA: Sage, 2011).

4. Dwight Conquergood, "Performance Studies: Interventions and Radical Research," *TDR/Drama Review* 46, no. 2 (2002): 145–56.

5. Bianca Spriggs, "Frank X Walker: Exemplar of Affrilachia," *Appalachian Heritage* 39, no. 4 (2011): 21–25.

6. William H. Turner, "Affrilachia as Brand," *Appalachian Heritage* 39, no. 4 (2011): 27–30.

7. Frank X Walker, "Playing It Now: Carolina Chocolate Drops Uphold Traditional Folk Music but Make It New," *Pluck! The Journal for Affrilachian Arts & Culture* 4 (2008): 38–40.

8. John R. Gold and George Revill, "Gathering the Voices of the People? Cecil Sharp, Cultural Hybridity, and the Folk Music of Appalachia," *GeoJournal* 65, nos. 1–2 (2006): 55–66.

9. Ibid., 62.

10. Ian C. Hartman, "Appalachian Anxiety: Race, Gender, and the Paradox of 'Purity' in an Age of Empire, 1873–1901," *American Nineteenth Century History* 13, no. 2 (2012): 229–55.

11. William Archer, "Jazz in the Mountains? One Town's Amazing Story," *Appalachian Heritage* 19, no. 4 (1991): 44–50.

12. Cecilia Conway, "Black Banjo Songsters in Appalachia," *Black Music Research Journal* 23 (2003): 149–66; Fred Hay, "Black Musicians in Appalachia: An Intro to Affrilachian Music," *Black Music Research Journal* 23 (2003): 1–19.

13. Hay, "Black Musicians in Appalachia," 8.

14. Ibid.

15. The performers often incorporate human beat boxing into their performances.

16. Jan Aart Scholte, "Globalization Debates" and "Defining Globalization," in *Globalization, a Critical Introduction* (New York: Palgrave, 2005), 13–47, 49–84.

17. David Held, Anthony McGrew, David Goldblatt, and Jonathan Perraton, "Rethinking Globalization," in *The Global Transformations Reader*, ed. David Held and Anthony McGrew (Cambridge: Polity, 2000), 60–67.

18. Paul C. Taylor, "Call Me Out My Name: Inventing Affrilachia," *Pluck! The Journal for Affrilachian Arts & Culture* 6 (2011): 1–2.

19. Mary Tess Barrett, "What Race Sounds Like: Perceiving American Music through the Carolina Chocolate Drops" (PhD diss., Wesleyan University, 2014).

20. Hope D. Johnson, "The Carolina Chocolate Drops Sensation," *Pluck! The Journal for Affrilachian Arts & Culture* 6 (2011): 97–103.

21. The managers of YouTube pages can set up the security so that a certain number of dislikes leads to the removal of the post from the thread.

22. Kerby A. Miller, "Scotch-Irish, 'Black Irish' and 'Real Irish': Emigrants and Identities in the Old South," *Irish Diaspora* (2000): 139–57.

23. Esther E. Gottlieb, "Appalachian Self-fashioning: Regional Identities and Cultural Models," *Discourse* 22, no. 3 (2001): 341–59.

24. William Hobart Turner and Edward J. Cabbell, *Blacks in Appalachia* (Lexington: University Press of Kentucky, 1985).

25. Barbara Ellen Smith, "De-gradations of Whiteness: Appalachia and the Complexities of Race," *Journal of Appalachian Studies* (2004): 38–57.

26. John Hartigan, "Whiteness and Appalachian Studies: What's the Connection?" *Journal of Appalachian Studies* (2004): 58–72.

27. Scott Romine, "Still Southern after All These Years?" *Southern Literary Journal* 30, no. 1 (1997): 128–36.

28. Stuart Hall, "Cultural Identity and Diaspora," in *Identity: Community, Culture, Difference,* ed. Jonathan Rutherford (London: Lawrence and Wishart, 1990), 222–37.

29. Richard Schenner, *Between Theater and Anthropology* (Philadelphia: University of Pennsylvania Press, 2010), 111–12.

3

Beyond a Wife's Perspective on Politics

One Woman's Expression of Identity in Western North Carolina in the Postwar Period

Amanda Zeddy

Scholars across the social sciences and humanities generally agree that individual and group identities are shaped by the socio-political categories of gender, race, class, sexuality, region, religion, and other salient constructions of social and economic relations, norms, and practices that frame the meanings and limits of political action and expression. Gender identities are one of the most pervasive constructs of social, economic, and political structures. Examining the narratives that constitute individuals' everyday experiences of gender identity can help to reveal the various and shifting ways in which patriarchy functions in different historical eras and political contexts. This chapter introduces key concepts of feminist social theory to analyze how these contexts shaped the political identity of Louise Broyhill in Appalachian North Carolina, who actively campaigned for her husband, US senator James Broyhill.[1]

Studies of individuals' political identities within southern Appalachian politics are uncommon and rarely address how the social and political categories of gender, race, class, sexuality, and religion function in spaces within Appalachia. Appalachian women have been an important focus within the field of Appalachian studies since the mid-twentieth century. Various scholars intentionally engage in this paradigm shift, but more studies are needed to examine the political dimensions of regional identities in the social contexts of political participation, political opinion formation, and beliefs about appropriate political behavior.[2]

To analyze the construction of Louise Broyhill's political identity through her engagements in high-level politics, I utilize a feminist social constructivist theoretical framework. Social constructivism serves as an interpretive framework in which to examine the identity constructions that influence the formation of "acceptable" understandings of politics and identity and the corresponding "acceptable" forms of political participation by one woman in western North Carolina from the post–World War II era until the late 1980s. Drawing from archival data of women's political engagement, I ask how patriarchical power relations, that is, male-oriented institutions, decision-making networks, and belief systems, impacted the formation of postwar political identities in the Appalachian South. I argue that patriarchal power relations influenced the boundaries of "acceptable" political behaviors in overt and subtle ways for an individual interacting in a historically specific socio-political climate. The first part of my chapter examines a feminist theoretical framework capable of analyzing the historical construction of gendered political identities in North Carolina. The second section narrows the focus to the conditions of patriarchy in this region of Appalachia. The final section applies these theoretical and contextual perspectives to analyze the political organizing work of Louise Broyhill.

Linda J. Nicholson notes that feminist theory from the late 1960s until the 1980s had a tendency to assume the perspective of white, middle-class women of the Western world, which excluded a wide range of lived experiences and perspectives of women from different social positions. Feminist scholars within third-wave feminism since the 1990s have made conscious efforts to move away from making generalizations in regard to human populations that universalize perceptions about the identity constructions of women. Third-wave, post-structuralist feminists have instead moved toward considering the wide variety of women's experiences of gender, sexuality, class, race, religion, and all other salient identities. This research uses an understanding of identity in which the self is multiple, layered, intersecting, and potentially not conscious of the internal contradictions that are triggered in any given context. Further, this perspective is inclusive of diverse claims of identity and takes into account the wide variance of women's social realities that come into existence due to differing social and political positions. Indeed, the material conditions individuals in western North Carolina experienced no doubt influenced how and from where they received and potentially acted upon the political information they were exposed to.[3]

Race, class, and gender as aspects of identity construction can be deployed together to create systems of domination and control in societies that shape and constrain the identity construction of individuals and how others perceive individual and group identities. Matt Wray in *Not Quite White* examines constructions of whiteness that intersect with class. The construction of "white trash" to refer to poor whites has historically been created and re-created as a stereotype that stigmatizes ("stigmatype") individuals based on their race *and* class. Stigmatypes of poor whites have been used as powerful symbols that have drawn social lines of exclusion, inclusion, and subordination. Anywhere in America where poor whites reside, including western North Carolina, will be affected by these stigmatypes to some extent due to the effect they have on the perception of poor whites by elites and the subsequent discriminatory institutional structures, norms, and rules created based on stigmatypes.[4]

I argue that the structures of patriarchy and other forms of social constraint function differently in different spaces, and therefore the identity construction and choices of individuals within different parts of Appalachia will vary based on each individual's positionality within social structures of power. To understand the ways in which individuals cognitively process political information, feminist post-structuralist theory that considers the social cognition literature will also be employed to enable a more detailed consideration of the internal workings of the mind in the construction of the self.[5]

In *Wealth of Selves* Edwina Barvosa explicates the cognitive processes that have an influence on the complex constellation of the construction of an individual's identity based on his or her lived experiences. More specifically, each individual will have a "set" of constructed identities as a result of experiences and interactions with others. For example, one person may have multiple understandings of him- or herself in relation to others: as a teacher, a person of color, a queer woman of color, a wife or husband, a transgendered woman, a mother or father. In the case of the study presented here, Louise Broyhill's experiences as a woman, mother, wife, and politically involved actor in western North Carolina shaped and influenced her understanding of her particular constellation of identity and therefore affected her political narratives.[6]

Each aspect of a person's identity will be supported by an arrangement of reinforcing frames of reference, to which one's cognitive processes will refer on a regular, daily basis to interpret the world. Therein, some facets of a person's identity will be more salient than others in particular contexts; some frames of reference and aspects will be activated over others depending on the situation and discourses being employed in that context. When some frames of reference are activated and others are not, a person "is more likely to accept messages and information that are compatible with their existing perspectives and to screen out and/or reject messages and information that are not."[7]

Patriarchy, racial supremacy, and heteronormativity as well as the frames of reference that support those normalizing systems of social control are included as internalized parts of individuals' identities and value schemas that can be activated in a variety of social and political contexts. Patriarchical frames of reference can become "chronically accessible" if discourses and constructs that are related to patriarchy are disseminated and repeated in a manner that is noticed and acknowledged more than other information. One person's identity constructions, frames of reference, and values in this way do not have to be internally consistent. A woman can espouse "feminist" values/frames of reference while also engaging in patriarchical values and frames of reference. This can be possible if these two contradictory value systems/frames of reference do not become activated at the same time, so an individual is never confronted with such internal contradictions of self.[8]

In summary, feminism and post-structuralism are useful theoretical frameworks in conducting historical cultural analysis since in these theories the human subject is constructed by both external environmental factors *and* internal cognitive processes. An individual's environment, cognitive processes, and learned behaviors are not factors independent of one another. Instead, these factors are engaged in a dialectic process wherein each variable changes over time and can affect other salient social categories. For instance, gender is not a stagnant social category. Gender is something that human beings *do*. As West and Zimmerman's "Doing Gender" elucidates, "gender must be continually socially reconstructed in light of 'normative conceptions' of men and women. People act with the awareness that they will be judged according to what is deemed appropriate feminine or masculine accounts of gender." Allowing for a deeper understanding of the effect that structures of power and social control have on women's identities and the way individuals cognitively process political information will provide a fuller, contextualized picture of why people behave and believe the ways they do. In this study, the theoretical frameworks outlined here will be used in evaluating archival and historical data.[9]

Historical analysis of western North Carolina using archival documents and secondary sources allows for the examination of social, economic, and political developments that affected people's everyday lived experiences. The following questions become central in this analysis: How have individuals in the region experienced and been controlled by institutions of power over time? How has this affected their sense of self? Through such historical analysis, we can trace the narratives and material contexts that affected the identity construction of individuals, mapping out how dominant narratives of patriarchy shaped perceptions about the limits of individuals' acceptable political engagement.[10]

Patriarchy, long a social force in the western region of North Carolina, has influenced imagined generalizations about an "Appalachian" identity. In his introduction to a 1973 history of western North Carolina by Van Noppen and Van Noppen, supported in part by the Western North Carolina Historical Association and academics at Appalachian State University, Cratis Williams claims that before that volume "no history of Appalachia has been written," especially a history that addressed "all facets in the lives of the people about which it is written."[11]

Although the book claims to discuss "all facets" of people's experiences of Appalachian North Carolina, it presents sweeping generalizations of men and women in a way that is overtly misogynist and offers an example of generalizing stigmatypes, or representations, of "the mountain man" and "mountain women." The "traditional" family units that are claimed to exist in western North Carolina since the Civil War are described thus: "Patriarchical. In them [family units] the men have been dominant, the women subservient. The men made the decisions, did 'men's work'; the women did the chores and the house work and often did not eat at the table with the men, especially if guests were present, but stood to serve men and guests." The description of the patriarchical nature of gender relations in family life justifies the subservience of women to men with the claim that women in these relationships were "loyal" and "not unhappy." Because they obeyed and served men without open defiance, women are portrayed as satisfied with their own position of subordination and relative social, economic, political, and sexual disadvantage.[12]

The authors of this history create a notion that women in the region are happily subordinated by patriarchy and relegated solely to the private realm of the household. Moreover, the identity constructions the book presents depict men and women alike in an essentialist manner that paints a perception of Appalachian North Carolinians as isolated and uninterested in political participation. Van Noppen and Van Noppen's elite narrative of "poor whites" demonstrates how cultural norms are constructed, norms that create stigmatypes of individuals in the region and shape others' perceptions of men and women in Appalachian North Carolina. Van Noppen and Van Noppen's perspective does not consider how structural hierarchies of power may influence the construction of men's and women's identities due to a unique constellation of social forces affecting how each individual processes and interprets his or her own lived experiences. A feminist poststructuralist analysis, in contrast, does consider the process by which each social context contains structural hierarchies of power that affect what identity constructions are accessible and seen as socially desirable, arguing that each human subject will have a different position and choices to make in relation to various power structures. Every individual will then experience the diverse sources of power exerted on him or her in different and shifting ways, and every individual will experience different intersecting constructions of identity.

A case study of western North Carolina that takes into account the lived experience and identity construction of subjects in the region must include *their* perspectives in a project to eliminate sweeping generalizations and stigmatypes. Van Noppen and Van Noppen's history is generally indicative of writing on Appalachia through much of the twentieth century. However, approaches in the study of Appalachia have broadened to provide narratives of the differences among the lived experiences within the region. I draw from this latter tradition in employing the narratives of Louise Broyhill, who lived and was politically active during the period in which Van Noppen and Van Noppen researched and wrote their history. My intention is to create a history that takes into account one woman's experiences, including her lived knowledge of patriarchy and other forms of social control that affect the construction of both gender and sexual identities *and* her own processing of her experiences.[13]

The broader historical context described here is meant to contextualize the time and place of Louise Broyhill's life and activities using the available historical statistical data and documents. Appalachian North Carolina is often mythologized as a premodern or marginally developed agricultural area composed of small family farms. Though western North Carolina has indeed been home to many small-scale subsistence farms, significant changes have taken place in the region over the course of the twentieth and twenty-first centuries. The production of cash crops such as tobacco became common in the early twentieth century, but this source of revenue has fallen off since the 1960s. Communities in the area have experienced modernization in the form of mechanized manufacturing, transportation, and information technologies. Western North Carolina occupies the number one position in the mining and production of mica, which is used in electrical insulation. Since 1950, many local businesses have disappeared, utility companies have tended toward becoming corporate-owned operations, second-home developments arrived in the 1940s and have continually expanded since, and universities and institutions of higher education have become some of the largest employers in otherwise rural communities. Beginning in the 1960s and 1970s, production industries such as furniture and textiles provided other nonagricultural work in the region. However, these industries have reduced their labor pool due to increased mechanization or by moving production facilities overseas. Many undereducated and low-skilled laborers are thus left to compete for the few service jobs available.[14]

Western North Carolina, though a resource-rich region, was and continues to be an area with historically low wages and sparse employment benefits. Statistics for Appalachian North Carolina in 1960 reveal that 40 percent of families lived below the poverty line. Public education in Appalachia remained underfunded, with only 29 percent of western North Carolinians completing high school. The cycle of poverty is alive and well in Appalachian North Carolina; the region is exploited by outside capital interests, such as those controlling mica mining and production, that have not invested in the necessary infrastructure to promote higher living standards. This lack of investment in infrastructure is reflected in high unemployment and poverty rates, poor education, and dilapidated housing structures.[15]

It is in this broadly described socioeconomic context that Louise Robbins Broyhill (1929–) operated as a political advocate for the Republican Party of North Carolina in the latter half of the twentieth century. She is the wife of James Thomas Broyhill (1927–), a member of the Broyhill furniture dynasty in Lenoir, North Carolina, who represented the Tenth District of North Carolina in the US House of Representatives from 1963 to 1986 and served as an appointee to the US Senate from July 14, 1986, to November 4, 1986. The Tenth District during Broyhill's tenure as representative was staunchly Republican and included Alexander, Avery, Burke, Caldwell, Catawba, Cleveland, Gaston, and Watauga counties after the 1960 US Census.

Louise Broyhill was born in Durham, North Carolina, and attended Hollins College and the University of North Carolina, Chapel Hill, but claimed ancestry in the mountains to the west. Her work as a political operative is indicative of how political identities are constructed through material experiences; Broyhill's chronically accessible frames of reference informed how she processed and subsequently engaged in social and political interactions and activities. For example, Broyhill was a participant in various women's political and social groups, including the Congressional Wives Club, the Republican Wives Club, and the Congressional Wives Prayer Group.[16]

Such groups are part of the social and political networks that characterize an entrenched history of political participation among the wives of US politicians, and they gave women access to engage in politics, albeit in limited ways—through supporting their husbands and fund-raising efforts. For instance, the Congressional Wives Club, established in 1908 by an act of Congress, affected Broyhill's lived experiences by allowing her to network with other women active in the political sphere; these social connections would have provided Broyhill with access to resources to engage as a public political speaker and fund-raiser. Broyhill's membership and activity in these organizations indicate the position of political privilege she held relative to most other women in western North Carolina.[17]

Her archived public speeches provide material for understanding how the identity constructions of gender, class, and race represent discursive frames of reference through which Broyhill can claim a political identity rooted in Appalachian place. Broyhill's speeches, which she delivered while working on her husband's political campaigns, construct a narrative of one woman's experience in northwest North Carolina and exemplify how an individual's lived experiences converge to construct a multiple identity.

At the Watauga County Rally on November 2, 1968, three days before Election Day during a presidential election year, Louise Broyhill gave a speech in her husband's stead since he was scheduled to speak at two other political rallies, in Catawba and Caldwell counties, that evening. Broyhill stated: "In the new counties [after redistricting], thousands of people have come forward to volunteer their time, their energy, and their imaginations in the Republican cause. Many of these people have never participated in politics before. They are doing all this for no reward other than a deep belief that good government demands work and attention of good people. They know the truth of the old saying that 'we must master the ways of politics or *be* mastered by those who do.'" These statements seem fairly ordinary for a political speech at a rally, with their underlying themes of patriotism, calls for citizens to participate in the election on the side of the speaker, and the notion of political liberation through participation.[18]

But Broyhill's words take on new meaning when later in the speech she discusses the inclusion of women in political participation:

We can now count the hours before the great decision will be made on November 5. All of us feel a special sense of urgency, but I suppose we women feel a special "something" this year that is difficult to describe. In recent days, I have campaigned with many women and I have talked with them about why they are making their contribution to politics. There was the mother in Alexander County. She is a busy woman already with many responsibilities. She runs a household for her barber husband and she is finishing her college degree as a full-time student. Yet she spent the last Saturday with me on a long tour through this county, meeting and talking to voters. She said to me, "Lots of my friends wonder why I do this, but it isn't hard to say why. For four years, I gave my husband in World War II and nearly lost him. My son is now in special combat training. It is important that I do what I can to make this a better world."[19]

Broyhill, a woman who achieved higher education degrees and was active in the public political sphere, embodied in some ways a basic feminist imperative: that women should be given the same opportunities as men to engage in social and political activities. Although not running for office herself, Broyhill was uniquely positioned to participate in the traditionally masculine realm of American politics through her social and political status as the wife of a member of Congress, and therein had the access and ability to connect and communicate with other women involved in politics. Broyhill occupied an elite position and therein had the resources to publicly encourage all women to become politically engaged, despite their traditional exclusion from the political arena in their communities in Appalachian North Carolina. However, Broyhill's discourse and activities also contain a contradiction to her call for involvement: women's roles in politics are different from those of men, and correspondingly women are to occupy and operate in separate spaces in the public political realm.

Broyhill is in effect reinforcing and sustaining patriarchical power structures rather than effectively resisting and transforming misogyny in public political practices.

Broyhill's identity can be understood as multiple: while she advocated for feminist strategies and issues, many of her social activities and narratives also upheld a perception of a woman's role as having as priorities to "run a household" for her husband and to raise children. In aiding her husband on the campaign trail, raising their three children, serving as PTA president, Brownie Scout leader, and Sunday school teacher, Broyhill showed a loyalty and commitment to her husband, family, and religious values. In a call for women to become more involved in public issues, Broyhill declared in a speech on May 3, 1986, "With women taking a more active role in politics, the face of Tarheel politics has changed dramatically. Republicans have won 9 of the last 13 statewide races—and with the 1986 Senate race, we hope—and will—make that 10 of 14!! If you are not already involved, get involved. If you are involved, stock the freezer and the pantry and get *more* involved." Here she is reminding women not to neglect their primary heteronormative duties and responsibilities to their husbands and families in the private sphere of the home while they participate in the public political sphere, which in effect places increasing demands on women's time, duties to family and society, and labor.[20]

Broyhill ends this particular speech with a quote from Charlotte Whitton—"Whatever women do, they must do twice as well as men to be thought half as good. Luckily this is not difficult"—implying that a woman can fulfill her home and public duties with ease. Here Broyhill is sustaining a discourse that can be seen as somewhat empowering to women since her claim is not only that women can engage in activities in a comparable manner to men, but they can do so with great success.[21]

In a 1968 speech, Broyhill addresses women's special position as guardians of morality. "They say that we women look at problems more emotionally than men. I think that is true and I am glad it is true. We are supposed to provide the security and moral tone of our homes and families. But we must also stand beside our men to help them provide a new moral tone for this nation—to do what we can to help America find its way, again." Broyhill is claiming that women are the moral gatekeepers in the private sphere, but then relegates to men most of the responsibility for holding political offices and making decisions in the public sphere, thus gendering and relegating responsibility of the space of the home to women while awarding decision making and political authority within the public sphere to men.[22]

Broyhill's public speeches are instructive of the feminist theoretical perspective introduced at the start of this chapter. The case of Broyhill indicates how theory can explain complex social relations and illuminate nuances that tell us much about the heterogeneity of regional and individual experience. It may be that Broyhill's experience of feminism is intricate: she internalized resistance to patriarchy in particular forms and functions *at the same time as* she held as part of her identity particular life activities and narratives that supported patriarchical norms and practices. Although she was politically active, caring for her husband and children was a salient part of Louise Broyhill's identity due to social forces that incentivized and sustained models of patriarchy. Recognizing the existence of these tensions rather than imposing unifying interpretations of political identity can help to advance our understanding of power, including the underlying dynamics of female political subjectivities in Appalachian and US political cultures. Broyhill's narratives about women and politics that seem contradictory can be reconciled in an understanding of the self that is multiple, decentered, and complex. Her socially constructed identity reflects her lived experiences of time, place, and social position. Thus, Barvosa's account of constructed, multiple, potentially contradicting identities can accommodate the contradictions contained within Broyhill's political narratives and activities, which encourage women to get involved in politics but in ways that support men's positions of authority and privilege. Broyhill's socialization and repeated lived experiences taught her and incentivized a sense of self that made patriarchical frames of reference chronically accessible to her in public political contexts. Broyhill might have never recognized any internal contradicting feminist/patriarchical frames of reference if the conflicts between these value systems did not become consciously activated at the same time.

In considering Broyhill's narratives in regard to women and politics, we must note her positionality; her agency and identity demonstrate an intersection of race, class, and gender that affected what were, or were not, understood as possible activities for her to engage in. Broyhill, as a member of an elite socioeconomic and political class, enjoyed relative advantage and greater access to resources and spaces in comparison with other women in the region. As such, it may have been relatively easy for her to issue calls for *all* women to participate politically without explicit consideration of the class and racial disadvantage that might limit some women's political access and participation.

I have argued that the boundaries of "acceptable" forms and understandings of politics for individual women were, and are, reflections of the dominant discourses and institutions of patriarchy that functioned in regional practices and affected the lived experiences and identity construction of individuals. Louise Broyhill's narratives show that her positionality and identity construction created boundaries between acceptable and not acceptable forms of political participation for women, based on her gendered understandings of politics. Although not complete, her relative freedom to participate in the political realm stands in stark contrast to the generalized, stigmatyped accounts of other women of her day in Appalachian North Carolina.

Notes

1. Sally Ward Maggard, "Will the Real Daisy Mae Please Stand Up? A Methodological Essay on Gender Analysis in Appalachian Research," *Appalachian Journal* 21, no. 2 (1994): 137; Joan Scott Wallach, *Gender and the Politics of History* (New York: Columbia University Press, 1999).

2. Many studies focus on rural, elite women running for elected office in the United States (see Susan Welsh, "Are Women More Liberal Than Men in the U.S. Congress?" *Legislative Studies Quarterly* 10, no. 1 [1985]: 125–34), or on women members of Congress who are elected from rural districts (see R. K. Sommers-Flanagan, "Do Rural Women Run? Factors Determining Where Women Represent" [honors thesis, Emory University, 2011]). The focus of these studies is not on political participation and attitudes within the Appalachian region, and they generally emphasize quantitative methods that are not able to capture the intricate social and cognitive processes that shape gender identities. See Elizabeth S. D. Engelhardt, "Creating Appalachian Women's Studies: Dancing Away from Granny and Elly May," in *Beyond Hill and Hollow: Original Readings in Appalachian Women's Studies* (Athens: Ohio University Press, 2005) and Judith Ivy Feine, "The Construction of Self by Rural Low-Status Appalachian Women," *Affilia* 6, no. 2 (1991): 45–60 for studies that adopt perspectives of Appalachian women's identities to consider complex social and cognitive processes and to address the political realities and engagement of women in Appalachia.

3. Linda J. Nicholson, introduction to *Feminism/Postmodernism*, ed. Linda J. Nicholson (New York: Routledge, 1990), 1.

4. Matt Wray, *Not Quite White: White Trash and the Boundaries of Whiteness* (Durham, NC: Duke University Press, 2006), 23.

5. Jane Flax, *Thinking Fragments* (Berkeley: University of California Press, 1990), 51.

6. Edwina Barvosa, *Wealth of Selves: Multiple Identities, Mestiza Consciousness, and the Subject of Politics* (College Station: Texas A&M University Press, 2008).

7. Ibid., 106.

8. Ibid., 106, 81.

9. Candace West and Don H. Zimmerman, "Doing Gender," *Gender and Society* 1, no. 2 (1987): 125–51; Francine M. Deutsche, "Undoing Gender," *Gender and Society* 21, no. 1 (2007): 106–27.

10. Pem Davidson Buck, *Worked to the Bone: Race, Class, Power, and Privilege in Kentucky* (New York: Monthly Review, 2001), 3.

11. Cratis Williams, introduction to *Western North Carolina since the Civil War,* by Ina Woestemeyer Van Noppen and John James Van Noppen (Boone: Appalachian Consortium, 1973), vii.

12. Van Noppen and Van Noppen, *Western North Carolina since the Civil War,* 62.

13. More recent work on Appalachian history does take into account a diversity of historical lived experiences, avoiding stigmatypes that perpetuate defaming, objectified, and universalizing constructions of Appalachian residents and communities. Examples are Henry L. Gates, *Colored People: A Memoir* (New York: Random House, 1994); and Abraham Verghese, *My Own Country: A Doctor's Story* (New York: Vintage-Random House, 1995).

14. Mary K. Anglin, *Women, Power, and Dissent in the Hills of Carolina* (Urbana and Chicago: University of Illinois Press, 2002), 119; John Alexander Williams, *Appalachia: A History* (Chapel Hill: University of North Carolina Press, 2002), 393; Thomas Carr, "Site Characteristics of Second Home Locations in Watauga County, North Carolina" (MA thesis, Appalachian State University, 1980), 6; Ronald Eller, *Uneven Ground: Appalachia since 1945* (Lexington: University Press of Kentucky, 2008), 203–4.

15. Eller, *Uneven Ground,* 31–32.

16. Louise Broyhill claimed that her "ancestors rest on a hill near Three Forks Baptist Church." Collection 101, Louise Robbins Broyhill Papers, 1968–1986, W. L. Eury Appalachian Collection, Appalachian State University, Boone, NC.

17. From 1945 until 1993 there was only one woman who represented North Carolina in Congress: Eliza Jane Pratt represented the Eighth District from 1946 to 1947. See the "Biographical Directory of the United States Congress: Pratt, Eliza Jane," in *Congressional Edition: United States Congress,* vol. 5226 (Washington, DC: Government Printing Office, 1908), 155, http://bioguide.congress.gov/scripts/biodisplay.pl?index=P000498 (accessed July 6, 2014).

18. Louise Robbins Broyhill Papers.

19. Ibid.

20. Ibid.

21. Ibid.

22. Ibid.

4

Intersections of Appalachian Identity

Anna Rachel Terman

In his 2012 Appalachian Studies Association keynote address, Si Khan asked, "How much of being a 'real Appalachian' do we attribute to place of birth, parentage, grandparentage, class, sexual orientation, occupation, ethnicity, language, physical ability, religion, race, culture, [and] education[?] Do you have to be born Appalachian? Can you decide to become Appalachian? Can you decide you no longer want to be Appalachian?"[1] These questions acknowledge the dual realities of the region; cultures are rooted in common traditions and histories, but the area is also part of a dynamic and mobile society. In Appalachian studies, numerous deconstructions and reconstructions of Appalachian identity make clear distinctions between popular culture stereotypes about Appalachia and scholarly understandings of the region and its people.[2] Regional identity is recognized to be a dialogic process rather than a fixed conclusion.[3] Nonetheless, a "mythical norm" version of Appalachian identity often remains present in our thinking.[4] Thus, practical ways of understanding Appalachian identity are still needed. In other words, how can we conceptualize an Appalachian identity that is heterogeneous, complex, and socially embedded in the context of efficient communication and research?

In this chapter I examine the complexities of regional identity in Appalachia through a lens of sociological research as a way of distinguishing and analyzing hegemonic and marginal notions of Appalachian identity. First, I introduce *intersectionality,* a feminist theoretical strategy that situates gender identities in the overlapping contexts of race, class, sexuality, age, ability, and other relevant categories of identity. Intersectionality is both a methodological strategy for including multiple voices and perspectives in research and an analytical strategy for developing an understanding of the politics and hierarchies involved in various social problems and issues in Appalachia. Second, I present the utility of intersectionality in the specific context of youth out-migration in the region based on my qualitative sociological research investigating the way gender, race, and sexuality affect sense of belonging among college-educated young adults in West Virginia. Here, intersectionality reveals not only the barriers to belonging in hegemonic contexts but also the potential for alternative forms of belonging in populations that seem to exist outside the norm. Intersectional analysis has been a part of Appalachian studies scholarship for some time, although the term is not often specified.[5] This chapter builds on this work to question how intersectionality can reveal new analytical perspectives and forge new paths for Appalachian research in twenty-first-century contexts.

What Is Intersectionality?

The term *intersectionality* was developed by feminist scholars of color to understand experiences of gender from more than one location. Black feminists have been the leaders of developing intersectional thought dating back to Sojourner Truth's speech "Ain't I a Woman?" which she gave at a women's rights convention in Akron, Ohio, in 1851, to the Combahee River Collective, in which the authors discussed oppression as an interlocking system of racism, sexism, heterosexism, and classism, to Kimberlé Crenshaw, who first used the term in the late 1980s and continues to contribute to this literature.[6] To be sure, women and men of other races and identities participated in developing these ideas as well and continue to do so.

In Sojourner Truth's speech, often cited as one of the earliest uses of intersectionality, she argued for women's rights by comparing the experience of white women to her experience as a black woman. She noted that sexism relied on the notion that women must be treated delicately because they aren't as strong as men and thus cannot be equals. Yet she explained that as a formerly enslaved black woman, she was not treated delicately and was expected to be strong enough to do manual labor. The rhetorical question "And ain't I a woman?" is used to reveal the faulty logic of sexism through the intersecting experiences of race and gender. Truth did not use the term *intersectionality*, of course, but over one hundred years later, black feminists started using it to talk about the ways sexism and racism worked together to create unique struggles for those at the intersection of marginalized gender and racial identities. It has become something of an academic buzzword, but it is widely and usefully employed in various disciplines to better understand gender, race, class, sexuality, and other identities together.

How Is Intersectionality Used?

At a basic level, intersectionality is a methodological and theoretical tool for centering the experiences of marginalized people and acknowledging that our identities are multifaceted.[7] This use is helpful in the Appalachian studies context when we analyze and discuss ideas about people in the region. People across Appalachia tend to have some commonalities: a relationship to land and the environment, cultural traditions, economic systems, and other social issues. However, the ways people experience these issues depend on gender, race, class, sexuality, age, and perhaps other relevant identities like religion and rural or urban identity. Awareness of the way intersectionality influences identity helps us understand that being an Appalachian is not a singular experience based on a stereotypical norm that relies on sexism, racism, classism, and heterosexism for legitimacy. For example, just as black feminists needed new language to express the intersectional experience of gender and race, people of color in Appalachia have also created language to express the intersection of place and race. Poet Frank X Walker coined the term *Affrilachian* to create a space and identity that acknowledge his place and race identities, which could otherwise be interpreted as mutually exclusive.[8] This intersectional expression gained popularity along with the development of an Affrilachian artist collective. Similarly, some people who identify as Appalachian and Asian use the term *Appalasian*.[9] In these and other cases, intersectionality is a helpful tool for mapping Appalachia across multiple identities and regional experiences. Although scholars in Appalachian studies continue to highlight identities that help inform our understanding of people and society in the region, intersectionality as a theory points us toward more possibilities for understanding the ways multiple identities together influence people in Appalachia.[10]

Intersectionality also provides a theoretical and methodological framework for better understanding the systems of power in our society.[11] Processes of oppression and stratification in society map our intersectional identities onto "appropriate" and "inappropriate" spaces and places of access. The political implications of the way identities and place intersect in Appalachia are at the core of many of the issues that continue to perpetuate the marginalization of Appalachian communities. For example, class and place intersect to create a complex system in which environmental disasters and daily environmental hazards are allowed to persist; gender and place intersect to reproduce regional masculinities and femininities tied to an unsustainable economic system, leaving men and women struggling to find satisfying and financially viable work; and sexuality and place intersect to divide rural and urban communities as dangerous or safe for lesbian, gay, bisexual, transgender, and/or queer (LGBTQ) people.[12] By highlighting these examples, I am suggesting how an intersectional approach to Appalachia offers a helpful and sophisticated way of mapping the various systems of power that manifest in the Appalachian context.

In addition to its use as a way of understanding Appalachian identities as multifaceted and Appalachian place as political, the concept of intersectionality is a potentially powerful tool for social justice in the region.[13] Much of the work being done both in Appalachian studies scholarship and Appalachian activism requires working across boundaries and identities. For example, there are people working across class lines to develop alternative energy production that alleviates job loss and environmental disasters, like those involved in Sustainable Williamson in Williamson, West Virginia; people working across racial and place divides to confront the prison industrial complex development in the region, like the Central Appalachian Prisoner Support Network; and writers, musicians, and visual artists who are creating new representations of Appalachia, like authors Crystal Good and Jeff Mann, and documentarian Elaine McMillion Sheldon, all of whom contribute to defying oppressive narratives about the region. Knowing more about how people are able to effectively negotiate these intersections is an important step in advancing these projects. Intersectionality is used in academia as a theory of identity and power, a methodological strategy, and an application of scholarship to social justice. As such, it is a particularly relevant theoretical and methodological strategy to employ in Appalachian studies, a discipline rooted in movements for social justice.

Intersectionality and Sense of Belonging among Young Adults in West Virginia

In her 2012 collection of poems, *Appalachian Elegy*, bell hooks says, "While I do not claim an identity as Appalachian, I do claim a solidarity, a sense of belonging, that makes me one with the Appalachian past of my ancestors: black, Native American, white, all 'people of one blood' who made homeplace in isolated landscapes where they could invent themselves, where they could savor a taste of freedom."[14] In a similar vein, hooks makes the connection between identity, belonging, and community in her 2009 book, *Belonging: A Culture of Place*.[15] hooks argues for creating a version of Martin Luther King Jr's "beloved communities" that includes belonging as an act of resistance to racism and dominator culture and as an act affirming inclusion and a culture of place. She describes her own return to Kentucky as the end result of her individual struggle to reconcile various aspects of her identity, including her sense of belonging. Thus, to hooks, beloved communities are places where people create more belonging among diverse people. As hooks notes, the goal is less about a quantitative measure of diversity and more about the qualitative accessibility of belonging. Fostering an Appalachian identity and/ or a sense of belonging in Appalachia must account for the intersectional experiences of people in order to be effective and just.

As an example of how intersectionality is applicable to understanding people and place in Appalachia, I offer qualitative data from two years of sociological research conducted in West Virginia on the ways gender, race, and sexuality affect sense of belonging and plans for migration among college-educated young adults. The qualitative data are based on a larger research project that included seven focus groups with a total of sixty-five current college students and twenty-seven individual interviews with college graduates under age forty in West Virginia. I organized the focus groups at three different schools in three different counties in the state, with collections of students based on their membership in gender-equality, LGBTQ, and African American student organizations. I developed the individual interview sample of college graduates through community- or identity-based organizations across twelve counties, specifically sampling for women, LGBTQ people, and people of color.[16] All names of people, schools, and places referenced below are pseudonyms. I purposely included people who had grown up in West Virginia and people who had moved to West Virginia from elsewhere in my sample, as both of these groups make up the population of young people in Appalachia. I chose to focus on the way gender, race, and sexuality intersect with place identities because I knew from my own experience working with youth in Appalachia that these identity categories are meaningful in relation to place. Furthermore, gender, race, and sexuality hold unique meanings in the historical and cultural context of Appalachia and are often used as fodder for stereotypes about Appalachian identity. In addition, a traditionally white, heteropatriarchal, working-class culture, in which heterosexual relationships form the basis of families and the male members of families hold the most power in society, is still symbolically, if not materially, relevant for people in the region.

The Intersection of Sexuality, Race, and Place in Appalachia

The experiences of Appalachia's LGBTQ community indicate how a connection to place is negotiated through struggles between internal ideas and external messages about Appalachia. For example, Joe, a white gay male college graduate, discussed the way he reconciles various aspects of his identity in relation to symbolic and material realities in Appalachia.

> I'm wearing a hoodie, a flannel shirt, a pair of skinny jeans, Kenneth Cole boots, and a scarf. This is my postmodern Appalachian hipster look. I always call them my costumes for the day. I love those traditional Appalachian, [not] like banjos and building skills, but my generation's traditional Appalachian activities. I like to go mudding; I like to go four-wheeling; I like to get dirty; I like to go dig ramps; I like all that stuff. And when I go to do that, I'm wearing coveralls and my work boots and all that sort of stuff. I have a million different camo things. If I'm meeting someone for coffee or something like this [interview], I'll put on an outfit closer to what I have on today. I do sort of do that transition back and forth thing. I think I'm always myself. I don't feel like I'm ever masking something. I feel like there's a piece of each of those groups in me, so when I'm with those groups, I access that in myself. I think that makes it easier. I think if people were able to do that, there would be a whole lot less global issues . . . it makes acceptance come much easier. I can absolutely go to the dirtiest, dingiest, roughest redneck bar and talk with the biggest, baddest redneck with the most tattoos of the Rebel flag and be fine with him by the end of the night.

As this quote illustrates, Joe described his ability to reconcile his intersecting identities throughout his interview. His experience corroborates the growing academic literature that disrupts the "metronormative" narrative of sexuality in the United States, which maintains that LGBTQ people must seek out urban communities in order to thrive.[17] Indeed, this metronormative assumption is based on an analysis of sexuality that does not take into account the intersection of sexuality and place identity.

Similarly, Erin, a white queer woman college graduate, talked about finding a place in an urban area outside Appalachia where her sexuality and place identity came together for the first time, which ultimately led her to move back to West Virginia.

> I got really, really into a gay country bar that I was a regular [at] for about a year and a half, and it was amazing. I feel sort of ridiculous when I talk about how important this country bar was to me, but I feel it was the first time that I found a space that was queer and sort of celebrated rural America. Even though it was in the city, but it was about country music. We were dancing with other queer people to songs about farming and songs about the South. I would get so emotional there sometimes; I would just tear up. I think I found some of that sense of belonging in terms of being queer and being out, but also in a way that wasn't like, "Oh, the South is fucked up."

Erin's experience shows that for many young people in Appalachia, the struggle to reconcile their intersecting identities can push people out *and* pull them into the region. In this way, gender, race, and sexuality identities can be oppressive in some contexts and privileging in others. The ability to negotiate these identities is a process that involves both internal and external factors.

In another case, intersectional analysis of African American experiences in Appalachia provides knowledge of the complex ways a minority racial status can hinder, empower, or affirm a connection to place in Appalachia. A woman interviewed from an African American student group at Allegheny University, who grew up outside Appalachia, described the intersection of race and place in the context of her family's ideas of West Virginia. "Every time I go home, my family, they kinda make jokes, but they're not funny jokes, they're like, racism jokes. They say, 'Oh, they gonna lynch you over there' and stuff like that. They really think that all West Virginia is like that." In this quote, the student expresses the tension between external and internal messages about place. Indeed, many students in this focus group who had grown up outside Appalachia mentioned being afraid, specifically using the language of "being lynched," when they first came to West Virginia. Some of them subsequently experienced positive aspects of the community, but others described negative experiences. One man in the student group said, "I kinda like it here. There's a lot of resources here that I've been able to take advantage of. I've met some people from the surrounding area, and they're not that bad. They'll help you in any way you need help." In this case, the student had been hired as an assistant sports coach at a local high school. On the other hand, the same student who recalled the "racism jokes" also encountered hostility to the idea that she belonged in West Virginia. She described being stopped at various places on campus and asked to show her student identification. During one incident, she was going to the campus recreation center when she was asked for identification and for her bag to be searched. She said, "I've never seen them check anyone's bag. . . . Why did he need to see my ID when there's other people that walked right past him?" Overall, these students' sense of belonging was very precarious; their relationship with place was hindered by stereotypes and lived realities of racism.

It is useful here to juxtapose the experiences of the Allegheny African American student group and the Lockwood African American student group, whose members overall reported more positive interactions with people in the community. This difference is contextualized by data from the Lockwood focus group in which students talked about developing connections to the community and area as part of the curriculum and school programs. One woman student explained,

You learn a lot about Appalachia, and in all my classes Appalachia comes up, and before I came here, I thought it was the Appal-eight-chian Mountains. It's the Appal-at-chian Mountains [*laughs*]. I was corrected, but Appalachia just has a unique culture, and I have a respect for the people. I have a respect for the diversity. People don't think diversity when they think Appalachia, but there's English, Scot-Irish; African Americans have had a huge impact in Appalachian culture and music, and it's crazy how much you learn, and I just didn't know that coming to West Virginia. Some of my friends were like, "Where's West Virginia? Oh, western Virginia?" No, it's a state [*laughs*]. There's just so much history and culture here, and the beauty and the environmental movement coming to West Virginia right now is gaining a lot of strength.

Here the student describes a feeling of empowerment gained through her association with Appalachia. Notably, she explains that she learned about the diverse identities that make up Appalachia. These data reveal how the intersectional experience of race and place for students can be highly influenced by their institutions and community. For the students at Lockwood University, their student group included established programs to integrate students into the community. In addition, education on the region and diversity within the region was available in the curriculum, which helped the student from the Lockwood group connect to the culture and community in West Virginia. The students in the Allegheny group, on the other hand, had some institutional support, but the programs seemed to be less established and connections between students and the community were less encouraged.

Data from the college graduates showed that the intersection of race and place could affirm and even strengthen a sense of belonging in Appalachia. For example, Christine, an African American and Native American heterosexual woman said,

I received more negativity when I would leave the state and people found out that I was from West Virginia. I went to DC once for a conference. I was the West Virginia representative for this conference. Someone came up to me, and it was a black man, an older black man, and he was peering at my neck. I remember asking, "What are you looking for?" He said, "Well, I'm looking for the rope burn." He was like, "Yeah, if you're from West Virginia, you must have some rope burns on you or something." I remember just being so angry and feeling so disrespected that not only someone would have the gall to say that to me, to my face, but it also would be another black person that would make a joke about someone trying to hang me just because I'm from West Virginia. It was just really upsetting, I guess, to realize that so many Americans were so, so biased and so, I guess, shallow, to think that there aren't black people in West Virginia. That makes me even more proud and happy to say, "Yes, I'm from West Virginia." It's okay for us to be here. It doesn't make me want to leave. It just makes me want to move more people in.

"You, come move here." If anything, I guess [through those experiences] my sense of belonging was stronger. I'd much rather be here, where I'm welcomed, than out there, thinking, like everyone else, that I'm not welcome.

When Christine says that she finds more belonging in West Virginia through her racial identity, it is because only here does she find the capacity for community through both her race and place identities. Her reaction to the experience at the out-of-state conference reflects the struggle for those outside the white, heteropatriarchal rural cultural norm to reconcile their intersecting gender, race, sexuality, and place identities.

The Intersection of Multiple Identities in Appalachia

Finally, it is important to note that although I focus specifically on sexuality, race, and place in the previous section, the study participants, like all of us every day, are experiencing multiple identities at once, not just two or three. Deidre, an African American and white biracial heterosexual woman college graduate, expressed the satisfaction she felt in being able to embody multiple binary identities.

I think for me there's definitely a sincere struggle in terms of being biracial, being an ambitious woman. . . . I think having a [city] influence makes me different than a lot of other "West Virginians," you know, but I still love that I grew up with motorcycles and four-wheelers and hunting season. . . . Right now I love the duplicity of my life, and I think that alone makes me unique—that I crave rural and urban, that I embrace being black and white, that I am a creative artist but also a business professional, and to me that's how I live my life.

As the experiences of Deidre and the other participants show, Appalachian identity is constructed through an intersectional process in which gender, race, and sexuality continue to play important roles. To be sure, these particular identities are not the only relevant categories of analysis in Appalachian studies. As scholars, we can use an intersectional approach to explore and determine which identities may be most relevant in specific contexts and which identities are most salient at different points in time. Related through the data above, intersectional methodology and analysis reveal the multiple identities that surround who is, who might become, and who might decide to no longer be "Appalachian." Furthermore, intersectionality helps us to better understand the systems of power, in this case surrounding gender, race, sexuality, class, and place, which affect the way people are oriented toward their communities and to Appalachia more generally.

Women, people of color, and LGBTQ people occupy a minority status and must negotiate their belonging in the context of the hegemonic, white, and heteropatriarchal working-class culture of West Virginia. I used an intersectional approach to bring the experiences of people of these identities to the center of analysis. However, Hae Yeon Choo and Myra Marx Ferree critique intersectional methodology and analysis that stop at merely "giving voice" to multiple identities or simply highlighting the places in the data where intersectional identities seem to matter in relation to a dominant norm.[18] They argue instead that intersectionality should be used to examine the systems that reproduce inequalities. Still, centering the experiences of marginalized identities leads us toward a process of redefining ideas about Appalachia. Feminist theorists suggest that applying an intersectional method allows us to analyze multiple identities together and confront the issue at hand more robustly.[19] When we center marginalized people in our analysis, we find information and solutions to problems that are not just particularly relevant but that can be universally applicable.[20] Although I focus on gender, race, sexuality, and class in the previous examples, underneath these categories are further intersectional identities based on age, education, and location. These particular intersections are relevant to the analysis of stereotypes and lived realities in the region. Specifically, intersectional analysis reveals that the idea that Appalachia is not a place for young people, educated people, women, people of color, and/or LGBTQ people is both a stereotype and a lived reality for many.

How Are Intersectional Identities in Appalachia Relevant to Social, Political, Environmental, and Economic Issues?

Broadly, intersectionality holds great potential in Appalachian studies as a tool for understanding what black feminist sociologist Patricia Hill Collins calls "the new politics of community."[21] Collins argues that as feminists have transformed our thinking about the family through questioning the gender roles and intersections of power within the family structure, we can also better understand the systems of power in communities, which she argues are too often assumed to be private-sphere, naturally occurring institutions rather than social constructs. Collins says, "Political leaders know that when people cease seeing themselves as part of a mass, a mob, a collectivity, a population, or a public, and instead claim a sense of belonging to a community, they are primed for political analysis and action."[22] Our communities in Appalachia hold power whether they are identity- and idea-based communities or place-based communities at the local, state, or regional level. Appalachian studies has given us a language for and orientation toward these various types of communities in the region, which has helped form an Appalachian political identity. Thus, fostering the development of an Appalachian identity can be a powerful strategy for growing sustainable communities through alternative economic systems, cultural traditions, and organizational and coalitional strategies; it is also a means of confronting poverty, environmental degradation, health risks, and educational challenges.

As Appalachian studies scholars Barbara Ellen Smith and Stephen L. Fisher point out, "Deliberate claiming of identity can be an act of resistance, a way of fighting back against Appalachian stereotypes, which in turn can undergird organizing against exploitation and discrimination in the region." However, they warn, "Place-based identity is always at risk of becoming place-bound, that is, insular and exclusionary. The tendency for place to be romantically conflated with 'community,' envisioned as a harmonious (and homogenous) space of shared interests and values, often informs such insularity." Smith and Fisher argue that only when place-based identity is "critical, relational, and extroverted" and used as a bridge that creates links among people and groups does it have the potential for transformative community building.[23] In other words, the work of redefining place-based identities and reassessing the roles of people in communities is an essential component of effective and socially just action. Similarly, Anna Carastathis argues that identity "coalitions" are an overlooked but key component of intersectionality.[24] Carastathis points out that identity-based groups are always intersectional and coalitional or potentially coalitional due to the fact that no group is completely homogenous. Collins, quoted above, notes that intersectional analysis remains underdeveloped in thinking through how communities, specifically, are sites for the perpetuation or disruption of social inequalities.[25] Appalachian studies scholars are well positioned to contribute to the development of this literature by using intersectionality to analyze the politics of community, particularly by identifying the ways privilege and oppression orient people to their communities.

It is precisely this political connection between identity and community (that is, a space where systems of power are reproduced and/or reduced) that makes the intersectional positions of people within (and in relation to) their communities a crucial component of realizing social justice in Appalachia. Katie Richards-Schuster and Rebecca O'Doherty discuss the role of youth in reenvisioning Appalachian communities: "Young people in central Appalachia face significant challenges becoming active participants in their communities and in making the decisions that shape their lives. They grapple with confusing messages and experiences that both celebrate and denigrate their culture and communities. At the same time, the history of resistance, the desire to connect to culture, people, community, and land, and the richness of culturally based assets have the potential to position youth in central Appalachia as talented and innovative change makers." Here, Richards-Shuster and O'Doherty reference the tension that exists between youth and communities. They conclude, "When young people re-envision themselves and their communities, they begin to create a movement of youth activists staying home and reconstructing Appalachia."[26] Supporting a movement of youth community activists in Appalachia is needed in light of regional youth out-migration and threats to community sustainability.

Si Kahn's questions with which I began this chapter, "Do you have to be born Appalachian? Can you decide to become Appalachian? Can you decide you no longer want to be Appalachian?" are provocative because the answers are at the crux of the politics of community and sustainability in Appalachia. We need knowledge about the relationship between identities and communities, and Appalachian studies can contribute significantly in the classroom, through research, and through activism. I conclude by returning to the assertion that scholarship and action rooted in intersectionality offer a rich and sophisticated model for those of us in Appalachian studies struggling to analyze race, gender, sexuality, and other identity issues. Incorporating intersectional thought into our scholarship helps us better acknowledge the methodological and theoretical traditions that continue to influence our understanding of the role of identity in Appalachia. Furthermore, intersectional analysis provides a path for moving beyond constructions and reconstructions of Appalachia and Appalachians to instead explore new and better ideas for engaging more people in solutions to issues facing the region.

Notes

1. Si Kahn, "Organizing, Culture, and Resistance in Appalachia: Past, Present, and Future," *Journal of Appalachian Studies* 18, no. 1 (2012): 21–22.

2. A few examples of this ongoing scholarship are Henry D. Shapiro, *Appalachia on Our Mind: The Southern Mountains and Mountaineers in the American Consciousness, 1870-1920* (Chapel Hill: University of North Carolina Press, 1978); Dwight D. Billings, Gurney Norman, and Katherine Ledford, eds., *Backtalk from Appalachia: Confronting Stereotypes* (Lexington: University Press of Kentucky, 1999); Barbara Ellen Smith, Stephen Fisher, Phillip Obermiller, David Whisnant, Emily Satterwhite, and Rodger Cunningham, "Appalachian Identity: A Roundtable Discussion," *Appalachian Journal* 38, no. 1 (2010): 56-76; and Emily Satterwhite, *Dear Appalachia: Readers, Identity, and Popular Fiction since 1878* (Lexington: University Press of Kentucky, 2011).

3. Alan Banks, Dwight Billings, and Karen Tice, "Appalachian Studies, Resistance, and Postmodernism," in *Fighting Back in Appalachia: Traditions of Resistance and Change,* ed. Stephen L. Fisher (Philadelphia: Temple University Press, 1993), 283–301.

4. Audre Lorde, "Age, Race, Class and Sex: Women Redefining Difference," in *Sister Outsider: Essays and Speeches* (Berkeley, CA: Crossing, 2007), 114–23.

5. A few examples are Barbara Ellen Smith, ed., *Neither Separate nor Equal: Women, Race, and Class in the South* (Philadelphia: Temple University Press, 1999); Elizabeth S. D. Engelhardt, ed. *Beyond Hill and Hollow: Original Readings in Appalachian Women's Studies* (Athens: Ohio University Press, 2005); Ancella R. Bickley and Lynda Ann Ewen, eds., *Memphis Tennessee Garrison: The Remarkable Story of a Black Appalachian Woman* (Athens: Ohio University Press, 2001); and Phillip J. Obermiller, M. Kathryn Brown, Donna Jones, Michael E. Maloney, and Thomas E. Wagner, "Identity Matters: Building an Urban Appalachian Movement in Cincinnati," in *Transforming Places: Lessons from Appalachia,* ed. Stephen L. Fisher and Barbara Ellen Smith (Urbana: University of Illinois Press, 2012), 63–77. In addition, there are numerous studies involving identity categories such as gender, race, or class in the context of Appalachian identity that are also intersectional analyses, although they may not explicitly connect these intersections with intersectionality in feminist thought.

6. Truth's speech can be accessed in multiple places. I suggest watching a video of author Alice Walker reading the speech in 2006: Alice Walker, *Alice Walker Reads Sojourner Truth,* 2008, https://www.youtube.com/watch?v=EsjdLL3MrKk (accessed January 4, 2016); Combahee River Collective, "The Combahee River Collective Statement," in *Home Girls: A Black Feminist Anthology,* ed. Barbara Smith (New York: Kitchen Table-Women of Color Press, 1977), 264–74; Kimberlé Crenshaw, "Demarginalizing the Intersection of Race and Sex: A Black Feminist Critique of Antidiscrimination Doctrine, Feminist Theory and Antiracist Politics," *University of Chicago Legal Forum* (1989): 139–67. See also Sumi Cho, Kimberlé Williams Crenshaw, and Leslie McCall,

"Toward a Field of Intersectionality Studies: Theory, Applications, and Practice," *Signs: Journal of Women in Culture and Society* 38, no. 4 (2013): 785–810.

7. Bonnie Thorton Dill and Ruth Enid Zambrana, "Critical Thinking about Inequality: An Emerging Lens," in *Emerging Intersection: Race, Class, and Gender in Theory, Policy, and Practice*, ed. Bonnie Thorton Dill and Ruth Enid Zambrana (Piscataway, NJ: Rutgers University Press, 2009), 5–7.

8. Mitchel L. H. Douglas, "What's in a Name?" in *The Affrilachian Poets*, http:// http://www.theaffrilachianpoets.com/history.html (accessed January 4, 2016).

9. Mikiko Crawford, "Autoethnography of an Appalasian" (paper presented at the Appalachian Studies Association Annual Conference, Huntington, WV, March 28–30, 2014).

10. Examples include Kathy Kahn, *Hillbilly Women* (Garden City, NY: Doubleday, 1973); Marilou Awiakta, *Selu: Seeking the Corn-Mother's Wisdom* (Golden, CO: Fulcrum, 1994); Mary Ann Hinsdale, Helen M. Lewis, and S. Maxine Waller, *It Comes from the People: Community Development and Local Theology* (Philadelphia: Temple University Press, 1995); John C. Inscoe, *Appalachians and Race: The Mountain South from Slavery to Segregation* (Lexington: University Press of Kentucky, 2001); and Jeff Mann, *Loving Mountains, Loving Men* (Athens: University of Ohio Press, 2005).

11. Dill and Zambrana, "Critical Thinking about Inequality," 7–11.

12. Shannon Elizabeth Bell and Richard York, "Community Economic Identity: The Coal Industry and Ideology Construction in West Virginia," *Rural Sociology* 75, no. 1 (2010): 111–43; Rebecca R. Scott, "Dependent Masculinity and Political Culture in Pro-Mountaintop Removal Discourse; or, How I Learned to Stop Worrying and Love the Dragline," *Feminist Studies* 33, no. 3 (2007): 484–509; Silas House, "Our Secret Places in the Waiting World: Becoming a New Appalachia," in *37th Annual Appalachian Studies Association Conference*, 2013, https://www.youtube.com/watch?v=ZR7A69yOL-k (accessed January 4, 2016).

13. Dill and Zambrana, "Critical Thinking about Inequality," 11–13.

14. bell hooks, *Appalachian Elegy: Poetry and Place* (Lexington: University Press of Kentucky, 2012), 4.

15. bell hooks, *Belonging, A Culture of Place* (New York: Routledge, 2009).

16. This sample structure is useful for using intersectionality as a basic way of understanding Appalachian identity as multifaceted. However, it is limited by the way that, especially in the focus groups, participants were more likely to discuss gender if they identified as women or transgender, race if they identified as black, African American, biracial, or multiracial, and sexuality if they identified as lesbian, gay, bisexual, or queer. Thus, experiences of being in the majority were less explicit. In addition, participants in my sample represent an educationally privileged group in Appalachia and one that may be predisposed to community participation. Nonetheless, the data describing experiences of marginal identities and the way they intersect with place reveal important information about the ways young adults negotiate Appalachian identity.

17. For examples, see Scott Herring, *Another Country: Queer Anti-urbanism* (New York: New York University Press, 2010); and Mary L. Gray, *Out in the Country: Youth, Media, and Queer Visibility in Rural America* (New York: New York University Press, 2009).

18. Hae Yeon Choo and Myra Marx Ferree, "Practicing Intersectionality in Sociological Research: A Critical Analysis of Inclusions, Interactions, and Institutions in the Study of Inequalities," *Sociological Theory* 28, no. 2 (2010): 129–49.

19. Leslie McCall, "The Complexity of Intersectionality," *Signs: Journal of Women in Culture and Society* 30, no. 3 (2005): 1771–1800.

20. For examples, see Andrea Smith, "Beyond the Politics of Inclusion: Violence against Women of Color and Human Rights," *Meridians: Feminism, Race, Transnationalism* 4, no. 2 (2004): 120–24; and Catherine MacKinnon, "Intersectionality as Method: A Note," *Signs: Journal of Women in Culture and Society* 38, no. 4 (2013): 1019–30.

21. Patricia Hill Collins, "The New Politics of Community," *American Sociological Review* 75, no. 1 (2010): 7–30.

22. Ibid., 12.

23. Barbara Ellen Smith and Stephen L. Fisher, "Conclusion: Transformations in Place," in Fisher and Smith, *Transforming Places,* 275.

24. Anna Carastathis, "Identity Categories as Potential Coalitions," *Signs: Journal of Women in Culture and Society* 38, no. 4 (2013): 941–65.

25. Collins, "The New Politics of Community," 24–25.

26. Katie Richards-Schuster and Rebecca O'Doherty, "Appalachian Youth Re-envisioning Home, Re-making Identities," in Fisher and Smith, *Transforming Places,* 78, 90.

Part 2

Language, Rhetoric, and Literacy

5

Appalachia Beyond the Mountains

Ethical, Community-Based Research in Urban Appalachian Neighborhoods

Kathryn Trauth Taylor

Introducing Urban Appalachia

Place-based researchers in Appalachian studies have argued that "virtually every place on the globe has long been shaped by and continues to participate in networks of relationships that stretch far beyond its boundaries."[1] As a third-generation Appalachian migrant growing up in Cincinnati, I sometimes felt disconnected from the larger Appalachian region. It wasn't until I took an undergraduate Appalachian literature course that I recognized my family and myself as Appalachian. In this course, I was introduced to local nonprofit organizations like the Urban Appalachian Council (UAC), which is devoted to bettering the lives of Appalachian migrants through social services, educational advocacy, employment training, and cultural programs. Thanks to the institutional efforts of the UAC and the artistic endeavors of many urban Appalachian and Affrilachian artists throughout the city, I became aware of the diverse, quilt-worked identity that Appalachians could create beyond the mountains. Volunteering at the UAC and following the Appalachian arts scenes in Cincinnati helped me understand the important role language can play in empowering people to "talk back" to cultural stereotypes and "own" their Appalachian identities. My research in the field of rhetoric and composition aims to harness the emotive and symbolic powers of place—especially for people upholding Appalachian identity in regions that aren't geographically Appalachian.

Rhetoric is a field of study that examines how language makes meaning, shapes conceptions, and inspires action. Undergraduate students often learn about rhetoric as part of their introductory composition courses, in which they write rhetorical analysis essays analyzing the impact of particular language choices in political speeches, literary works, and even advertisements. As an art form and an area of study, rhetoric has roots that date back to ancient Greece; Aristotle defined rhetoric as the art of finding the available means of persuasion in a given situation. Today, rhetoricians trace literacy and language practices across cultures, analyze the political implications of media representations, conduct qualitative research within diverse discourse communities, and perform a number of other research strategies to assess the power of language to shape people's lives.

In this chapter, I examine how rhetoric shapes the identities of people within a diverse urban community of Appalachian migrants where ties to Appalachia are sustained through writing stories of homeplaces, performing old-time music, and rhetorically naming themselves "urban Appalachians." My chapter offers a methodological model for conducting community-based research that builds ethical relationships among researchers, artists, and community residents and helps generate respect for groups whose identities are often disrespected. After sharing preliminary findings from a yearlong community-based research study, I conclude the chapter with suggestions for conducting ethical research within local identity-based communities.

As I began developing a dissertation project in the field of rhetoric and composition, I was drawn to advocacy efforts happening within urban Appalachian neighborhoods in Cincinnati. Because I wanted to obtain a broad view of Appalachian advocacy outside the geographic region, I developed a site-based study at the nonprofit Urban Appalachian Council. My study involved an analysis of three types of rhetoric: (1) the institutional rhetorics in the UAC's public documents (the organization's website, professional resources, research efforts, and historical archives), (2) the everyday rhetoric used by community residents who utilized the services of the UAC, and (3) the artistic rhetorics emerging from diverse writers, poets, and musicians at the UAC and around Cincinnati. My goal was to triangulate these

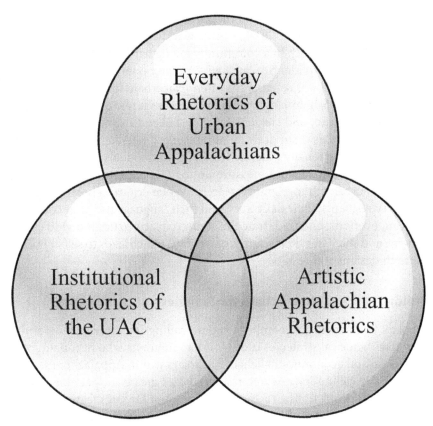

Figure 5.1. Three groups of study at the Urban Appalachian Council

data sets to see how different groups understand and represent their urban Appalachian identities. In so doing, this study methodologically demonstrates how the study of rhetoric makes clear the process of place-making, as individuals and groups construct their identities, and thus place, through language (see figure 5.1).

Most representations of Appalachians have ignored the diverse reality of the population, focusing more on stereotypes than on the lived realities of everyday life. In the 1950s, Berea College's Roscoe Giffin argued at a conference presentation that southern Appalachian migrants came from a "dysfunctional mountain culture" that starkly contrasted with "the modern 'rational' model of city living."[2] Today, decades after the largest migration waves, Appalachian migrants and their descendants continue to face such stereotypes while living in "multiethnic, working-class neighborhoods in and around Cincinnati."[3] In a community facing harsh economic struggle, claiming Appalachian identity can lead to greater oppression.

In literacy studies, researchers often exacerbate these challenges by comparing Appalachian language to school standards, drawing attention to residents' illiteracy and lack of education.[4] Ellen Cushman has observed that literacy scholars often draw on phrases like "illiterate," "primarily oral cultures," or "functionally illiterate" to "define individuals by what they do not have, do not do, do not measure up to."[5] She cites this as a common problem in urban ethnographic research: "When critical scholars describe inner city residents, their daily lives, and their language use, they too often demean, overlook, and underrate the commonplace tactics individuals use to name and challenge their sources of trouble," which leads to self-fulfilling research designs and results.[6]

Building Ethical Research Methodologies

Scholars in rhetoric and composition are calling for more studies of the everyday rhetorical strategies used by urban migrants who negotiate complex social and economic challenges.[7] Scholars within Appalachian studies are similarly calling for research that generates greater respect for diverse Appalachian peoples.[8] The research methods and findings featured in this chapter reveal some of the everyday rhetorical struggles and strategies of urban Appalachians, and the institutional and artistic rhetorics that support or intensify those struggles. Before reporting preliminary findings, I offer an overview of the research methods used in this study and discuss some strategies for building research methodologies that generate respect for groups struggling to gain it.

How might academic research help generate respect for groups offered "little or no respect" in order to "help people to improve their current conditions"?[9] I developed this question by merging calls for community-based advocacy in Appalachian studies with the concerns Ralph Cintron articulated in his ethnographic study of a Latino migrant community near Chicago and the issues explored by indigenous writer Linda Tuhiwai Smith in her book *Decolonizing Methodologies*. Reflecting on her experiences with academic researchers, Smith has expressed frustration: "At a common sense level research was talked about both in terms of its absolute worthlessness to us, the indigenous world, and its absolute usefulness to those who wielded it as an instrument. It told us things already known, suggested things that would not work, and made careers for people who already had jobs."[10] Based on these problems and inequalities, I argue that ethical, community-based research methodologies should

1. provide space for participants' voices and reflections in research analyses;
2. question the implications of the representations created through their research;
3. accept roles created for them by participants, even if that includes work not directly beneficial to writer-researcher-professors;
4. respond to participants with awareness and generosity; and
5. reflect upon power and difference in scenes of research.

Such research methods aim to empower research participants. To build these methods into my own yearlong research study, I first invited participants into the process of defining research questions, selecting data and stories that should be analyzed and shared, and making final cuts and edits to their reflections, life experiences, and other data. Second, participants' reflections written from their own points of view were incorporated into the data analysis as well as my interview and observation results. As Amy Clark and Nancy Hayward state in their recent book, *Talking Appalachian: Voice, Identity, and Community* (2013), "Neither research studies nor creative works alone can begin to cover the depth and breadth of what there is to know about the varieties of Appalachian English."[11] As you read the following research findings, I hope you also discover that the creative pieces "tell the story that research cannot."[12]

Growing Individual Empowerment from Institutional Rhetoric

In a community already undergoing significant economic hardship, maintaining Appalachian identity can result in increased stereotyping and individual oppression. However, because the advocacy efforts of the Urban Appalachian Council are bound to a shared sense of identity, interviews with community residents revealed that claiming Appalachian identity within this particular institutional context can become an empowering move.

Eighteen residents and leaders at the UAC agreed to participate in my research study, and of these, I selected five female students, two instructors, and the UAC education director for more detailed interviews and observations. Findings from my study suggest that residents' positive associations with their Appalachian heritage is encouraged through many of the institutional rhetorics that circulate at the UAC. Before sharing residents' perspectives, I will provide a few examples of the UAC's institutional rhetoric.

In the 1990s, the UAC developed an intake protocol to introduce incoming residents to Appalachian migration and culture. Instructors show newcomers a map and list of Appalachian counties and cities and ask them to point out their (or their families') place of origin or birth. In addition, the UAC provides documents about respecting diverse cultural identities, information about the historical migration of Appalachians into cities across the midwestern United States, and bibliographies of Appalachian documentaries, films, and books. In other words, both geographic and cultural materials are presented to residents to promote the community's identification with Appalachian culture and heritage. Institutional rhetorics have a direct impact on community residents' everyday rhetorics and cultural identities. Nearly all the participants interviewed in my study discovered their Appalachian heritage as part of the Urban Appalachian Council's cultural and educational programs.

Two women in particular, Sharon and Patty, linked the UAC's institutional rhetorics with their shared Appalachian identities. Sharon grew up in Price Hill in an urban Appalachian family. Her grandfather was born in eastern Kentucky but migrated north to find work. He and her grandmother found a home on River Road in Cincinnati when Sharon's mother was little. After dropping out of school in the eighth grade, Sharon had a decent job with a cleaning service until she was laid off in 2009. Her first instinct was to get her GED, but government regulations wouldn't allow her to receive unemployment and welfare (which would support her to go back to school) at the same time. Knowing that she needed a GED to be employable, she eventually "had to go on welfare to do my GED." Thus Sharon came to the UAC in 2009 to attend GED classes, hoping also to "prove to my daughter that the GED and education is very important." She was not aware of her Appalachian heritage before she started classes, which was around the time that her grandmother was nearing death. Sharon then discovered that she had over 150 relatives living in Tennessee. They attended the funeral and told stories about her grandma playing the banjo on the porch of their mountain shack in her youth. Sharon laughed during our interview, "It was very surprising to all of us!"

Patty was born in an urban Appalachian neighborhood in Cincinnati. Her mom remembers the neighborhood before it became industrialized; she recalls picking blackberries in a field where there is now a large mall. During her childhood, Patty's family frequently moved to different parts of the city following her grandfather's job on the railroads. She recalls her mother giving food to the "hobos who would jump trains from our back-yard near the tracks." Eleven years ago, when her son was four months old, Patty moved to Price Hill. She didn't know she was Appalachian until she arrived at the UAC and she was asked about her family roots. Her grand-parents were from Wolf County, Kentucky, and moved to Cincinnati for railroad work.

Hillbilly stereotypes keep many community residents like Sharon and Patty from claiming their Appalachian heritage to avoid assignment to a socially undesirable regional group. When I asked both women to reflect on stereotypes associated with being an Appalachian in the city, the follow-ing conversation emerged:

> Sharon: I got a funny one. I lived on Ehright in Price Hill, and I used to walk barefoot in the summer. One day I was walking my sister out to her car and she started pulling out of the driveway kind of fast. Well, this guy driving down the street slammed on his brakes and yelled, "You damn hillbilly!" [*laughs*]. I was so mad I ran down the street barefoot yelling, "I ain't no damn hillbilly!" [*laughs*].
>
> Patty: My mom always complained about wearing shoes. My neighbors said, "Look at these hillbillies." I was only ten but I remember thinking, "There's ain't no damn chickens in our yard" [*laughs*].

The shared sense of identity Sharon and Patty expressed in this interview—and the casual laughter they now use to combat name-calling and harass-ment from outsiders—reveals the importance of back-talking together about social struggles and creating community in light of stereotypes. Their relationship is a powerful example of institutional rhetoric at work; by introducing community residents to Appalachian identity and culture, the UAC provides a supportive space for residents to talk back to negative representations of Appalachians. A similar theme emerged in nearly every interview I conducted: most residents discovered their Appalachian heritage at the UAC, thanks to the many institutional rhetorics that were developed to support that identity.

Describing experiences similar to Sharon's and Patty's, a self-identifying urban Appalachian woman named Debbie explained during her interview that she never claimed her Appalachian heritage when she was a child because other kids on the school bus made fun of her clothes, her "weird" packed lunch, and her family's laundry hanging on a line outside their city house. Those kids on the school bus made her life so miserable that she eventually dropped out in the tenth grade and got her GED instead. After getting a degree in medical transcribing from a nonaccredited college and finding the work unsatisfactory, Debbie went to the University of Cincinnati for her associate's degree in social services technology. There she met a professor who was involved at the UAC—and who changed her career path and sense of identity:

> I loved my professor. . . . She was very nurturing, understanding, and always had time to talk to you. I found out about UAC because I had to do a service/practicum. I then went to work for the UAC two years after that, which is the first time I really learned about Appalachian culture. I didn't realize how rich and interesting the culture really was. I mean, it was everything my mother was. She was barefoot. She cooked the Appalachian foods that those kids would make fun of us for eating—like cornbread. And she was thrifty: if she had a piece of meat in the house, we all would eat it—make it stretch. Our family values lined up with Appalachian cultural values too. When I learned about the culture, I thought, "Wow. I'm home."

Like Debbie, many other community residents explained in our interviews that they learned about their Appalachian identity through the UAC. The organization supports such identity building. When residents first decide to enroll in the UAC's free educational programs or social services, UAC instructors collect information about residents' last school grade completed, family structure and income, and racial/ethnic background, including whether or not the resident is Appalachian. According to instructors and the UAC education director, most residents express uncertainty about what it means to be an Appalachian during this intake process.

By introducing residents to Appalachian heritage and migration—looking at maps of the Appalachian region, pointing to where they're from, reading UAC materials about Appalachian identity, and discussing Appalachian identity in a positive way—UAC instructors work to define a sense of people-hood and group identity for Appalachian migrants and their descendants. Sara, a first-generation Appalachian woman, explained in our interview: "I didn't know I was Appalachian until I came here! I walked into the UAC to pick up my welfare check, and they told me about GED classes. Once I signed up, they asked if I was Appalachian and I didn't know how to respond. They showed me a map and asked me to point out my hometown. It wasn't until then that I realized that I'm Appalachian!" In Sara's example we see how identity literally becomes tied to place, as heritage or Appalachian cul-tural identity is unlocked by locating her place on the map. Now that Sara is an AmeriCorps instructor at UAC, she guides residents through this pro-cess and teaches them about their Appalachian heritage. Debbie expressed a similar commitment to empowering urban Appalachians to accept and claim Appalachian identities: "My goal now is to enlighten others about the culture through my teachings and the Appalachian Festival, and the cultural things we've done in our classrooms [at the UAC]—like making corn-silk dolls, quilting, wood carving, writing and capturing people's stories. In their stories, you can hear the culture and how their lives are so connected."

The Urban Appalachian Council is unique among other local social ser-vice agencies and nonprofit organizations in Cincinnati not only because of its institutional rhetorics that focus on Appalachian identity, but also because of the dialect and language practices that resound within the center. All four instructors at the UAC speak Appalachian English; there is an audible Appalachian dialect in their voices. A shared cultural identity—expressed through vernacular similarities—leads to more productive learning experi-ences at the UAC. According to the UAC education director, adult students view instructors who speak with Appalachian dialects as more accessible and caring, which helps sustain student attendance in the GED education program: "We've had teachers come in who are highly educated, trained in the parochial school style—and the students just don't respond to it. Sara and Nancy are more inclusive teachers who teach at the students' levels. They just feel more comfortable and they can relate."

Dialect is one of a few key external indicators that can *place* a person as Appalachian for outsiders, and at the same time, *secure* a sense of belong-ing for insiders. While other institutional settings criticize Appalachian and rural dialects, the UAC very intentionally empowers rural language—situ-ating Appalachian English practices as an educated and intelligent "sound" by selecting instructors who are from the local community. Such positioning contrasts with cultural stereotypes that Appalachian dialects indicate ignorance and a lack of education.

To illustrate the exceptionality of this reversal, Debbie shared the following narrative, which took place years after she realized her Appalachian heritage and began working at the UAC: "You know, my daughter went to Walnut Hills High School and one day, her teacher started telling a hillbilly joke in class. Well, because of the UAC and the cultural programs I'd exposed her to, my daughter stood up in class and said, 'That offends me. I'm Appalachian.' And then an African American male student stood up and said, 'That offends me too. I'm Appalachian.'"

These and other examples of confronting stereotypes reveal the powerful role that diverse and inclusive institutional rhetorics can have on an individual's sense of community and self-worth. Rhetoric, in other words, plays a central role in generating dynamic senses of peoplehood (as tied to place) for Appalachians and their neighbors. What seems most important to urban Appalachian identity today is a commitment to respecting diverse experiences that emerge within shared spaces and building a sense of community that acknowledges those differences.

Creating a Shared Sense of Peoplehood

Community residents also built a sense of peoplehood by sharing poems and stories during a creative writing program called "Write to Education," which incorporated weekly creative and essay writing workshops into the UAC's GED curriculum. My research involved collaborating with AmeriCorps instructors at the UAC to develop and implement lesson plans for the writing program, help cohost workshops, and assist instructors and adult students as they used computers—sometimes for the first time—to type their written texts and create a final group anthology. The preliminary findings outlined here suggest that writing together helps diverse community residents create a complex, dynamic "sense of peoplehood."

During one workshop, "Memory," a woman with four young kids wrote about the very recent murder of her husband. A man wrote about his experience overcoming the alcohol addiction that had kept him from being a better father. In fact, the writing in this particular workshop was so intense that one student eventually asked: "How many people in this room have seen someone get killed firsthand?" Five of the twelve people in the room raised their hands. On many days, we attuned the curriculum to meet participants' immediate needs, using composing as a way of facing struggle: we wrote arguments for walkable streets; developed ideas for community summer programs; and composed complaint letters to landlords asking for healthier apartment buildings.

During a workshop called "What We Carry," we wrote about the literal things we carry (like bills or kids) or the intangible things we carry (like pain or hope). After writing individually on this topic, we compiled our favorite lines into a group poem:

What I Carry

I carry the love I have for my family
even when things aren't right with us.
I carry thinking of my mom,
how she did things with me.
I carry her small body and weakness,
times ten when I look at my children.

I carry my children to a happier life,
Up, happy, in a good mood—
I share things with my children.

I carry my tears, cascading down a rocky cliff,
to write down the feelings,
to be a role model and lead by example,
and follow through.
Who knew poems could weigh so much?

In the beginning, I had to get over the past, and I did—
protecting myself and my dignity.
I carry everything I'm meant to carry,
taped up tight, collected into each other.
I have no choice but to carry it.

During the follow-up group interview at the end of the program, one urban Appalachian woman explained, "It's been ten years since I let out my emotions. It was hard for me to process all of the stuff going on in my community. I felt like I needed therapy or something! But sitting here now and writing really helps me feel better and get out those emotions. This is such a blessing, you know?" An African American woman who had recently migrated to Cincinnati from the Appalachian city of Pittsburgh shared similar thoughts during an individual interview with me: "Writing is like therapy for me. It helps me cope. All the things I've been feeling in the past year [*pause*]—I can get it down. When I get home, I get out my laptop, listen to beats, and write to it. It kills time, so I know I love it. It helps me from stressing and crying and worrying about money and everything else."

As another urban Appalachian woman explained, "Writing helps me heal and share with others too." By composing together, adult students at the UAC connect with one another and build a shared cultural identity—a dynamic sense of peoplehood—that stretches across the categories of race and place. However, through their shared composition the women are building more than a shared identity; they are using rhetoric to reconstruct understandings, both theirs and others', of the Appalachian region and people.

Creating Ethical Research Projects

Based on these examples of institutional, everyday, and artistic rhetoric circulating within an urban Appalachian community, we can identify the powerful role that rhetoric can play in building a sense of community for diverse residents. By introducing residents to the Appalachian region and supporting creative arts programs, the Urban Appalachian Council creates spaces where community residents can share a sense of Appalachian identity—even beyond the mountains. Such community-based research efforts build cultural respect for groups who aren't often offered respect.

More and more colleges and universities are emphasizing the importance of students getting outside the classroom and conducting research and service within local communities. I conclude this chapter by sharing one of the most powerful moments of my own undergraduate life, which came during a "research road trip" that I took during my Appalachian literature course. In the course, we read a collection of poems and stories on mountaintop removal mining called *We Went to the Mountaintop but It Wasn't There.*[13] We talked about how many Appalachian communities felt conflicted about this dramatic method of mining because it offered needed jobs and produced needed energy but simultaneously destroyed local landscapes. Our last major assignment was to write a research paper on any topic from our course. As I started imagining the many potential topics I might write about—including cultural stereotypes, literary trends, and the changing racial and ethnic aspects of Appalachian identity—I felt drawn more and more powerfully back to the topic of mountaintop removal mining (MTR). I wondered what communities looked like after nearby mountains were flattened. I wondered how residents felt about the changes to their landscapes. I wondered how activists were fighting against the mining companies, and how coal miners felt about community activism against their employers.

As these curiosities churned in my head, I distinctly remember one moment that changed my view of myself as a student and learner: my professor, after hearing that I wanted to know more about MTR, energetically but unaggressively said, "Why don't you just go there? Why not call up the nonprofit organization that works on this topic and see if you can visit? Why not make the three-hour drive to eastern Kentucky over an upcoming weekend and see for yourself what MTR looks like? Why not speak with residents directly affected by it? You don't need permission to do that work. You can just do it on your own—inspired by your own interests and curiosities. Then you can write a research report on your journey." That early college road trip to eastern Kentucky later inspired me to go to graduate school, conduct engaged research in urban Appalachian neighborhoods, and begin a career as a college professor. Indeed, this experience helped me to map my place as an academic researcher.

I conclude with this story to emphasize the important relationship among academic research, ethics, and activism. Similar to my earlier college research road trip, the ethical research methods used within my dissertation study encouraged me to move beyond the walls and landscaped gardens of my university and meet face-to-face with local community residents. I heard their stories, wrote about their experiences, and published their words alongside my own. In the process, I learned about all the diverse ways individuals and communities can create senses of peoplehood and support one another. Research, in other words, could create space for people to reflect upon their similarities and differences—to reflect upon their identities. Analyzing the relationship between diverse kinds of rhetoric (such as institutional, individual, and artistic rhetorics) is one way that researchers, students, and community members can identify the rhetorical strategies and research methods that generate respect for groups struggling to gain it. Conducting community-based research and encouraging a critical awareness of local struggles are ways that researchers—whether professors, students, activists, or community members—can attune themselves to local issues and make a difference in communities beyond the classroom.

Notes

1. Stephen L. Fisher and Barbara Ellen Smith, eds., *Transforming Places: Lessons from Appalachia* (Urbana: University of Illinois Press, 2012), 269.

2. Phillip J. Obermiller, M. Kathryn Brown, Donna Jones, Michael E. Maloney, and Thomas E. Wagner, "Identity Matters: Building an Urban Appalachian Movement in Cincinnati," in Fisher and Smith, *Transforming Places,* 68.

3. Ibid., 65.

4. Kathleen P. Bennett, "Doing School in an Urban Appalachian First Grade," in *Empowerment through Multicultural Education,* ed. Christine E. Sleeter (Albany: State University of New York Press, 1991), 27–48; Shirley Brice Heath, *Ways with Words: Language, Life, and Work in Communities and Classrooms* (Cambridge: Cambridge University Press, 2003); James Moffett, *Storm in the Mountains: A Case Study of Censorship, Conflict, and Consciousness* (Carbondale: Southern Illinois University Press, 1988); Victoria Purcell-Gates, *Other People's Words: The Cycle of Low Literacy* (Cambridge, MA: Harvard University Press, 1995).

5. Ellen Cushman, *The Struggle and the Tools: Oral and Literate Strategies in an Inner City Community* (Albany: State University of New York Press, 1998), xix.

6. Ibid., xviii, xix.

7. See Deborah Hicks, "Class Readings: Story and Discourse among Girls in Working-Poor America," *Anthropology & Education Quarterly* 36, no. 3 (2005): 212–29; Erica Abrams Locklear, *Negotiating a Perilous Empowerment: Appalachian Women's Literacies* (Athens: Ohio University Press, 2011); Barbara Ellen Smith, "De-gradations of Whiteness: Appalachia and the Complexities of Race," *Journal of Appalachian Studies* 10, nos. 1-2 (2004): 38–57; Katherine Kelleher Sohn, *Whistlin' and Crowin' Women of Appalachia: Literacy Practices since College* (Carbondale: Southern Illinois University Press, 2006).

8. Dwight B. Billings, Gurney Norman, and Katherine Ledford, *Back Talk from Appalachia: Confronting Stereotypes* (Lexington: University Press of Kentucky, 2001); Wilburn Hayden Jr., "Appalachian Diversity: African-American, Hispanic/Latino, and Other Populations," *Journal of Appalachian Studies* 10, no. 3 (2004): 293–306; John Inscoe, ed., *Appalachians and Race: The Mountain South from Slavery to Segregation* (Lexington: University Press of Kentucky, 2001).

9. Ralph Cintron, *Angels' Town: Chero Ways, Gang Life, and Rhetorics of the Everyday* (Boston: Beacon, 1997), x; Linda Tuhiwai Smith, *Decolonizing Methodologies: Research and Indigenous Peoples* (New York: Edwards Brothers, 2012), 3.

10. Smith, *Decolonizing Methodologies,* 3.

11. Amy D. Clark and Nancy M. Hayward, *Talking Appalachian: Voice, Identity, and Community* (Lexington: University Press of Kentucky, 2013), 7.

12. Ibid., 13.

13. Kristin Johannsen, Bobbie Ann Mason, and Mary Ann Taylor-Hall, *Missing Mountains: We Went to the Mountaintop but It Wasn't There* (Nicholasville, KY: Wind, 2005).

6

Digital Rhetorics of Appalachia and the Cultural Studies Classroom

Jessica Blackburn

This chapter is devoted to the praxis of teaching digital media studies in the Appalachian studies (or Appalachian-focused) classroom. My goal is to explore the pedagogical nuances and rhetorical affordances of critiquing Appalachian community websites in the regional studies classroom. Conversations about systematically teaching an Appalachian studies curriculum began in the 1970s and continue to this day; however, the majority of this literature does not address the pedagogical potential of bringing Appalachian cyberspace into the classroom.[1]

Complementing traditional Appalachian literatures, teaching critically about the region through e-Appalachian representations of place enables students to apply rhetorical, political, environmental, and cultural theories to current texts that not only claim to represent regional identities but often *capitalize* on those identities through the commodification of a digitally constructed Appalachian ethos. The spread of Internet technologies is considered to offer Appalachian communities "the potential for economic renaissance and community development," yet "the obstacles to full or even moderate integration into the new information economy are formidable" in rural areas of the region.[2] Appalachia's "digital divide" is not significantly different than that of America's other rural areas in this regard; however, left underexplored is the critical issue of understanding how small Appalachian communities use Internet resources when they are available to promote economic and community development.

To investigate this dynamic, I have chosen two chamber of commerce websites for neighboring towns in northern Appalachia: Salamanca, New York, and Ellicottville, New York. (These Appalachian places are more than virtual to me; I am also writing from the experience of living and teaching in this area of the region for four years.) These two community websites can be treated in the Appalachian studies classroom as rich textual artifacts around which traditional academic rhetorical criticism might be performed. Furthermore, by querying the online narratives of these two communities, we open a dialogue allowing contemporary Appalachian studies to include old *and new* sources enabling us to keep a watchful eye and active stance on the politics of regional identity, voice, and representation.

I have chosen these two communities and their websites to illustrate my pedagogical approach to Appalachian digital rhetorics because while these two neighboring northern Appalachian towns are *geographically* similar, their online presence could not be more *digitally* dissimilar in terms of rhetorical framing. By focusing on "rhetorical framing"—that is, the subversive and/or overt methods used to suggest, narrate, imply, evoke, define, or attach sociocultural meaning to an idea, event, person, location, and so on—one can teach about regional identity and digital rhetorics in the context of community websites and their (ab)use of Appalachian identity politics, including the strategies used to narrate each community's cultural commodification. In choosing these specific community websites, both the pedagogical concerns of rhetorical theory and the academic objectives of Appalachian studies are addressed. Additionally, unlike the canonical literature and vastly important and widely celebrated authors of the region (for example, Lee Smith, Ron Rash, Wilma Dykeman, Barbra Kingsolver, Denise Giardina, and Silas House), these websites are alternative examples of "Appalachian texts" that are situated within the recognizably modern, sociopolitical contexts of today's Appalachian studies students. Such an inclusion of digital rhetorics in the Appalachian studies classroom allows us to perform the traditional academic exercises of close reading, explication, and rhetorical criticism. Focusing on community websites encourages us to explore the rhetorical situation of modern-day Appalachia; relevant, current, cultural metanarratives surrounding Appalachian identity; the impact of rhetorical framing; and the influences of economic pressures felt by Appalachian communities that are writing their way into their online identities. Likewise, it often comes as a great relief to students when the Appalachian (Web) text we ask them to critique is one with which they identify individually and collectively, thereby destabilizing the classroom hierarchy of knowledge and authority, which is a primary concern of mine in any classroom but especially so in Appalachian classrooms, which are often made up of students who are "insiders" in terms of regional cultural narratives yet "outsiders" regarding academic cultural norms. However, before we look at the rhetorical elements of these websites, we should first establish a basic foundation of rhetorical theory and then examine the context that engenders the websites: a context that Appalachian studies students might enjoy researching and certainly one around which meaningful classroom discussions can occur.

Theory

To begin, I like to turn my students' attention to Barry Brummett, rhetorician and author of *A Rhetoric of Style*. Brummett reminds us that "having an identity does not mean being unique, it means being aligned with a social category."[3] When practicing rhetorical criticism, it is important to consider the associated social category of a text. And when practicing rhetorical criticism with cultural studies in mind, we see how concepts like "identity" become even more important to our research. So when we approach digital rhetorics of Appalachia, it becomes especially worthwhile to explore the social categories with which community "home pages" rhetorically align themselves by framing the community's identity and promoting the community's material and cultural capital.

    According to rhetorician Kirk Hallahan, to look at how something is "framed" is "a rhetorical approach that focuses on how messages are created. . . . Framing is conceptually connected to the underlying psychological processes that people use to examine information, to make judgments, and to draw inferences about the world around them."[4] When we deconstruct cyber Appalachia and consider how community websites "frame" their communities, it is important to note that "semiotic analysis of the elements and signs of a website advertisement shows that individuals belonging to different cultural groups create meaning in different ways."[5] In other words, when practicing rhetorical criticism of community websites, it is important to examine the semiotics (or signs and symbols) behind all multimodal elements used to frame a community's cultural style (image, font, color, language, sound, and so on) as well as their cultural and/or hegemonic perceptions. To get to the bottom of how a community website frames itself and aligns itself with a social category, I always ask my students to look closely at what/who is on the page(s) as well as what/who is missing from the "design spaces that engage and manipulate people in certain ways."[6] That is, I ask students to think about websites as cultural epistemes and sites of socially constructed meaning. This means that community websites function as more than commercialized microphones enabling communities to voice themselves online; websites also function as the site or location in which *readers* come to form their knowledge and understanding of a local community, which is always and forever understood as representing both the individual town itself *and* the region as a whole. In other words, "Appalachia" is so loaded with culturally prescribed meaning that any town carving out its online identity will always be faced with the challenge of being distinct: either distinctly *Appalachian* or distinctly *different*. All regions come with preexisting cultural contexts. In the case of Appalachia, any tourism-based town must consider the region's historic cultural context when rhetorically framing the community's website in an effort to best represent the community *and/or* generate tourism interest and dollars. When we look to the cyber rhetorics of Appalachian community websites, we see how towns are faced with the choice of whether or not to (1) fall into the (stereo)typical narrative of antiquated hillbillies and mason jars, (2) carve out something altogether different in terms of Appalachian identity, or (3) attempt to blend the old and the new in *distinct* ways. However, whatever rhetorical framing and community aligning strategies are chosen, the website must always balance the town's perception of itself with the tourism industry's perception of Appalachia—always seeking to create the community website that best appeals to consumers. After all, there is little sense in a chamber of commerce building a community website without the local economy in mind, and it is this authoring of Appalachian identity that interests me the most from a digital rhetorics perspective. Furthermore, as Mark Warschauer and Douglas Grimes point out in "Audience, Authorship, and Artifact: The Emergent Semiotics of Web 2.0," "From a broader historical perspective [websites] represent a continuation of much older trends from plain text to multimedia, from static to dynamic content, from authorship by an educated elite to mass authorship, and from high costs of entry into the public sphere to low ones. The torrid pace of development and participation in new online genres is likely to present applied linguists with ever-new challenges for understanding how humans communicate via digital media."[7] As Warschauer and Grimes explain, "new" media are based in old rhetorical practices. And this applies to the "new" Appalachia—the Appalachia we find online.

Figure 6.1. Website funded by the Appalachian Regional Commission

Now that we have a basic understanding of rhetorical framing and its role in constructing a community's cyber identity, we should contextualize that theory within modern Appalachia. We don't have to look too deeply into a community website before we bump into that community's framing and its acceptance or rejection of some type of mountain ethos. Ethos, as rhetorician and compositionist Nedra Reynolds defines it, is "the individual agent as well as the location or position from which that person speaks or writes . . . like postmodern subjectivity, [ethos] shifts and changes over time, across texts, and around competing spaces."[8] When it comes to digital Appalachia, websites often expose an online ethos located around a mountain narrative in response to tourism, including reproductions of "hillbilly" imagery. In other cases, such as the Appalachian Regional Commission's tourism website, we see the "historic homestead" promoted for public consumption: images of antique malls, soda shops, Civil War reenactments, and seed-spitting contests (see figure 6.1).

In other cases, we might find a complete rejection of anything and everything "mountain." In still other cases, we find a narrative that embraces the mountains geographically but (re)narrates the "mountain" ethos as something altogether fresh—almost in defiance of the tired and intentionally parochial images featured in "reality" television shows like *Buckwild, Duck Dynasty, Hillbilly Handfishin'*, or *Rocket City Rednecks* (to name just a few). This cyber Appalachia offers communities the opportunity to multimodally frame, invent, narrate, or translate their town's style or niche(s) through digital rhetorics. What is most interesting in the cultural studies classroom, though, is the application of critical concepts like Judith Butler's concerns over language, identity, and the "power to name oneself and determine the conditions under which that name is used."[9] Specifically, we see how cyber Appalachia functions as a digital extension of a community, but that extension may or *may not* reflect the actual identities (or the internal or external perceptions of those identities) existing within those real communities. Instead, we see that some Appalachian home pages are intentionally designed to connect with externally located consumers in order to sell a narrative to online browsers who are searching the Web for the community that most accommodates their expectations of an "Appalachian" town to visit and patronize with their tourism dollars.[10] In other words, in the case of cyber Appalachia, the community website is the text and the rhetorical situation is directly attached to the moment when someone sits down to plan a trip to the region and begins by googling the term *Appalachian vacation*.

This Appalachian virtual reality is entirely dependent upon the way(s) in which a community or that community's appointed webmaster responds to external expectations of an *Appalachian experience*. What does one expect when visiting the region? What does it really mean to "take a walk back in time" in a "historic downtown" located in the heart of "Old Timey Appalachia"? How does one historic town distinguish itself from all the other historic downtowns and successfully lure tourism into its local economy? Furthermore, how does one town frame itself in a way that aligns with the desired social category of "historic and quaint"—especially if that desired social category is from the past (that is, obsolete except for the purpose of nostalgic tourism)? How is any of this possible if the website relies on the dubious notion that Appalachia is "old-timey," with its premodern towns that circumvent modernity (that is, the Internet)? In any case, we see that looking closely at cyber Appalachia allows for fruitful and progressive discussion, as we increasingly find ourselves looking at community websites that are more often than not an "imaginary figure, which, just like the soul, the shadow, the mirror image, haunts the subject like his other, which makes it so that the subject is simultaneously itself and never resembles itself again."[11]

Context

While it is worth mentioning that fiscal productivity alone hardly renders a community "successful," it is useful to examine how a community shapes its website as well as how a community is shaped *by* its website—especially when we are considering local economies of the region. Two northern Appalachian towns that exist side by side geographically but worlds apart digitally are Salamanca, New York, and Ellicottville, New York. These towns and their websites offer an especially rich opportunity to compare (e-)Appalachia's cultural significance. In fact, I've selected these towns because of their contrasting local economies, although they are in the same county, which is designated as "transitional" by the Appalachian Regional Commission (ARC). According to the ARC, "Transitional counties are those transitioning between strong and weak economies. They make up the largest economic status designation. Transitional counties rank between the worst 25 percent and the best 25 percent of the nation's counties."[12]

Especially interesting is that one of these towns, Ellicottville, successfully attracts tourists, while its neighbor Salamanca, with similar resources and attractions, fails to do so to the same degree. Is it possible that their *differing* cyber rhetorics might play a role in this outcome? Ellicottville and Salamanca are eleven miles apart. Yet these two towns are represented online through entirely disparate framing tactics, and their comparative share of tourism dollars reflects this. According to the latest census data, from 2013, Salamanca's population is 5,683, Ellicottville's 380 (that is *not* a typo).[13] We also learn from the census data that Salamanca enjoys a per capita income of $18,013, with 25.9 percent of residents below the poverty line. Conversely, Ellicottville's per capita income stands at $63,420. Salamanca's median house/condo value is $66,600, while Ellicottville's is $232,828. The difference in income and poverty levels between these two communities is astounding, especially considering their proximity—both towns are in the same county and in the same stretch of the Allegheny Mountains. Both communities have easy interstate and highway access to the exact same resources. And both communities exist under the same economic pressures of upstate New

York—a climate rife with competing hydraulic fracturing pressures and environmental concerns.

Essentially, when we look at these two communities, we see nearly *identical* potential for local economic stability, yet one community has achieved it while the other is in utter economic distress. This is deeply compelling when we consider that both communities house a major tourism draw: Salamanca is home to the Seneca Allegany Casino and Hotel, and Ellicottville boasts the Holiday Valley and Holimont ski resorts. Both towns are a stone's throw from the Allegheny National Forest; Buffalo, New York; Erie, Pennsylvania; the renowned Lake Erie; and the beautiful wine country of the Finger Lakes. Both towns enjoy the access of Highway 219 running directly through their downtown; in fact, Salamanca exists within the crossroads of 219 and I-86. In other words, isolation is not a contributing factor, despite the mountainous location. Other than the noteworthy distinction of Salamanca's 16.9 percent Seneca Nation population, both towns are predominantly populated by folks who identify as "white alone, not Hispanic, or Latino." So with Salamanca being more than fourteen times the size of Ellicottville's meager one square mile and population of 380, what keeps Salamanca from at least *remotely* keeping pace with the seemingly booming economy of neighboring Ellicottville? With their almost identical potential for economic growth and community stability, what keeps one town afloat while the other struggles just to tread water? Could it really be as simple as a deeply contrasting Appalachian community profile that draws folks into one town and away from another—contributing to and even buoying one tourism-based economy while sinking the other? When we look closer at the local economy, the numbers speak pretty loudly.

According to the city's census data, between 2008 and 2012, Ellicottville's most prominent industry was accommodations and food services (that is, hotels and restaurants), with 34 percent of jobs coming from this sector.[14] This alone tells us that Ellicottville's economy relies on the tourism industry bringing folks into the town's hotels, B&Bs, resorts, inns, restaurants, brewery, coffee shop, and so on. Salamanca's predominant industry is also accommodations and food services, but the sector represents only 11.6 percent of the jobs in that town. It is not that one town boasts a significant advantage in terms of its base tourism industry: Ellicottville is dominated by the ski industry while Salamanca, a Seneca reservation, features a gambling casino and Native museum. Yet the tourism industry *triples* its impact on Ellicottville's economy compared to Salamanca's. So what is it that brings folks to Ellicottville's hotels and restaurants but not Salamanca's? What is it that brings folks (in some cases) up Highway 219 right *through* Salamanca on their way to Ellicottville? What keeps these communities from enjoying financial symbiosis, given the proximal opportunity for tourists to bounce back and forth between the two towns, enjoying both the casino and the slopes? Or the trails and the rivers? Or the restaurants and the galleries? What brings the masses to Ellicottville, leaving neighboring Salamanca as quiet as a ghost town?

The mystery becomes less baffling when we look at these communities' websites. Once we begin to read the semiotics of these websites, we discover two distinctly different framing methods. One town frames itself as nostalgic, historic, and sentimentally rooted in the past, while the other frames itself as *both* sentimentally historic *and* progressively cosmopolitan. One town's website features its past, while the other blends its history with its future. It takes little guesswork to figure out which town seems most "attractive" to consumers in the end.

The Digital Texts

The tourism website for Cattaraugus County, home of the towns of Salamanca and Ellicottville, opens with a home page explicitly telling tourists to "think again" if they are expecting to find modern New York in this region. Instead, this website describes a quaint region of rolling farms, plush forests, and fresh rivers. In fact, it is little coincidence that this home page rhetorically attaches its county's identity to the "glaciers of the Ice Age." Inviting tourists to imagine themselves "in a simpler way of life," this website depicts an Appalachia replete with solitary dirt roads and Amish buggies, away from the "tall buildings, bright lights and cement, the bustling crowds of people and noisy traffic [of] Madison Avenue and Wall Street." The language alone suggests an Appalachia for tourists seeking an antisocial and isolated region, a place someone would go to be alone—removed from modernity.

Delving deeper into the tourism websites of Salamanca, a tribal territory of the Seneca Nation, and Ellicottville, we see a sharp divide between the promotional strategies of each town. Salamanca leans toward tradition. Yet it is a natural heritage, not the cultural heritage of the Seneca Nation, that features most prominently. The website creates a false binary in which tourists are encouraged to choose Salamanca when choosing between two types of vacation destinations: either a fast-paced, loud, and crowded modern town or the "other side" of life. While links to the Seneca Nation are listed on Salamanca's home page, the city primarily references itself as the "gateway to the Allegany State Park." The website's visual rhetoric depicts a tourism destination for visitors who want to step back in time in intentional opposition to the populated streets of cosmopolitanism: old buildings and river views, not indigenous culture or gaming, are featured front and center. On this website, as on the Cattaraugus County site, Appalachia is framed as a disconnected corner of America that is still independent and true to its roots—free from the influences of modernity. Salamanca's Appalachia becomes the place tourists go when they want to get away from it all. In this way, this website casts its town as "the perfect vacation and tourist destination situated in a time past, tethered to a time 'outside' of today's *reality*, reliving and re-performing a history only made possible by such tucked away, authentic, and sentimental mountain communities."[15] Web page visitors read that the city is "filled with country charm. Salamanca is the only city in the United States that lies almost completely on an Indian Reservation," yet nothing else is revealed about this cultural history; instead the site puts forward a more generic description of the city's proximity to other municipal areas and the presence of a local hardwood industry.[16]

Further framing Appalachia as historic and *nostalgic,* the county's related website suggests that tourists take a tour of the countryside surrounding Salamanca. Thus, this website amplifies and privileges the assumed tourism draw of isolationist Appalachia by foregrounding rural imagery. It is particularly striking that the Seneca Nation's casino, located on the edge of the city, does not feature in the city's site, although it is linked under the "Events" tab of the county's site. But the emphasis is decidedly on rurality in Cattaraugus County. The website goes so far as to describe the area as even more old-fashioned and antediluvian than "other Amish communities" by framing the New Order Amish as too progressive: "Experience the Old Order Amish Community with a trip along New York's Amish Trail, located in the western portion of the Enchanted Mountains. Unlike other Amish communities, there is no commercialization and life is still carried on without modern conveniences. Follow their hand-painted signs to their businesses, usually located in their homes. You can stop at their shops and purchase quilts, furniture or baked goods any day except Sunday. Take a drive through Amish country, step back in time and enjoy the simpler things in life along New York's Amish Trail."[17] Tourists are thus invited to visit an

Appalachian town tied intentionally to the past and rejecting the future—including all of its modern conveniences.

When we compare Salamanca's website to that of neighboring Ellicott-ville, we see an immediate difference in the rhetoric used to advertise and sell each town: a picture of insulated, disconnected Appalachia versus a representation that frames a balance between old and new ways of life. Celebrating Appalachia's cosmopolitanism *as well as* the region's cultural heritage, small-town appeal, and historic architecture and landscape, Ellicottville's website suggests the town offers the best of both worlds.

Ellicottville's website is in almost complete opposition to Salamanca's isolationist framing and visual rhetoric: whereas Salamanca's site features a single person with his back to the camera, ruminating about days gone by, Ellicottville's foregrounds images of packed sidewalks and bustling storefronts. Whereas Salamanca warns tourists not to come expecting Wall Street and Madison Avenue, Ellicottville intentionally resists the status quo assumptions about historic rural appeal and "sleepy town tourism," instead showcasing a town packed with people experiencing all the community has to offer. Displaying the architecture of a historic building to the left of the screen and shops with open doors to the right, this home page metaphorically illustrates a town with its doors open to the world—certainly not shutting out modernity. This visual rhetoric strikes a balance between old and new as the tabs overhead direct tourists to categories of "What to Do," "Events," "Where to Stay," "Where to Eat," and "Where to Shop." Ellicottville's website frames its community's identity as a blending of down home with haute couture. When tourists click on the "Where to Eat" tab, they find descriptions such as "Built in 1895, The Barn has been in use as a stable, temporary jail, and blacksmith shop. Now it boasts a warm, relaxing atmosphere, complete with a stone fireplace, where couples, friends, and families with children can come in and enjoy fine, casual dining."[18] And just across the street from this relaxed, "comfort food" restaurant, tourists find the new Ellicottville Winery and tasting room. In its balance between old and new, Ellicottville's website successfully manages to locate itself in Appalachia geographically but *not* stereotypically or ideologically.

In short, we see Ellicottville blending the region's romanticized history with the contemporary needs and interests of today's tourists. Savvy marketing strategies allow this Ellicottville website to rhetorically situate itself within a celebrated rural history while also highlighting cultural attractions—it is certainly not coincidental that when the town's website describes Ellicottville as "progressive," it quickly balances that modernity with the description that the town also "cherishes our past." Like Salamanca, we see Ellicottville's website aligning itself with the Allegany State Park, but unlike the other town, Ellicottville claims associations with the Cattaraugus County Arts Trail, fine dining, ski slopes, and the vineyards of the Finger Lakes. These cosmopolitan aspects contrast with the isolationist rhetoric of Salamanca's website, which features an Appalachian-*ness* that insulates potential tourists.

In illustrating these distinctions, the intent is not to suggest that one town is better than the other, nor to imply that Salamanca's ultimate goal *should be* to attract tourism. However, make no mistake about the goals of a town's chamber of commerce or its website: any town with a website uses that as a vehicle to frame its community and forward its notions of identity. These two towns share the same Appalachian identity, but they are narrated as cultures apart, expressing their identity with two very different rhetorical frames. Put simply, we see their Web presences complementing as well as complicating long-standing Appalachian stereotypes of the down-home isolated town tucked away and out of sight.

Conclusions for Teaching Appalachian Digital Rhetorics

In 2008, David Jolliffe and Allison Harl published the results of their study of college reading habits, "Studying the 'Reading Transition' from High School to College: What Are Our Students Reading and Why?" in *College English*. Jolliffe and Harl provide great insight into the reading habits of today's college students in general, but perhaps most important is their claim that students are motivated by and engaged with reading, but "the texts that they interact with most enthusiastically are technologically based . . . technology purposes overlap in many ways that relate to academic study . . . faculty members need to teach students explicitly how to draw the kinds of connections that lead to engaged reading, particularly text-to-world and text-to-text connections. . . . As they read, students need to be walked through demonstrations of mature, committed, adult readers who draw connections to the world around them, both historical and current, and to other texts."[19]

With the emergence of cyber Appalachia, we see a new and relatable venue for modern cultural studies in the regional studies classroom, and we see a new discourse genre worthy of in-depth and complicated critique. Within the college classroom, we often find rhetorical analysis to be simultaneously one of the most difficult critical reading skills to teach yet one of the most liberating, enlightening, and empowering to *learn*. And what is the field of cultural studies if it does not include rhetorical analysis? The twenty-first-century Appalachian studies classroom has access to a communication tool that both reflects and shapes the region, and including this rhetorical space in our critical examination of the region is essential to fully understanding the past as well as the future of Appalachian rhetorics and identity politics. For these reasons, Appalachian studies teachers might consider closely critiquing texts such as community websites with their students. In doing so, we provide our students, who are digital natives, with the opportunity to share classroom authority while still meeting the important demands of exposing them to sociohistorically rich and stylistically complicated cultural artifacts—albeit contemporary artifacts.

As with all textual selections that we place on our syllabi, we have an obligation to offer rich and dynamic material to our students. With the proliferation of cyber Appalachia, we have a vast body of digital texts, from which we may seek websites, videos, blogs, and so on that demonstrate complex rhetorical strategies. While these texts may not fit neatly into our current categories of "regional culture," we are certainly witnessing the unveiling of cyber Appalachia, and this new frontier is worthy of critical awareness—especially in the Appalachian studies classroom as our students participate in the consumption and (very likely) the production of Appalachia's online presence in various spaces. As we see with the websites described above, students have much to gain from critically reading and deconstructing the sophisticated nuances found in Appalachian digital rhetorics. And while many of the available cyber Appalachian texts may not compete with the aesthetics of belletristic prose found in the traditional anthology of Appalachian literature, there are numerous digital texts available that do employ rhetorical devices worthy of critique in the cultural studies classroom. Furthermore, these multimodal texts provide us the pedagogical opportunity to reconsider our definitions of Appalachian culture and broaden our understanding of the region's geographic borders—borders that are being made increasingly complicated (if not arbitrary) by cyberspace.

Notes

1. An example of the early literature is Jim Branscome, "Annihilating the Hillbilly," in *Colonialism in Modern America: The Appalachian Case* (Boone, NC: Appalachian Consortium Press, 1978), 211–27. A recent example is Theresa L. Burriss and Patricia M. Gantt, eds., *Appalachia in the Classroom: Teaching the Region* (Athens: Ohio University

Press, 2013). See the Digital Library of Appalachia (http://dla.acaweb.org/) for an outstanding collection of electronic resources for researching and teaching Appalachian studies.

2. James Bohland, Anita Puckett, and Jean Plymale, "The Decline of Space and the Ascent of Place: Internet Technology in Appalachia," in *Pittsburgh and the Appalachians: Cultural and Natural Resources in a Postindustrial Age,* ed. Joseph Scarpaci (Pittsburgh: University of Pittsburgh Press, 2006), 156.

3. Barry Brummett, *A Rhetoric of Style* (Carbondale: Southern Illinois University Press, 2008), 96.

4. Kirk Hallahan, "Seven Models of Framing: Implications for Public Relations," *Journal of Public Relations Research* 11, no. 3 (1999): 206.

5. Danai Tsora, Marius Janson, and Dubravka Cecez-Kecmanovic, "Marketing on the Internet: A Semiotic Analysis," in *Proceedings of the Tenth Americas Conference on Information Systems* (New York, 2004), 4219.

6. James Paul Gee, *What Video Games Have to Teach Us about Learning and Literacy* (New York: Palgrave Macmillan, 2007), 38.

7. Mark Warschauer and Douglas Grimes, "Audience, Authorship, and Artifact: The Emergent Semiotics of Web 2.0," *Annual Review of Applied Linguistics* 27 (2007): 18.

8. Nedra Reynolds, "Ethos as Location: New Sites for Understanding Discursive Authority," *Rhetoric Review* 11, no. 2 (1993): 326.

9. Judith Butler, *Bodies That Matter: On the Discursive Limits of Sex* (New York: Routledge, 1993), 227.

10. Jessica Blackburn, "[E]ppalachia: Rural Ethos, Online Discourse, and Cyber-Frontiers," *Appalachian Journal* 41, nos. 3–4 (2014): 214–30.

11. Jean Baudrillard, *Simulacra and Simulation* (Ann Arbor: University of Michigan Press, 1994), 95.

12. Appalachian Regional Commission, "Source and Methodology: Distressed Designation and County Economic Status Classification System, FY 2007–FY 2013," n.d., http://www.arc.gov/research/SourceandMethodologyCountyEconomicStatus-FY2007FY2013.asp> (accessed October 20, 2014).

13. US Department of Commerce, "State and County Quick Facts," US Census Bureau, n.d., http://quickfacts.census.gov/qfd/index.html (accessed September 1, 2014).

14. Ibid.

15. Blackburn, "[E]ppalachia," 220.

16. "About Salamanca," http://salum.com/about.htm (accessed July 1, 2015).

17. "Enchanted Mountains Activities," http://enchantedmountains.com/activities (accessed September 12, 2014).

18. "Where to Eat," http://www.ellicottvilleny.com/directory-category/restaurants-bars/ (accessed September 1, 2014).

19. David Jolliffe and Allison Harl, "Studying the 'Reading Transition' from High School to College: What Are Our Students Reading and Why?" *College English* 70, no. 6 (2008): 612.

7

Continuity and Change of English Consonants in Appalachia

Kirk Hazen, Jordan Lovejoy, Jaclyn Daugherty, and Madeline Vandevender

When the general public reflects on English in Appalachia, people reach out to traditional hillbilly stereotypes popularized by such comic-strip franchises as *Li'l Abner* and *Snuffy Smith,* both of which were read by millions of people over decades. These popular characterizations propagate and rely on stigmatized dialect features. For example, in *Li'l Abner,* Daisy Mae says, "Whut wif all th' soshul an' politikul de-velpments," which, among other features, highlights the vernacular stigma of *with* as *wif.*[1] Snuffy Smith brings vernacular -ING variation to light when he says, "We still do a lotta prayin'!!"[2] Despite these traditional stereotypes of static language features and their continued foregrounding in reality TV shows about Appalachians such as *Coal* and *Buckwild,* a closer examination of speech in Appalachia indicates that while some vernacular dialect features remain in the region, dialect diversity and language change are the norm. This chapter analyzes social and linguistic effects that contribute to the ebb and flow of language variation in the West Virginia region of Appalachia. Using a quantitative approach to key sociolinguistic variables, this chapter demonstrates the continuity of diversity and change of English in Appalachia. Employing sociophonetic methods, we reconsider consonant continuity and change in West Virginia speech and what they mean for cultural stereotypes and identity in the region. We detail the methodology and careful analysis required in sociolinguistic research, remapping the fluidity of language change over time through selected examples. Our chapter focuses on West Virginia to examine the reality of dialect variation and language change in contemporary Appalachia. In the process we identify problems with regional language stereotypes and demonstrate the need for renewed scholarly study of language and life throughout Appalachia.

We approach English in the Mountain State from the field of sociolinguistics, specifically the quantitative study of language variation. Sociolinguistic research questions primarily focus on either linguistic or social qualities, although both dimensions are included in studies in the field.[3] The variationist branch of sociolinguistics dates back to the early 1960s and has developed research methodologies adopted from dialectology.[4] As part of the West Virginia Dialect Project (WVDP), we work within variationist sociolinguistics to explore dialects and language change in West Virginia. In past studies, the WVDP has examined dialect features such as *a-* prefixing ("We were *a*-walking the dog"), demonstrative *them* ("But *them* girls like him"), leveled *was* ("We *was* out late"), and pleonastic pronouns ("My sister, *she* was loud").[5] In this chapter, we focus on the sound qualities of consonants to illustrate the kinds of continuity and change developing in the sound system of English in Appalachia. Specifically, we examine two consonant features involved in synchronic variation, H-lenition and the merger of word-initial W/WH sounds.

To study these sound changes, we employ methods from sociophonetics to analyze the acoustic qualities of sounds in a scientific manner.[6] Most sociophonetic studies have concentrated on vowels, and our own studies have involved some vowel analysis, but the kingdom of consonants is underexplored and certainly deserves detailed investigation.[7] The focus here is on the variation in the pronunciation of *wh* words such as *which, whale,* and *wheat* (WH variation) and variation in *h* words such as *heart, huge,* and *history.* After illustrating the origin of these forms, their diachronic developments, and their synchronic states, we explain how the range of variation in their modern forms leads to both continuity and change of the English spoken in Appalachia.

Background and Methods

For the investigation of sociolinguistic variation in Appalachia, the WVDP conducted sociolinguistic interviews with 183 Appalachians. From these interviews, sixty-seven speakers, born between 1919 and 1989, form the basis of the West Virginia Corpus of English in Appalachia (WVCEA). The sixty-seven speakers were chosen because of the quality of their interviews and their demographic classifications. The corpus was designed to determine a baseline of English variation in Appalachia and comprises over 630,000 words. The primary social classifications were age, region, and sex, and the number of speakers was originally balanced for each of those.[8] A secondary set of social characteristics was also selected as potentially influential in sociolinguistic variation: social class, ethnicity, rurality, and the social-class-related factor of educational mobility.[9]

These speakers are divided into three age groups. World War II was the most significant social event in the twentieth century for West Virginia, as it contributed greatly to out-migration, both to the military and to cities in northern states, and this boundary divides the older and middle-aged speakers. The younger speakers are divided by economic and educational changes that took place in the region at the end of the 1970s. Each age group is fairly evenly divided by region and sex. Of the sixty-seven speakers, six are African American.[10] The speakers were either born and raised in West Virginia (sixty-four) or near the West Virginia borders in Appalachia (three), but they all have parents from West Virginia, and most of their family ties with the state date back multiple generations.

For our limited social analysis, we do not analyze a single community of people who know one another; instead, we provide a sample from across the state. A sampling of this type allows us to assess broad trends and litmus-test variables (such as -ING), ensuring that we have a good social distribution of the population.[11]

From these interviews, the WVDP team manually transcribed each interview from the audio file. Each transcribed word aligns with the time it is uttered, so that when the interview is played, the written words flow along with the sounds. This alignment was done in Praat, software designed for acoustic analysis.[12] Each time-aligned interview is divided into thousands of utterances, and the boundaries of each utterance are marked at any pause of .06 seconds or longer. Each utterance can then be considered a "sound slide," and these sound slides can then be analyzed with computer software to assess their acoustic qualities, producing quantitative results. With the statistical analysis of sounds, researchers no longer "play it by ear" in terms of making judgments. For example, instead of guessing whether the [l] in *coal* is more of a consonant or more of a vowel, modern software produces quantitative results that are reproducible from study to study and allow comparison across speakers and communities. The time-aligned transcripts and audio files are stored on the Sociolinguistic Archive and Analysis Project (SLAAP) database at the North Carolina State University Library.[13] These sound slides can be searched based on the standard orthographic spelling of words spoken within the audio file; there is no attempt at phonetic transcription. The WVDP team worked from this corpus to analyze words containing tokens of the variables.

The first variable we examine is H-lenition. This variable has been part of the English language from the beginning and is still found in some varieties of English around the world. The term *lenition* represents the loosening of the constriction in the vocal tract that produces a sound. Here we are interested in the range of variation between a fully voiceless consonant, [h],[14] and a complete absence of an [h] sound at the start of words like *heart, huge, human,* and *help.* This dialect feature was perhaps most famously portrayed by Eliza Doolittle in the movie *My Fair Lady,* from Shaw's *Pygmalion:* "'Urricanes 'ardly ever 'appen." H-lenition occurred in several linguistic environments in Old English, particularly those with H before consonants; the Old English words *hraven* (raven), *hnutu* (nut), and *hlavord* (lord) all underwent H-lenition. In modern dialects of England, the H-less forms are strongly correlated with lower social classes.

Although the spelling of English can only show either the full *h* or its absence (for example, *huge* versus *'uge*), the reality of language offers up a fine gradient of reduction between 100 percent and 0 percent. The acoustic methods of sociophonetics are well suited to handle these kinds of fine-grained details. Our unit of study was the combined [h] + following vowel. Unlike orthography, there are no boundaries demarcating where an [h] stops in relation to the vowel, so the entire section was measured: in [hɛlp], the [hɛ] section would be measured (see figure 7.1).

In words such as *huge* and *human,* any intervening glides were also included: in [hjudʒ] the entire [hju] would be measured. For H-lenition, we measured the duration and percentage of glottal pulsing—the vibration of the vocal folds in the larynx. Duration is measured in seconds, although it should be noted that few of our tokens were longer than half a second: the mean was just below 0.2 seconds. Glottal pulsing was assessed through a Praat voice report by the fraction of locally unvoiced frames: these are the percentage of sections of time with or without glottal pulsing. We use glottal pulsing to represent voicing, although it should be recognized that voicing actually comprises several qualities.[15]

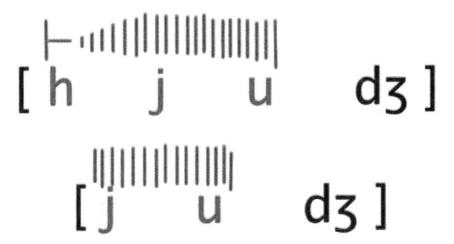

Figure 7.1. Gradient voicing of H dropping

The second variable we examine is the WH/W merger. Here we are interested in the extent to which word-initial WH sounds are similar to word-initial W sounds. As discussed below, the history of English leads us to believe that these two variables were orthographically distinct for some time. However, it appears that many speakers today have the same pronunciations for the initial consonants in words such as *whet* and *wet*. As with H-lenition, the range between a distinctive WH and W is a gradient, and we measure duration and glottal pulsing to assess the length and extent of voicing for these segments. We also measured the combined consonant and vowel sections of words, as there is no delineating boundary between the word-initial consonant and the following vowel. For example, in words like [wɛt] we measured duration and glottal pulsing for [wɛ] (see figure 7.2).

In Old English, there appears to have been a solid distinction between the two sounds, for example, in the words *hwelc* (which) and *wicca* (witch). The Old English word *hwelc* transitioned in spelling over time to *wheche, weche,* and *wyche*—an orthographic trend usually taken to indicate a loss of voicelessness. Note that the original spelling of *hw* is another instance of word-initial H before a consonant that was altered after Old English, similar to *hnutu* and *hraven*.

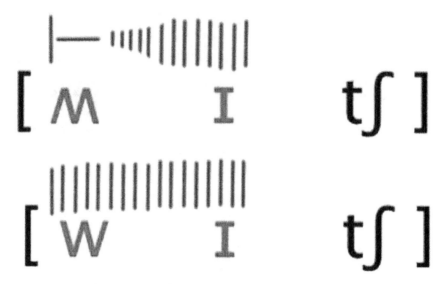

Figure 7.2. Gradient voicing of voiceless W

The Range and Flux of West Virginia Consonants

Several other trends in consonants have previously been investigated by the West Virginia Dialect Project, and their patterns illustrate the range of language variation that exists in Appalachia. The first of these is called coronal stop deletion and involves the deletion of -*t* or -*d* from words like *past* and *braised*. The second is -ING variation, where the final nasal of -ING can be rendered as either an alveolar [n] or a velar [ŋ]: This variable is popularly referred to as *g*-dropping, although no [g] sound is actually dropped in the pronunciation of -ING. The other consonant variable noted in stereotypical renditions of English in Appalachia is the production of voiceless -*th* as [f] in words like *birfday*.

Coronal stop deletion has long been studied in sociolinguistics, and this feature is alive and well in West Virginia. A previous study by the WVDP shows that coronal stops have an average rate of 66 percent deletion and that surrounding sounds have the largest influence—particularly those that follow the coronal stop.[16] For example, deletion is much higher (90 percent) before following consonants (for example, *best cart*) than before following vowels (30 percent; for example, *best apple*). Although there is frequent orthographic representation of this feature in literature on all kinds of vernacular varieties, including

English in Appalachia, there is little social marking, or stigmatization, of this variable. Ethnicity and age are two examples: despite some differentiation in ethnicity and age within the English of Appalachia—African Americans and younger speakers having a slightly higher rate—the range of social variation is small and seemingly incidental. It could develop as a socially important variable in the future, but as of the end of the twentieth century, it had not.

-ING variation has been a staple feature of sociolinguistic study since the inception of the field and has also been studied by the West Virginia Dialect Project.[17] Despite the variation involving two nasal consonants, the linguistic constraints on the -ING variable are not phonological. In other words, the surrounding sounds do not influence whether an alveolar [n] or a velar [ŋ] appears in a word like *walking*. The linguistic factor that does influence this variable is the grammatical status of the word in the sentence: gerunds, as in the sentence "Walk*ing* is fun," have higher rates of [ŋ]; progressives, in an example such as "She is walk*ing*," have higher rates of [n]. On the social-class front, there are sharp divides in English, and have been for centuries. The alveolar [n] form is more stigmatized. In West Virginia, upper-middle-class speakers had a rate of 38 percent [n] compared to the working-class rate of 73 percent; additionally, speakers from the southern half of West Virginia had a higher rate than those from the northern half.[18] Despite these social and linguistic differences, -ING is not undergoing language change, and neither is coronal stop deletion.

In terms of types of variation, H-lenition and the WH/W merger are more similar to coronal stop deletion than to -ING variation, as this last variable is not affected by surrounding sounds but the first three are.

One consonant variable the WVDP had hoped to investigate was a change of the voiceless *-th* [θ] to [f], as in *birfday*, a feature often used in older stereotypical characterizations of Appalachian speech, as in *Li'l Abner* and *Snuffy Smith*. Yet it was difficult to find more than a few examples in our corpus, as its presence in West Virginia has greatly diminished. The inner workings, social markings, and directions of change are different with all three of the variables reviewed here and thus indicate the range of continuity and change of consonants in English.

H-lenition

We included the first variable, H-lenition, in our study because our undergraduate research assistants observed it in the speech of West Virginia natives with words like *huge*. The WVDP research assistants, without whom the WVDP would not exist, join our research effort because they are attuned to language and the role it plays in their lives, providing native expertise and rigorous scholarly effort to our enterprise. They are adept at analyzing language and help contextualize and describe its social range in West Virginia. Research assistants helped to make the major decisions about classifying the social groups in our corpus, and results from sociolinguistic analysis fully supported their assessment.

As mentioned previously, the main acoustic qualities we focused on were the duration of the H + vowel section of a word and the degree of glottal pulsing in that section. We will refer to the absence of glottal pulsing as the percentage of *voicelessness*. Voicelessness can be seen most prominently when people whisper, as the vocal folds are held stiff, and there is no glottal pulsing. It should be noted that voicelessness is actually more complex and comprises other qualities also.

For the H + vowel segments, the percentage of voicelessness represents how much of that combination lacks glottal pulsing. Were the H tokens half the length of the measured segment, the H + vowel segment would have 50 percent voicelessness: half voiced vowel and half voiceless consonant. If we have a token with 10 percent voicelessness, the H would be quite short in comparison with the vowel. We were surprised by an overall low percentage of voicelessness for H + vowel segments among all the speakers. We had expected that the mean would be around 50 percent voicelessness. Instead, the mean for our speakers falls at 15 percent voicelessness (see figure 7.3).

It is unclear how this compares to other dialect areas, as this sociophonetic approach has not been applied to H-lenition before (previously it was counted as reduced or not reduced). It could be that such scant voicelessness would mark many of the instances as vernacular for other regions of the United States, but without conducting perception tests we are merely speculating. Yet with half the tokens falling below 15 percent voicelessness, it is safe to say that for these speakers there is little [h] in the *h*-initial words. The only linguistic factor that had a statistically significant effect on voicelessness was the duration of the H + vowel segment. As the duration increased, the degree of voicelessness also increased (see figure 7.4). We consider that the duration provides extra "canvas" on which people can paint their voicelessness; as the length of the H + vowel sequence decreases, the vowel, an essential element of the word as a whole, appears to crowd out the *h*.

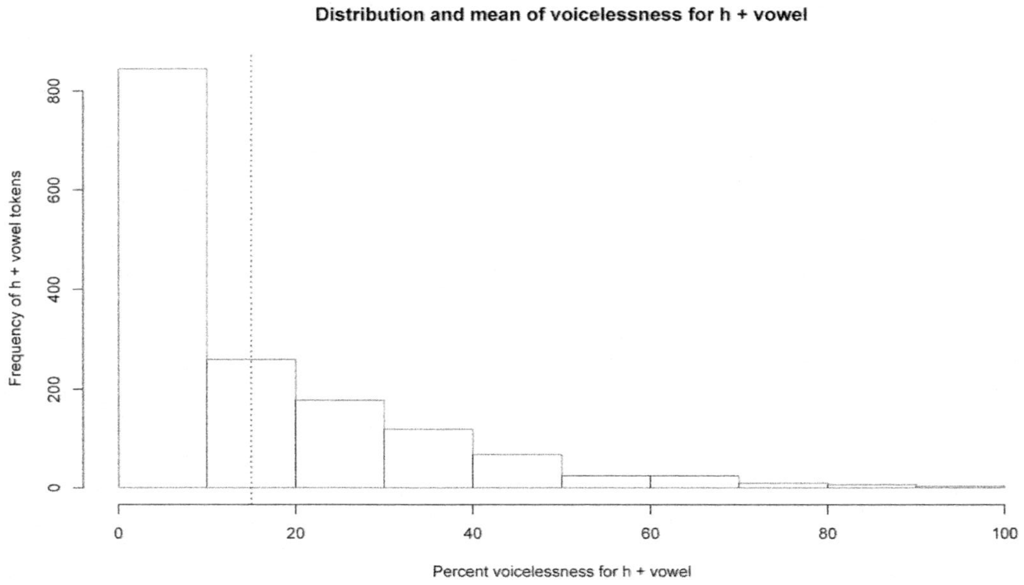
Distribution and mean of voicelessness for h + vowel
Frequency of h + vowel tokens
0
200
400
600
800
0
20
40
60
80
100
Percent voicelessness for h + vowel

Figure 7.3. Frequency of voicing for H words

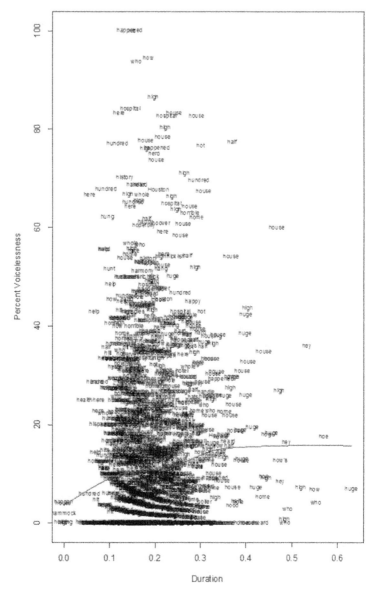

Figure 7.4. Duration by percent voicelessness with H words as data points

With respect to social factors, we found that speakers with postsecondary educational experience, regardless of age, appear to have higher degrees of voicelessness. Older speakers also tend to have slightly higher mean durations for H + vowel segments compared to speakers in the middle and younger age ranges. There was also an increase in the percentage of voicelessness from older northern to younger northern speakers, thus implying that the former have a more prominent vowel sound in their H + vowel segments. Thus, they had more H-lenition than younger northern speakers. Given the correlations between college experience and age, in addition to the change over time for the northern speakers, we can hazard the guess that short H duration might have some social stigma. Unlike in England, H-lenition in West Virginia does not appear to be strongly stigmatized.

WH/W Merger

Our second variable is the WH/W merger. As mentioned previously, the main acoustic qualities we focused on were the duration of the consonant + vowel section and the degree of glottal pulsing in that section. Although we are comparing two historically different word classes, those spelled with *wh* and those with *w*, the measurable segments are essentially the same. Both segments contain a bilabial glide transitioning into a vowel, though historically the *wh* would be a voiceless bilabial glide [ʍ] and the *w* would be a voiced bilabial glide [w]. Today, while some speakers do maintain the distinction between the two sounds, English as a whole is on its way to a full merger, in which there is no distinction in the pronunciations of *which* and *witch*. Our results reflect that trend.

In terms of linguistic factors, voicelessness is more variable for WH/W, whereas duration is not as variable as it was with H-lenition. To first sketch the landscape for this variable, figure 7.5 provides the distribution of all WH and W tokens for voicelessness. The mean percent of voicelessness is 12, even lower than that of H.

From figure 7.5 and a mean voicelessness of 12 percent, it is safe to state that these speakers have little voicelessness in these measured segments. Yet, when considering the word-class's effect on voicelessness, WH words (13 percent) did have significantly more voicelessness than W words (10 percent) for the entire data set. As can be seen from the previous means, the effects are slight and not uniform for every speaker, but even when taking into account random variations by the speakers and the words themselves,

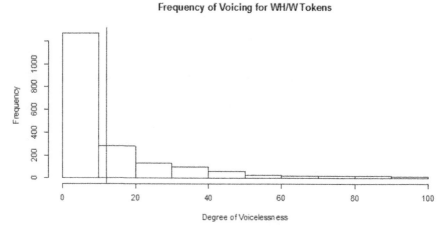

Figure 7.5. Frequency of voicing for WH and W words

there is still enough historical echo to distinguish WH words from W words in terms of voicelessness. Duration does vary among the speakers, with a mean of 0.12 seconds for the WH/W + vowel segment, but unlike *h*, there was no correlation between duration and the amount of voicelessness.

Other linguistic factors do play a role in the degree of voicelessness, but most of these appear to be related to the effects of assimilation, wherein a neighboring consonant makes the WH or W more similar to it. For example, in a two-word combination like *wet wipe*, we would normally expect the [w] of *wipe* to be fully voiced. Yet our data indicates that a preceding voiceless sound, like the [t] of *wet,* strongly correlates with increased voicelessness of the [w] of *wipe.*

Several different social factors appear to correlate with increased voicelessness for both WH and W words. For example, college-educated speakers born between 1940 and 1989 had W and WH as distinct variants, yet both forms became consistently more voiced over time. Speakers with no college education never had the distinction, however, and both variants were predominantly voiced. It is not always easy to discern *why* such results have occurred. In this case it could be that those with the desire for further education are more focused on spelling pronunciations of words, hence giving effort to distinguishing between WH and W, but such explanations are ad hoc and not based on any social observations of speakers in their speech communities. For W words, region was significant for voicelessness, with southern West Virginians in our sample favoring increased voicelessness as compared to their northern counterparts. There is no historical reason in terms of linguistic precedent as to *why* southerners have higher rates of voicelessness with W words. It could be that this period is the start of social differentiation for this variable, but without further assessment in southern West Virginia communities, that is merely conjecture.

Overall for WH and W, we find that speakers vary widely in terms of their mean voicelessness. In figure 7.6, the speakers are ordered from left to right by the difference between their mean WH and their mean W. If everyone had a more voiceless WH than W, all the values would be positive. If WH and W had the same voicelessness for these speakers, all their values would be 0. Instead, we see the wide distribution of figure 7.6.

Three patterns should be noted here. First, there is gradual shifting among the speakers: there are not long plateaus where numerous speakers have the same difference between WH and W. This kind of gradual cline is normal for phonetic variation. Second, there are both positive and negative values, indicating that a portion of the population has more voiceless Ws than WHs, a historically unsupported trend. Third, few speakers have equivalent values for WH and W: it appears that distinguishing the two word classes is the norm.

Overall for WH and W words, the historical trend of WH voicelessness persists, but only by a small margin, and some speakers have completely reversed the traditional pattern. For either kind of speaker, the range of variation allows for social correlations to develop over time.

The Future of H-lenition and the WH/W Merger

The patterns we see for WH/W and H-lenition have evolved from historical trends first begun during the Old English period. Although changes in vowels can take decades to complete, changes in consonants can take centuries. Whether or not changes to consonants are ever "complete" is an open question. It is doubtful that all the varieties of English worldwide will lose their word-initial [h], but some varieties have already lost many of them in certain contexts. The variable nature of consonants is front and center when considering synchronic variation. With the bilabial glides WH and W, their distinction in Old English was sharply contrasted: there were few, if any, true minimal pairs, or two words differing by one sound in the same place (such as *sue* and *zoo*), where the WH and W were needed to distinguish two words. Our findings indicate that the voicelessness distinction is small, but histori-

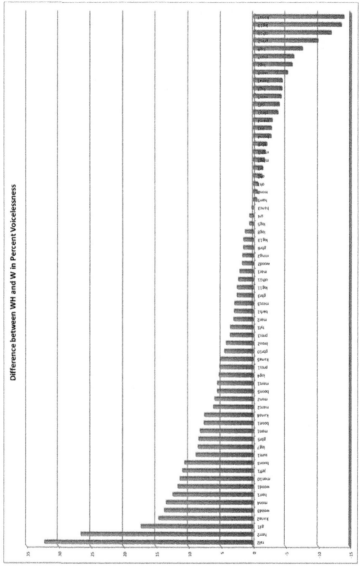

Figure 7.6. Percent voicing difference between WH words and W words by speaker

cally WH words do have slightly more voicelessness than W words. Yet there are other speakers who have more voiceless Ws. Whether or not this wide range continues is yet to be seen, although some variation in voicelessness for word-initial bilabial glides seems to be the norm. With both H-lenition and WH/W, West Virginians might well use these envelopes of variation for social marking in the future, but these language variation patterns do not seem to have any assigned social meaning at this point.

Given the results of our analysis, it is clear that consonants are a natural, renewable resource, and shifts in their patterns do not portend extinction for them. The future of English may show a depletion of word-initial H and WH forms, whereby only a few varieties use them regularly. Regardless of the future, however, the spelling of the words is safe, as English spelling is highly conservative and represents consonants that have not been spoken regularly in centuries, such as the [k] in *knight*.

The study of sociolinguistics encompasses several fields and allows for the examination of language patterns within the social constraints that buffet them about through time. Although vowels have often been a significant focus of sociolinguistic investigation, consonants also show dialect variation—at times resulting in cumulative changes in the language.[19]

Several different consonant variables are reviewed in this chapter, including coronal stop deletion, -ING variation, H-lenition, and WH/W merger. -ING variation demonstrates strong social correlations with certain variants in the same ways as in other English-speaking communities around the world, specifically the inverse correlation for the rate of [ɪn] with social class.[20] Other kinds of consonant variation, such as coronal stop deletion, show little social variation, as is the norm in other speech communities in the United States.[21] The two main variables under study are most similar to coronal stop deletion in having little social variation. Both H-lenition and WH/W demonstrate some constraint on their voicelessness by social factors, but the range of this variation is small and does not appear to be used for overt social marking. Linguistic factors, such as the duration of the segment for H-lenition and the phonological environment for W, do affect the extent of voicelessness for these variables.

With such variables, the Appalachian speakers we study are more similar to speakers in other communities than traditional stereotypes recognize, and the reality of their variation is also more complex. One damaging quality of dialect stereotypes is that they present a limited range of variation, as

if everybody in West Virginia spoke with phrases like *I ain't goin' a-fishin'
today.* As a result, when West Virginians travel outside the state, it is common for them to hear, "You don't sound like you are from West Virginia." In
fact, our student authors of this chapter have frequently been told this line
not only outside the state but also within it. Although non-Appalachians,
it seems, are working from stereotypes, native Appalachians also enforce
these speech differences based on regional differences in West Virginia.
When spoken by northern West Virginians, "You don't sound like you are
from West Virginia" means "You don't sound like you are from *southern*
West Virginia," and the stereotypes are strengthened. With a study like this
one on consonants, we are better able to portray not only the average type
of sound but also the range of sounds that make up the West Virginia linguistic landscape.

There is wide variation in certain speakers' consonants, but there is
little cumulative directional change from our oldest speakers to our young-
est. These two variables are continuing their fluctuating path, providing two
realms for the creation of social meanings by West Virginians. These realms
do point toward language change in West Virginia speech, but our Appalachian speakers also retain some of the dialect variation that distinguishes
them. West Virginia speech is changing, matching language trends outside the
region, but it is also maintaining its diversity as a dialect within the English
language. As Appalachian speech developments show both continuity and
change, representations and portrayals of that speech should do the same.

Notes

The authors would like to thank the National Science Foundation for support of this
research (BCS-0743489, BCS-1120156). We also want to thank all the WVDP research
associates for their hard work.

    1. Steve Stiles, "Li'l Abner," *Potrzebie* (blog), January 2, 2012, http://potrzebie
.blogspot.com/2012/01/al-capps-lil-abner-came-to-end-on.html (accessed March 20,
2014).

    2. Sidney Lova, "Snuffy Smith," *The Daily Funnies V* (message board), October
13, 2007, http://setiathome.berkeley.edu/forum_thread.php?id=42953 (accessed March
20, 2014).

    3. Kirk Hazen, "A Historical Assessment of Research Questions in Sociolinguis-
tics," in *Research Methods in Sociolinguistics: A Practical Guide,* ed. Janet Holmes and
Kirk Hazen (Malden, MA: Wiley Blackwell, 2014), 7–22.

    4. Kirk Hazen, "The Study of Variation in Historical Perspective," in *Sociolinguistic*

Variation: Theory, Methods, and Applications, ed. Robert Bayley and Ceil Lucas (Cambridge: Cambridge University Press 2007), 70–89.

5. Kirk Hazen, Paige Butcher, and Ashley King, "Unvernacular Appalachia," *English Today* 104.26, no. 4 (2010): 13–22; Kirk Hazen, Sarah Hamilton, and Sarah Vacovsky, "The Fall of Demonstrative *Them*: Evidence from Appalachia," *English World-wide* 32, no. 1 (2011): 74–103; Kirk Hazen, "A New Role for an Ancient Variable in Appalachia: Leveling and Standardization in West Virginia," *Language Variation and Change* 26, no. 1 (2014): 1–26.

6. Erik R. Thomas, "Phonetic Analysis in Sociolinguistics," in Holmes and Hazen, *Research Methods in Sociolinguistics,* 119–35.

7. Kirk Hazen, "Mergers in the Mountains," *English World-wide* 26, no. 2 (2005): 199–221.

8. Such demographic classifications do not replace studies of how speakers construct their social identities, but given the current state of the scholarship on English in Appalachia, we do not know enough about the sociolinguistic variations of the region to be able to study how Appalachians construct social meaning. This project must be saved for a later day. The word totals for each subpopulation (for example, middle-aged southern males) were brought into line with each other, and hence a few speakers were added to certain subgroups. There are four age groups, but the oldest age group (group 1) is unbalanced for sex and region and is not part of our current work.

9. Speakers were divided into those with any postsecondary educational experience and those with none. In previous work, this factor group was found to be highly significant. See Kirk Hazen, "(ING): A Vernacular Baseline for English in Appalachia," *American Speech* 83, no. 2 (2008): 116–40.

10. According to the 2000 US census, West Virginia had an African American population of only 3.2 percent. In the WVCEA, African Americans represent 9 percent of the speakers.

11. Hazen, "(ING)."

12. Paul Boersma and David Weenink, "Praat: Doing Phonetics by Computer" computer program, version 5.3.67, http://www.praat.org/ (last modified March 28, 2014).

13. Tyler Kendall, "On the History and Future of Sociolinguistic Data," *Language and Linguistics Compass* 2, no. 2 (2008): 332–51.

14. Square brackets indicate the phonetic representation of sound in the International Phonetic Alphabet: http://www.internationalphoneticalphabet.org.

15. Thomas C. Purnell, Joseph Salmons, Dilara Tepeli, and Jennifer Mercer, "Structured Heterogeneity and Change in Laryngeal Phonetics: Upper Midwestern Final Obstruents," *Journal of English Linguistics* 33, no. 4 (2005): 307–38.

16. Kirk Hazen, "Flying High above the Social Radar: Coronal Stop Deletion in Modern Appalachia," *Language Variation and Change* 23, no. 1 (2011): 105–37.

17. Hazen, "(ING)."

18. Ibid.

19. William Labov, Sharon Ash, and Charles Boberg, *Atlas of North American English* (The Hague: Mouton de Gruyter, 2006).

20. William Labov, *Principles of Linguistic Change,* vol. 2, *Social Factors* (Oxford: Blackwell, 2001).

21. Hazen, "Flying High."

Part 3

Economy and Environment

8

Frackonomics

Jacqueline Yahn

After the 2012 reelection of President Barack Obama, Robert E. Murray, the CEO of Murray Energy, the largest coal-mining company in the United States, penned these words for publication in the *Wheeling Intelligencer*:

> Dear Lord:
>
> The American people have made their choice. They have decided that America must change its course, away from the [principles] of our Founders. And, away from the idea of individual freedom and individual responsibility. Away from capitalism, economic responsibility, and personal acceptance.
>
> We are a Country in favor of redistribution, national weakness and reduced standard of living and lower and lower levels of personal freedom.[1]

This prayer is contextualized by the months leading up to the 2012 election, during which prominent members of the coal industry vehemently insisted that a vote for President Obama was a vote for the War on Coal. This belief arose during the first years of Obama's presidency as the federal government strengthened its oversight of the coal industry. Curiously, at the same time the Obama administration was advocating for the natural gas industry's growing use of hydraulic fracturing as a means of exploiting domestic shale plays. In the eyes of the coal industry, this was the ultimate betrayal. After all, for nearly two centuries coal mining was the sweetheart of America's energy industry, enjoying tax breaks and weak environmental regulations. For men like Murray, Obama was their Brutus.

Although Murray's prayer reads as a eulogy for the nation's economic prosperity and an incrimination of the president, in actuality it reinforces the growing consensus that coal, often dubbed king of the Appalachian region, will have to abdicate its throne to its regional challenger, natural gas. Americans no longer view coal as their only option. It is the political equivalent of ending a relationship with the explanation "It's not you, it's me." In the case of energy production, coal is still a viable suitor, but another resource, natural gas, touted for its abundance and cleanliness, is tugging at the nation's heartstrings.

For a contemporary coal baron like Murray, who made his fortune because he inherited access to millions of acres of minerals cheaply purchased, in most cases, more than a century ago, it is sobering to learn there are still minerals in the northern Appalachian plateau that you do *not* own. Particularly when those minerals, known to the public as the Marcellus shale, harbor years' worth of natural gas and are embedded in the state's plan for energy independence.[2]

In this chapter I examine the landscape that is home to the Marcellus shale, northern Appalachia, considering the implications of hydraulic fracturing ("fracking"), a technique used alongside horizontal drilling to access deep pockets of shale that were once inaccessible within the historical, political, and economic context of natural resource extraction in the region. To fully understand why fracking is so widely supported by politicians and private citizens alike, this discussion begins with a reexamination of the popular ideology of American exceptionalism and its ties to *placemaking* in America. *American exceptionalism,* as defined by historian of the American Revolutionary period Gordon Wood, is the belief that America is unique among the world's nation-states: the only one founded upon egalitarian principles that ensure the protection of individual liberties, the only one that promotes the humane treatment of all peoples, and the only one to secure its citizens' right to economic prosperity as a birthright.[3] This chapter argues that America's steadfast belief in its own exceptionality has led to the nation-state promoting decades of dominance by the coal and steel industries that has left Appalachia's northernmost corner in a weakened civil state, vulnerable to further restructuring by yet another extractive industry. Within this discussion the term *frackonomics* is developed as a way of explaining the economic implications of the shale rush in northern Appalachia. I conclude with a discussion of the unaccounted-for costs for northern Appalachians by pointing to the alarming similarities between the practices of mountaintop removal (MTR) and hydraulic fracturing, suggesting that fracking, like MTR, threatens to inflict further environmental harm, cause economic distress, and instigate civil disobedience.

The Makings of Place in America

A central aim of *Appalachia Revisited* is to help readers reexamine the place Appalachia *is* as opposed to the place it is often *imagined* to be. As Schumann explains in his introduction to this volume, the meanings of *place* are inevitably influenced by the demands of the human condition within specific environmental/cultural/historical contexts. America, as historian Gordon Wood observes, began as a collection of ideas shared among our founders.[4] In fact, Americans are the first human beings in the modern world to establish and maintain a democratic government purposefully founded with the betterment of the human condition in mind. It is for this reason that this chapter suggests that American exceptionalism explains why a nation of people, purportedly concerned with the human condition, willingly allows energy corporations to turn places within the nation into sacrifice zones. On a macro-level, this ideology of exceptionalism is often used to justify the nation-state's protection of extractive industries such as coal and natural gas that thrive by exploiting rural areas.

Within these sacrifice zones, corporations pillage natural resources at low cost to the state but high cost to the place. Natural resource extraction is a place-based business, which means corporations must engage in a coy form of place-making in order to maximize their profits, all the while endearing their companies to the nation-state. Batteau suggests that this form of corporate-led place-making led to the political invention of Appalachia. He explains that presenting Appalachia's land, people, and customs as the foil of cosmopolitan America (Appalachian otherness) justified the exploitation of the region's resources. The public is able to reason that resource extraction in Appalachia not only allows for maintenance of the American standard of living, it also serves as a way of assimilating Appalachians into cosmopolitan society and affording them the opportunity to pursue the American Dream.[5] As Hedges and Sacco point out in their *Days of Destruction, Days of Revolt*, corporations employ this strategy with their own profit in mind, giving little concern to the long-term well-being of the places they are sacrificing. The deception works because the corporations employ a local labor force; this simultaneously minimizes costs, thus pleasing the nation-state with a product that is cheap and abundant, and subdues the local people by providing a modicum of prosperity. The nation-state, Hedges and Sacco argue, has morphed into a *corporate-state*.[6]

The development of fracking, the use of horizontal drilling techniques to more easily access natural gas trapped tightly within shale beds, allows corporations to turn northern Appalachia into a sacrifice zone.[7] This shale was once too costly to access, meaning an abundance of it still remains hidden beneath our national surface. Analysts now predict that widespread employment of fracking means US gas production will grow by approximately "47 percent through 2035."[8] As a result, not only will the US companies be able to produce natural gas for domestic use, they can export the product globally. The industry will thus garner the protection of the nation-state, which sees natural gas as a means of maintaining both economic prosperity and national security, even as extraction reshapes portions of America's rural landscapes.[9]

America Revisited

This chapter, which focuses on the northernmost corner of Appalachia, argues that the construction of Appalachia's extraction economy was a joint scheme of the nation-state and extractive industries. A review of the history of extractive industries in Appalachia and America reveals how the current urge to institute frackonomics, that is, the prioritization of economic development in Appalachia's northern tier around the demands of the gas industry, is accepted by many American citizens as a necessary way to maintain our exceptional standing as *the* world power.

After the Civil War, America refocused its nation-building efforts, leading to the industrial booms of the nineteenth and twentieth centuries; throughout this time new technology allowed the United States to tap into the nation's natural resources, transforming the country from an agrarian society to an industrial civilization.[10] America engaged in what is known as frontier-based development, a particularly successful strategy of acquiring exclusive access to land and natural resources needed to build the economy.[11] The nation's productivity increased as it expanded its railways, built urban infrastructure, and encouraged its workforce to relocate to cities. As farms mechanized and subsistence agriculture steadily declined, rural America became the supplier of the nation's workforce as its residents out-migrated to cities. While rural America's population declined, corporate presence in rural regions burgeoned as the extraction of natural resources such as coal, timber, oil, and natural gas was integrated into the scheme of nation building.[12]

As America embraced the ethos of progress, its citizens came to believe that history favored the land of the free. Members of the growing urban population became accustomed to their mobility, access to goods and services, and increased leisure time; this progress encouraged more Americans to support the idea of exceptionalism, first proposed by our founders, which is the steadfast belief that America as a nation-state is a benefactor of exceptional opportunities not only for its own people but for the global community.[13]

Terry Eagleton, author of *Ideology: An Introduction,* asserts that citizens come to accept ideologies such as exceptionalism through lived experiences that reinforce the dominant belief. The more Americans attributed their personal successes and freedoms to their American citizenship, the more power the nation-state and leading capitalists were able to gain.[14] This belief in exceptionalism is a form of what agrarian scholar and political scientist James Scott calls high-modernist ideology, thinking that favors the conveniences of industrialization. As Scott explains, nation-states gain power by establishing a widespread belief among their citizens that they would be substantially worse off without the state's protection and economic support. In the case of natural resources, the state's intent is to pave the way for extractive practices by creating opportunities for large corporations to efficiently retrieve resources.[15] As America transitioned from agriculture to industrialization, resources such as Appalachia's coal moved to the top of the nation's priority list.[16]

America's focus on domestic energy extraction, particularly natural gas, is at a heightened level of intensity as scholars continue to predict a coming age of resource scarcity. Political leaders are keenly aware that the rapid depletion of our domestic coal and oil reserves coupled with the volatility of the international energy market could mean a paradigm shift in the way the world does business; lack of fuel would demobilize the world, which runs on cheap energy. Localization, as Howley explains, is a possible consequence of natural resource decline, although it is deemed unimaginable by leaders of our nation-state who derive their political influence by maintaining a centralized power structure for energy policy and who maintain a worldview in which America is seen as the defender of democracy and the free market.[17] Citizens who support this centralized power structure because of the securities it provides make the current fracking boom possible. Many proponents of high modernism insist that sacrificing portions of our rural lands is a necessity in the twenty-first century, the salient belief being that humanity cannot transgress from vast energy consumption and live to tell the tale.[18] Yet frackonomics still requires the consent of northern Appalachian landowners whose homesteads, businesses, and public agencies rest atop the Marcellus shale. Consequently, their consent is depicted as a patriotic donation of portions of the region's natural equity, suggesting that northern Appalachians can balance the nation's energy budget while earning some reserves for their personal accounts.

Revisiting the aims of the nation-state and the ways in which its partnership with extractive industries has secured its power helps to explain why fracking the nation's shale seems like a logical next step. Americans have adapted to a globalized society in which mass production, global trade, and affordable transportation are essential components of our lifestyle; it follows that a lack of centralized control over energy resources would threaten the well-being of millions of Americans. At present, therefore, many American citizens remain enamored by the short-term benefits of increasing our domestic natural gas extraction, which include a sense of stability in comparison to other world nations and regions. Just as important, proponents of fracking promote shale development as an opportunity to bring economic relief to one of the poorest areas of the United States.[19]

Northern Appalachia Restructured

The overarching argument of this chapter is that the northern Appalachian economy and landscape are both currently being restructured in order to favor the goals of the nation-state and the natural gas industry in preference to the interests of American citizens. Both entities use scientific logic to support their confidence in the Marcellus shale's ability to aid the United States in transitioning to a more sustainable energy future, therefore justifying their actions in northern Appalachia. Englender expounded this belief at Villanova's *Environmental Law Journal*'s symposium in a talk titled "'Shale' We Drill? The Legal and Environmental Impacts of Extracting Natural Gas from Marcellus Shale." It was Englender, a Penn State University geologist, who first theorized that the Marcellus shale contained trillions of tons of recoverable gas, leading the industry to allocate millions of dollars to land acquisition, exploration, and drilling throughout Appalachia's northernmost states. Before his fellow panelists discussed the current environmental and legal impacts of natural gas drilling throughout the Marcellus shale, Englender opened the symposium by explaining why fracking is occurring at this particular point in human history. Fracking is not just a logical choice, he argued; it is really the only choice left now that peak oil has occurred. It is also, as he explains it, a cleaner fuel than coal, which produces two times the amount of greenhouse gases that natural gas does when burned. Most important is Englender's assertion that horizontal drilling and hydraulic fracturing are economically feasible forms of resource extraction.[20]

While fracking undoubtedly has short- and long-term benefits for the nation-state, what about the outcomes for northern Appalachia? Company-generated literature goes to great lengths to secure local assent for fracking, needed since the vast majority of recoverable natural gas rests beneath private and publicly owned lands, and these lands are divided into much smaller parcels than are landholdings in the western United States, where shale rests beneath government-owned lands or large tracts of land held by ranchers. Thus the industry publishes and promotes literature that focuses on personal benefits for private citizens and collective benefits for local communities. Publications written from the company's vantage point provide a simplified explanation of the process: landowners negotiate leasing agreements with natural gas companies that give the companies permission to access the shale beneath their land. Sometimes this includes erecting a well pad or holding pond on the owner's property. In return, the company pays to lease per acre and agrees to pay a specific percentage of royalties to the landowner throughout the duration of gas production on the property. It appears that almost everyone in the local area has an opportunity to benefit from fracking: landowners earn royalties from their lease; workers can acquire a higher-paying job; business owners enjoy an increased customer base. Moreover, public agencies will have more money to spend on services for the community such as education, road construction, and public safety.[21]

Unsurprisingly, natural gas companies are much less eager to discuss the negative impacts of their presence in the region. One of the most dangerous impacts, the possibility of misuse of the region's water resources, is often dismissed as illogical; the industry touts the safe technologies employed to protect water sources located near well sites, holding ponds, and disposal plants. Yet fracking requires approximately "5.6 million gallons [of water] per well in the Marcellus Shale," most or all of which comes from local water sources. Moreover, it is improbable that safety features at well sites can ensure complete protection from the environmental risks natural gas extraction poses to local people.[22] To counter these concerns, the nation-state and natural gas companies reinforce the notion—through literature, public forums, and mass media—that if we frack northern Appalachia today, the nation's citizens collectively will enjoy a safer and, most important, prosperous tomorrow. This wisdom is being formed in spite of our knowledge that resource extraction often weakens rural areas, turning them into mono-economies that will face dire economic and environmental circumstances when the boom gives way to the bust.[23]

Exceptionalism, an Economic Faux Pas

The notion of American exceptionalism elicits widespread skepticism. As Barbier has pointed out, expansion across a vast frontier and the mass expenditure of natural resources is no longer a feasible plan. Wendell Berry observes that America's penchant for nation building has "unsettled" the nation, polarizing rural and metropolitan America.[24] While America has undeniably formed the wealthiest society on earth, this required the sacrifice of resource-rich places, mined for their energy sources, building materials, and cheap labor.

As Hazlitt explains in his seminal work *Economics in One Lesson*: "The art of economics consists in looking not merely at the immediate but at the longer effects of any act or policy; it consists in tracing the consequences of that policy not merely for one group but for all groups."[25] Jared Diamond illustrates this concept in his notable work *Collapse: How Societies Choose to Fail or Succeed* by examining the ways in which nations sacrifice their long-term interests in environmental and financial contexts in order to make short-term gains.[26] The natural gas industry, the nation-state, and landowners are, like others before them, tempting economic fate by advocating, although perhaps at times subconsciously, a focus on short-term outcomes that benefit only certain parties. They may assert that their decisions take long-term planning into account, but they do little to explain how. Englender may argue that natural gas is a holdover fuel for the United States, but he refrains from projecting what it is we're holding out for, observing that that is a dilemma for the "next century."[27] Likewise, landowners may report they are leasing their lands for economic advantage, but they overlook the long-term property damage they will incur.

Barth, an economist researching the financial projections tied to increased natural gas extraction, echoes Hazlitt in explaining that predictions of the wealth natural gas extraction will bring are based on contingencies that may never come to fruition. According to Barth, those forecasting favorable results fail to consider that negative impacts—for example, loss of tourism or agricultural production—are inevitable. More alarming, rosy projections are made in spite of the knowledge that evidence from recent experiences in New York actually refutes such claims. Worst of all, they commit the economic faux pas of focusing on short-term benefits for a marginal portion of the global population, the selected regions of America that heavily depend on high modernism.[28]

The Short and Long of It

While this chapter cannot address in their entirety all short- and long-term outcomes of the fracking boom, it does aim to give readers an overview of the possible effects for the region, the nation, and the world.

In *The End of Country,* a seminal text on the local response to natural gas drilling, McGraw offers readers a personalized account of his family's experiences during the early days of northern Appalachia's gas boom. McGraw pointedly describes the economic and personal stresses western Pennsylvania's residents have experienced as steel production, dairy farming, and coal mining continue to decline. By engaging in both research and informal discussions with neighbors and industry leaders, McGraw works to grasp what outcomes—positive and negative—natural gas drilling may bring to the region. As an owner of farmland, McGraw provides an inside view of the economic stress many area residents experience. His account reflects Batteau's important observation that Appalachia today is in many ways an economic and political invention born of nineteenth- and twentieth-century endeavors of the nation-state. Northern Appalachia, as its current residents know, still bears physical and financial scars from America's frontier-based development. This tier of the region, with its rusting steel mills, vanishing dairy farms, and declining coal industry, serves as an example of the long-term economic consequences of industrialization. McGraw, like many northern Appalachians, is all too aware of the long-term consequences of natural gas drilling—a landscape devastated by previous episodes of industrialization gives a foreboding hint. Yet, like dozens of his neighbors, he and his family find that their short-term economic needs trump the threat of future environmental instability in the region, preventing them from making decisions that would safeguard the land for the generations that will inherit it.[29]

The short of it is that fracking northern Appalachia requires local landowners to lease their lands. As Eric Olen Wright explains, it's not unusual for the working class to sacrifice long-term needs such as a healthy ecosystem and sustainable economy (as McGraw's family elected to do) in order to ensure short-term economic security.[30] Many citizens and public agencies need the revenue from natural gas drilling to alleviate current economic stress; a particularly salient example of this is found in Ohio's Appalachian region, where rural schools, struggling financially because of the state's funding structure (which is based on property taxes) are leasing their grounds to natural gas companies to keep pace with the financial demands of new state and federal mandates. Unfortunately, this relief is likely to be temporary, eventually leaving the region worse off. Such situations echo the historical circumstances that characterized coal mining in central Appalachia: impoverished farmers sold their land to the industry only to inflict poverty upon future generations of landless people.[31]

At present, northern Appalachians are leaving much of the discussion of how future generations will reclaim their land, water, and air for another day. Local governments are focused on building infrastructure to support the current economic growth; maintaining services such as safety, health care, and education; and regulating new industrial dilemmas. Similarly, citizens are engrossed in the legal workings of leasing lands to drilling companies; working toward becoming part of the skilled workforce needed in the new industry; and capitalizing on their newly acquired wealth. As Wright observes, living in the midst of such intense change makes it hard for residents and local government officials to surmise about the future.[32]

Elsewhere, the price of energy continues to rise, leading the natural gas industry to quicken its pace as current prices make fracking economically feasible. At the same time, the nation-state is giving the industry the green light as political tensions in the Middle East threaten the stability of the world's oil supply. Current rates of fracking in northern Appalachia and other shale-bearing regions are promoted as the best way to provide security for the nation *tomorrow*.[33] This centralized plan is designed by the nation-state and the industry, neither of which give attention to the negative economic, environmental, and social impacts rural regions so often incur during booms in natural resource extraction. Yet fracking promises to reshape not only the northern Appalachian landscape but also its economy. Much of the literature promoting the economic benefits of the current fracking boom is published by the natural gas industry, which has little interest in a future Appalachia it is unlikely to be a part of.

In contrast, more thorough discussions of the future exist in literature resulting from research conducted by state extension agencies and by university and independent scholars. Pennsylvania's state extension service, in partnership with Penn State University, has worked throughout the boom to publish literature to assist landowners with long-term planning should they choose to lease, including a thorough explanation of the environmental impacts of well pad and holding pond construction on their land. Other studies have examined the potential long-term impacts on public institutions, including school districts. Scholars of the region have also joined together to work independently from state-run agencies and universities, holding panels focusing on a localized view of natural gas drilling and publishing papers that closely examine the viewpoint of local communities. This scholarship recognizes the negative economic impacts industry literature tends to overlook and makes recommendations for long-term economic planning beyond the boom years.[34]

Natural gas companies are primarily concerned with the immediate restructuring of northern Appalachia's mineral rights, which allows them to quickly acquire access to shale. These companies are interested in making a place for their production, but not in what they will make of the place they extract from. With this in mind, Weidner explains that companies offer landowners standard leases, meaning that if landowners are not persistent in their negotiations, they will inevitably sign binding agreements that favor company interests. All landowners, local business owners, and local governments have submitted to a process whose long-term economic, environmental, and service delivery impacts are unclear.[35]

Even the nation-state itself is unlikely to remain unscathed. Even the boom's most staunch supporters recognize natural gas drilling as a temporary fix. Without a long-term energy plan, not only will rural areas suffer, so will the nation as a whole. And finally, to paraphrase Weisman, while our world would recover without us, we're much less likely to survive without it.[36]

The Wide Reach of Appalachia

In 2012, months before Murray's prayer hit the presses as the president was elected for his second term, the Appalachian Studies Association held its first conference in the region's northernmost tier. At the roundtable on fracking, it became evident that coal, as Murray would later assert to the local press, had a competitor. More striking to conference participants was the widespread environmental degradation hydraulic fracturing was likely to incur. Water contamination and exposure to toxic chemicals were two hot-button topics the panel addressed.[37] These issues were familiar to scholars and lifelong residents of the region, as was the civil disobedience emerging in pockets of the region with the highest volume of fracking activity. As invested parties knew, before the nation-state fracked northern Appalachia's hills, it moved central Appalachia's mountains. In a recent interview, Scott explained that if we want to grasp the potential outcomes of fracking northern Appalachia today, we should look back at the history of coal mining in the region.[38]

Until recently, coal was the region's most important natural resource, often given the sobriquet *king* to characterize its economic and political dominance throughout the region and the nation. Nationally, coal served as a benevolent monarch, extending portions of its earnings to the outstretched hands of some of the nation-state's most powerful economic and political stakeholders, and investing its energies in the nation's upward and outward expansions. But with each handshake and exchange, Appalachia became more environmentally and economically strained as it was asked to stretch its resources just a little further to feed the nation's energy hunger. The flaw in this economic model is that it supported the long-term interests of the monarch and its ally, the nation-state, while disregarding the needs of the place known to the world as Appalachia.

In their widely hailed pop culture text on economics, Levitt and Dubner suggest, "Morality, it could be argued, represents the way that people would like the world to work—whereas economics represents how it actually *does* work."[39] A conventional wisdom is forming that by supporting fracking, northern Appalachians are enlisting in a patriotic act and a moral cause that will keep our nation united and free. The reality is that the widespread support for frackonomics is directly tied to the needs of the nation-state, which requires increasing amounts of fuel in order to produce the energy required for maintaining its power structure and satisfying its citizens. And if economics tells us something about the inner workings of the nation-state, then Hazlitt is right and northern Appalachia today is a reflection of yesterday's economic and environmental choices—a weakened civil state coercively positioned to partake in frackonomics to regain its economic strength. If we keep this in mind, we understand that the Appalachia of tomorrow, too, will reflect the costs of today's choices, meaning the newest expenses of the nation's exceptionalism will be charged to Appalachia's northern peoples.

Notes

1. Robert E. Murray, "Murray Prays for America," *Wheeling (WV) Intelligencer,* November 8, 2012.

2. J. David Hughes, *Drill, Baby Drill: Can Unconventional Fuels Usher in a New Era of Energy Abundance?* (Santa Rosa, CA: Post Carbon Institute, 2013), 48–77.

3. See Gordon S. Wood, *The Idea of America: Reflections on the Birth of the United States* (New York: Penguin, 2011), 273–90.

4. Ibid.

5. See Allen W. Batteau, *The Invention of Appalachia* (Tucson: University of Arizona Press, 1990).

6. See Chris Hedges and Joe Sacco, "Days of Revolt," in *Days of Destruction, Days of Revolt* (New York: Nation Books, 2012), 225–71.

7. Ground Water Protection Council, *Modern Shale Gas Development in the United States: A Primer* (Oklahoma City: US Department of Energy, 2009), 8–11.

8. Quoted in Hughes, *Drill, Baby, Drill,* 24.

9. See, for example, Russell Gold, *The Boom: How Fracking Ignited the American Energy Revolution and Changed the World* (New York: Simon and Schuster, 2014); Daniel Yergin, *The Quest: Energy, Security, and the Remaking of the Modern World* (New York: Penguin, 2011).

10. Ruth Schwartz Cowan, "Industrial Society and Technological Systems," in *Society, Ethics, and Technology,* 2nd ed., ed. Morton E. Winston and Ralph D. Edelbach (Toronto: Wadsworth, 2003), 54–71.

11. E. B. Barbier, *Scarcity and Frontiers: How Economies Have Developed through Natural Resource Exploitation* (Cambridge: Cambridge University Press, 2011), 368–428; Joel Kotkin, *The City: A Global History* (New York: Random House, 2005), 90.

12. See, for example, Cynthia M. Duncan, *Worlds Apart: Why Poverty Persists in Rural America* (New Haven, CT: Yale University Press, 1999); Osha Gray Davidson, *Broken Heartland: The Rise of America's Rural Ghetto* (Iowa City: University of Iowa Press, 1996), 13–46.

13. See Christopher Lasch, *The True and Only Heaven: Progress and Its Critics* (New York: Norton, 1991), 40–81; William J. Bennett, *America, the Last Best Hope,* vol. 1, *From the Age of Discovery to a World at War* (Nashville: Nelson Current, 2006), 434–74.

14. Terry Eagleton, *Ideology: An Introduction* (New York: Verso, 1991), 221–24.

15. J. Scott, *Seeing Like a State: How Certain Schemes to Improve the Human Condition Have Failed* (New Haven, CT: Yale University Press, 1998), 87–102.

16. See Batteau, *The Invention of Appalachia;* Jeff Biggers, *The United State of Appa-*

lachia: How Southern Mountaineers Brought Independence, Culture, and Enlightenment to America (Emeryville, CA: Shoemaker and Hoard, 2006).

17. See Robert Heinberg, *The Party's Over: Oil, War and the Fate of Industrial Societies,* 2nd ed. (Babriola Island, BC: New Society, 2005); Craig B. Howley, "The Coming Vitality of Rural Places," *Eğitim Bilimleri Araştırmaları Dergisi—Journal of Educational Sciences Research* 3, no. 1(2013).

18. Mark Lynas, *The God Species: Saving the Planet in the Age of Humans* (Washington, DC: National Geographic Society, 2011), 229–44.

19. Consider the regular supply of promotional information about Appalachia's regional economy disseminated by the industry-sponsored Marcellus Shale Coalition. See http://marcelluscoalition.org/ (accessed April 20, 2015).

20. Hughes, *Drill, Baby, Drill,* i–iv; Todd Aagard, Terry Englender, and Hannah Wiseman, "'Shale' We Drill? The Legal and Environmental Impacts of Extracting Natural Gas from Marcellus Shale," *Villanova Environmental Law Journal* 22, no. 2 (2011): 189–224; Seamus McGraw, *The End of Country: Dispatches from the Frack Zone* (New York: Random House, 2011).

21. Jannette M. Barth, "The Economic Impacts of Shale Gas Development on State and Local Economies: Benefits, Costs and Uncertainties," *New Solutions* 23, no. 1 (2013): 85–101.

22. Quoted in Myron Arnowitt, Robert E. Bishop, David J. Lampe, Brian W. Okey, and Tom Wilber, "'Fracking': A Roundtable," *Journal of Appalachian Studies* 18, nos. 1–2 (2012): 36; see also Robert E. Bishop, "Chemical and Biological Risk Assessment for Natural Gas Extraction in New York," State University of New York College at Oneonta, Department of Chemistry and Biochemistry, 2011.

23. Barth, "The Economic Impacts of Shale Gas Development"; Stratford Douglas and Anne Walker, *Coal Mining and the Resource Curse in the Eastern United States* (Morgantown, WV: Social Sciences Research Network, 2013).

24. Barbier, *Scarcity and Frontiers;* W. Berry, *The Unsettling of America* (San Francisco: Sierra Club Books, 1977).

25. Quoted in Henry Hazlitt, *Economics in One Lesson* (New York: Harper and Brothers, 1946), 5.

26. See Jared Diamond, *Collapse: How Societies Choose to Fail or Succeed* (New York: Penguin Books, 2005).

27. Quoted in Aagard, Englender, and Wiseman, "'Shale' We Drill?" 16.

28. Janette M. Barth, *Unanswered Questions about the Economic Impact of Natural Gas Drilling in the Marcellus Shale: Don't Jump to Conclusions* (Hudson, NY: JM Barth, 2010).

29. McGraw, *The End of Country;* Batteau, *The Invention of Appalachia,* 1–8.

30. Eric Olen Wright, *Class, Crisis and the State* (London: Verso, 1978), 61–108.

31. See Craig B. Howley, Aimee Howley, Megan Eliason Rhodes, and Jacqueline Yahn, "Three Contemporary Dilemmas for Rural Superintendents," *Peabody Journal of*

Education 89 (2014): 619–38; Ron Eller, *Uneven Ground: Appalachia since 1945* (Lexington: University Press of Kentucky, 2008).

32. Jeffrey Jacquett, *Energy Boomtowns and Natural Gas: Implications for Marcellus Shale Local Governments and Rural Communities* (University Park: Northeast Regional Center for Rural Development and Pennsylvania State University, 2009), 1–24; Wright, *Class, Crisis and the State,* 61–108.

33. See Englender's discussion in Aagard, Englender, and Wiseman, "'Shale' We Drill?" 190–93; Ground Water Protection Council, *Modern Shale Gas Development,* 3–10.

34. See Krista Weidner, *Natural Gas Exploration: A Landowner's Guide to Leasing Land in Pennsylvania* (University Park: Penn State Extension Agency, 2013), 10–18; Kai A. Schafft, Leland L. Glenna, Yetkin Borlu, and Brandon Green, *Marcellus Shale Gas Development: What Does It Mean for Pennsylvania Schools?* (University Park: Penn State Extension Agency, 2012); Arnowitt et al., "'Fracking,'" 31–47; Jason L. Weigle, "Resilience, Community and Perceptions of Marcellus Shale Development in the Pennsylvania Wilds: Reclaiming the Discussion," *Sociological Viewpoints* (2011): 3–14.

35. Weidner, *Natural Gas Exploration,* 10–11; Jacquett, *Energy Boomtowns and Natural Gas,* 46–56.

36. Aagard, Englender, and Wiseman, "'Shale' We Drill?" 204; Alan Weisman, *The World without Us* (New York: Picador, 2007), 369.

37. See Arnowitt et al., "'Fracking,'" 31–47, for a thorough discussion of the round-table proceedings. See Bishop, "Chemical and Biological Risk Assessment" for discussion of environmental and health risks.

38. For discussions of coal mining, particularly mountaintop removal, in central Appalachia, see Michele Morrone and Geoffrey L. Buckley, eds., *Mountains of Injustice: Social and Environmental Justice in Appalachia* (Athens: Ohio University Press, 2011); and Erik Reece, *Lost Mountain: A Year in the Vanishing Wilderness* (New York: Riverhead Books, 2006). For Scott's complete interview, see Jacqueline Yahn, "The Affectionate Agrarian: An Interview with James Scott," 2014, Ohio University Institute for Democracy in Education, https://www.ohio.edu/education/centers-and-partnerships/centers/institute-for-democracy-in-education/research-initiatives.cfm (accessed April 20, 2015).

39. Quoted in Steven D. Levitt and Stephen J. Dubner, *Freakonomics: A Rogue Economist Explores the Hidden Side of Everything* (New York: Harper Perennial, 2005), 11; Hazlitt, *Economics in One Lesson,* 4.

9

Revisiting Appalachian Icons in the Production and Consumption of Tourist Art

Kristin Kant-Byers

Scholars in Appalachian studies commonly acknowledge that discourses of Appalachia as a region of backwards, primitive, and isolated mountain folk are invented stereotypes of a more complex reality. Yet regional stereotypes remain pervasive, persuasive, and consumable—especially icons produced in the tourism industry. As an anthropologist, I wanted to know why stereotypical icons persist. So I examined the cultural, social, political, and economic dynamics within tourism that sustain and reproduce stereotyped Appalachian icons. I was not concerned with evaluating the authenticity of Appalachian cultural forms; my focus, rather, was on how and why individuals see these forms as more or less meaningful. My first step was to establish a pattern of iconography in a particular tourism destination in order next to understand the meanings underlying the persistence of icons. Once I had established a pattern of iconography, I then used interviews, free listing, participant observation, and surveys to collect data about the associations artists and tourists make about Appalachian culture. I discovered through this project that stereotypical icons persist because artists and tourists hold similar notions about Appalachian culture, notions that have been informed by a long history of media representation, linkages to economic interests, and emotionalized experience of place.

In this chapter I describe the sorts of images available in an art market located in a tourist destination within the Appalachian region—a place I call Mountainville.[1] Mountainville, a small, socioeconomically diverse town of thirty-five hundred residents, is characterized by high levels of tourist activities—over 10 million tourists visit annually—and high concentrations of art production and art consumption.[2] Efforts to promote this town as a "mountain" tourist destination increase the likelihood that Mountainville produces stereotypes in the marketplace. Indeed, Mountainville may not be representative of Appalachia at all, yet it is a place people go to consume and experience Appalachia.

In this chapter I use social science methods to explore the production of knowledge about Appalachia's regional iconography. In this case, the primary method I used to obtain data on icons was a *content* analysis—the systematic classifying and quantifying of the frequencies of visual representations.[3] Systematically analyzing visual representations of Appalachia offers valuable insights into the cultural values and practices of the producers and consumers of regional icons in specific spaces of social and economic exchange. I specifically selected paintings and reproduced prints of paintings because this art medium contains recognizable symbols easily manipulated to convey cultural meanings and ideas. Moreover, paintings are popular with tourists because they are easy to transport and display. I determined by visiting or phoning over a hundred arts and crafts galleries that approximately thirty-eight galleries in Mountainville carried original paintings and prints. Of these, I randomly selected ten galleries to conduct the content analysis. Gallery sizes ranged from a one-person operation in two hundred square feet of exhibition space that attracted on average three visitors a day and reached yearly sales of $10,000, to an establishment with seven employees in seven thousand square feet that hosted two hundred visitors a day and achieved annual sales of over $600,000.

Study Methods

Content analysis. To create a representative sample of tourist art in Mountainville, I catalogued every third painting in ten galleries, resulting in a data set of 455 paintings produced by twenty different artists.[4] For each of these paintings or prints I recorded price, physical dimensions, title, artist, and content. I noted when images were repeated as prints throughout the gallery. These prints were catalogued as separate entries, often because they contained differences in price and/or dimensions. I labeled each painting

Table 9.1. Content analysis results

Types of subject	Number of paintings	Percentage
Buildings	135	29.7
Landscapes	77	16.9
Florals	74	16.3
Wildlife	68	14.9
People	62	13.6
Still lifes/nautical	39	8.6
Total	455	100

with a one-word code capturing its primary subject: "barn," "cabin," "river," "mountain," "deer," and so on.[5] I then used the primary subject as a basis to group the paintings into seven larger categories: buildings, landscapes, florals, wildlife, people, still lifes, and nautical.[6] Table 9.1 shows the number and percentage of paintings with these types of subject images.

Correlation of catalogued images to conceptualizations of Appalachia. Once I had catalogued the images in paintings, the next task was to evaluate how the images compared to Appalachian stereotypes and icons. To make this comparison, I used the following working definitions: *images* are simply visual representations of something, someplace, or someone; *cultural stereotypes* are understood to be assumptions and essentialized conceptualizations made of a group of people, their lifestyle, beliefs, behaviors, values, material culture, and the like; *icons* are defined as images imbued with stereotypes or visual representations of stereotypes. Delineating terms enabled me to see icons as the conduit between mental conceptualizations of a group of people and the visual representations made of that group.

Free listing stereotypes. I gathered data about stereotypes perceived by Mountainville artists and gallery owners as well as community leaders via interviews. Each interviewee was asked to *free list,* or to brainstorm, any and all stereotypes he or she associated with Appalachian culture. Then I asked each to free list icons or imagery he or she considered to represent Appalachian culture. This order presented the responder with time to consider his or her notions of Appalachia and how these notions might be visualized. After I collected the free lists, I coded and categorized the responses. I tallied the number of responses to indicate predominance of icons in the interviewees' perceptions of Appalachian representation. The free listing exercise was conducted to determine the relationship between what participants, particularly artists, perceived as Appalachian icons and what subjects they painted.

Thirty-one interviewees participated in this written exercise. Because most of the participants were not from Appalachia but had moved to Mountainville from other places in the United States, this exercise helped determine their understandings of regional cultural assumptions and factual knowledge about the Appalachian region and culture. Many participants admitted that some stereotypes they listed were misrepresentative and others they considered accurate. The results show participants are aware of stereotypes referring mostly to *character and personality traits* of Appalachian people (48 responses). Positive traits like "neighborly," "helpful," and "friendly" as well as "honest," "hardworking," and "gentle" rank highest in responses, but culturally negative traits like "lazy," "stubborn," and "racist" were also mentioned. Since these responses reflect traits of individual persons, the participants may have been influenced by their personal experiences with neighbors and acquaintances they perceive as more representative of Appalachia than themselves.

The second-largest category concerned *educational stereotypes* (22 responses) such as "ignorant" and "inarticulate." Another large response group (21) referenced *material culture and landscapes,* ranging from "trucks" and "porches" to "whisky" and "wagons." The remaining categories of stereotypes emerging from the artists' and gallery owners' responses are *isolated* (20), *traditional* (19), *body image* (18), *caricatures* (15), *poverty* (9), and *environmental landscape* (4). These categories reflect cultural traits. That the participants listed wider cultural traits indicates the deep enculturation of stereotypes of the Appalachian region and culture—even among people who live and work in Appalachia!

Free listing iconography. In addition to a free list of stereotypes associated with Appalachian culture, I also asked interviewees to free list Appalachian iconography—the image forms that Appalachian stereotypes might take. This created a second list to which correlations might be made between images catalogued in galleries and conceptualizations of Appalachia. Nineteen individuals participated. Because this question was less well understood, I elaborated by asking participants to think of images or pictures of Appalachia or what they might expect would be in a painting employing Appalachian stereotypes. I categorized responses according to the codes used in the painting content analysis. Using the same codes helped to make a more valid comparison of images participants perceived to be Appalachian and what images were actually produced for the tourist art market.

As with the first free list, artists and gallery owners overwhelmingly ranked the material landscape and the built environment as representative of the region. Interviewees most often listed moonshine, clothing (overalls, straw hats, torn shirts, hanging laundry), tools (shotguns, water barrels), and handmade objects (brooms, corncob pipes, pottery, woodworking, woven items) as images of Appalachian stereotypes. Participants also recorded images of buildings representing Appalachia, including cabins, outhouses, barns, and churches. Buildings make the second-largest category of responses. The tendency of artists to visualize Appalachia through buildings resonates with the high frequency of building images in the body of paintings catalogued through the content analysis.

Comparing the interviewees' lists of stereotypes to their lists of icons yields two noteworthy observations. First, when listing icons and images of Appalachia, a significant number of participants listed images of buildings, yet building structures were not listed as stereotypes. Cabins, churches, barns, and so on were not listed by participants asked to provide their sense of Appalachian stereotypes. Yet such buildings, according to the data from the content analysis, are used to visualize "Appalachian" scenes and do rank high in catalogued gallery paintings. The reason such icons are present in paintings as well as artists' conceptions of Appalachia may have more to do with artists' experiences in the local landscape of Mountainville's tourism industry than with the general region of Appalachia. Because an adjacent national park has preserved several nineteenth-century dwellings and outbuildings, many residents and tourists see and experience these structures. Because these buildings are popular local tourist attractions, over time kindred images have become features of the art of the area. Thus artists, acting as consumers of images and meaning, incorporate the local representations of Appalachian culture in the production of art.

The second significant observation that arises from comparing the free listing of stereotypes to the free listing of icons of Appalachia is that the "character traits" category, which comes first in the list of stereotypes, is third in the list of icons. Because of the difficulty of painting abstractions like personality traits and mannerisms, character traits are simply more readily verbalized than visualized. This logistical dilemma may explain why artists, when picturing the poverty of the region, were quick to cite images of dilapidated mailboxes, leaky roofs, and old cars. Some personality characteristics are too abstract to convey visually in an art world dominated by a realistic style.[7]

It is not surprising that interviewees can easily list Appalachian stereotypes and iconography. As members of the American cultural mainstream, the artists, gallery coordinators/workers, and community members I interviewed are enculturated with institutionalized ideas of Appalachian culture. Although many artists admit that such ideas are inaccurate and nonrepresentative, they nevertheless utilize them in order to sell paintings. An inquiry into the prevalence of stereotypes of Appalachian culture tourists visiting Mountainville hold offers some insight into why artists as producers of local imagery feel compelled to paint images and icons constricting true understandings of Appalachia.

Buyers', non-buyers', and artists' survey. In four locations throughout the 2005 summer and fall seasons, I conducted surveys with gallery visitors after they exited the gallery. One hundred twelve surveys were collected from eighteen art buyers and ninety-four non-buyers. Survey questions asked visitors to provide up to four responses detailing what they know about people living in Appalachia. The responses were coded (to correspond with the codes used to analyze the free lists of stereotypes provided by artists, gallery owners, and community leaders), categorized, and tallied. The ranking of categories provides a peek into the kinds of stereotypes tourists associate with people from Appalachia.

Stereotypes relating to individual personality traits ranked highest with all three groups (tourists who bought art, tourists who browsed but did not buy, and artists). Traits like "friendly" and "hardworking" were most frequently cited by surveyed gallery visitors as characteristic of Appalachian people. All three groups also see poverty and undereducation as key elements of Appalachian culture.

Comparisons between the tourists' and artists' categories of stereotypes yield some small but interesting differences. For example, artists are generally more visually oriented and subsequently associate culture with objects and personal appearance. The stereotype depicting Appalachian people as craftspeople using handmade tools to produce necessary goods is ranked higher by tourists, but is not significant in artists' accounts. That this survey was conducted in Mountainville's arts and crafts community immediately following a tourist's visit to a gallery and his or her immediate experience with craftspeople may explain why tourists perceive Appalachian folk to be craft producers more so than do the artists themselves.

However, despite some occasional subtle differences, tourists and artists seem to make congruent and consistent associations about Appalachian culture. Why such homogenous perceptions of Appalachian culture are perpetuated may have much to do with the sociohistorical construction of Appalachia as a distinct culture and the enculturation of this view in the public mindset. Because artists generally believe they must produce art that connects with tourists who expect and experience deeply embedded Appalachian cultural essentializations, these essentializations become a part of the artists' repertoire of images and icons. Although some artists may not believe such icons are representative of Appalachian culture, they still contribute to the perpetuation of stereotypes because stereotypes sell. Thus, structural forces like the tourist market are the main impetus for the consistency of stereotyping embraced by artists and tourists. This is not to say individual artists are duped into believing cultural propaganda, but rather that they select culturally (mis)appropriated images while at the same time maintaining the integrity of their individual artistic vision.

Sociohistorical Construction of Appalachia

To understand how the Appalachian region is construed as culturally distinct, this section examines the ways Appalachia has been talked about, written about, and visualized in public media, providing an intellectual history of Appalachian images. Establishing a historical pattern of cultural distinction sets the stage for understanding the formation of tourists' perceptions of Appalachian culture.

Images of Appalachia suggesting cultural difference have been projected to Americans since the 1800s. Tales of Daniel Boone and Davy Crockett seemed to affirm notions of the wild mountainous areas as places of danger yet tamable by people who were perceived to have the right amount of wits, stamina, personal and moral honor, and resistance to authority figures.[8]

During a period when much of the United States was experiencing post–Civil War economic growth, reports and images of violence and family feuds in the mountains of Kentucky and West Virginia were presented and interpreted in the national press as signs of lawlessness and ignorant mountain folk. As Waller suggests, stories and images of Appalachian family feuds allowed members of the American middle class "to distance themselves from the potential for family violence."[9] Moreover, the violent icons of

Appalachia legitimized the interference of regional outsiders in local politics and resource extraction.[10]

Images of violence in the late 1800s and early 1900s were replaced in the 1910s to the 1940s by representations of Appalachians as childlike, displaying qualities of irresponsibility and obliviousness. Images of rural subsistence-based poverty in the regions were projected in cartoons, comic books, movies, and literature. Depictions of lazy, barefoot men and women in worn and ill-fitting clothing, the men sporting black and scrubby beards, living in shabby shacks and carrying shotguns embodied mainstream America's fear of economic instability, a public warning of the consequences of Americans losing access to wealth and resources.[11] Additionally, these images were of white-only characters, conveying notions of race as an influx of eastern European and Asian immigrant labor in the northern industrial belt led the middle and upper classes to regard the white Anglo-Saxon ancestry of many Appalachian people to be the purest form of Americans.[12] In the US context of racialized thinking and racial unrest, images of Appalachians as white were comforting and proved advantageous to those trying to develop lines of financial support connecting poor Appalachians and the wealthier northern upper classes.[13] Such images reflected cultural beliefs and attitudes valuing economic order and stability, patriotism, and racial purity.

Cultural beliefs and attitudes toward poverty in Appalachia were further influenced by the War on Poverty campaigns of the 1960s. While some parts of the country experienced an economic boom, Appalachia's legacies of outside capital development were reflected in poor living conditions, few opportunities for enhancement and empowerment, and little control over local resources. National television, newspaper, and magazine stories disseminated images of people in extreme poverty. Middle-class volunteers across America arrived ready to rally and fight for improved conditions. Movies from this era represented Appalachian people as "helpless victims of greed" in need of saving by virtuous citizens from the modernized and urbanized upper classes in the more economically successful northern states.[14] Such perceptions led to stereotypes of Appalachian people as poor, lazy, and backwards by their own fault. Thinking about Appalachian people in terms of these stereotypes dangerously ignored the roots of poverty, disguising the power structures and ideology that had resulted in Appalachians' absent access to resources, to control, and to opportunity.[15]

Other media representations, such as the film adaptation of James Dickey's *Deliverance* (1972), recast the hillbilly as menacing and violent.

This Appalachian icon, molded from the "local" characters in the movie, represented a rebuff of backwardness in a society coveting urban sophistication and technical advancement. The urban icons in the movie stood for masculinity and heroism overcoming the wild violence of nature represented by the local and rural characters.

Other projects, such as the Foxfire book series (beginning in 1972) and the *Waltons* (1972–1981) television show, emphasized simple lifestyles and strong kin connections as regional cultural traits.[16] These nostalgic images became emblematic of perceived Appalachian values of family and place. Nostalgia is also at the center of more recent work. Catherine Marshall's *Christy*, a novel, musical, television movie and, most widely seen, a 1994–1995 television series, presented pioneeresque landscapes and material culture in the story of an upper-class young teacher as she interacts with and tries to understand a mountain community distrustful of outsiders.[17] In the twenty-first century, films such as *Songcatcher* (2000) and multimedia events like *Cold Mountain* (2003) indicate continued changes in how the American public understands and consumes regional images. Some of these changes, coupled with a sense of cultural distinction and nostalgia, are reflected in Mountainville's tourist industry.

Historical Patterns and Individual Consumption

The commonalities between the public configuration of Appalachian culture and the expressions of culture embedded in Mountainville gallery paintings demonstrate the direct relationship between the structural projection of ideas on a societal scale and assimilation of those ideas on an individual scale. In other words, these commonalities help to explain the persistence of Appalachian stereotypical icons. According to anthropologist Marushka Svasek in her discussion of art and cultural production, "We attribute values to objects, but are also influenced by the ideas or values they express."[18] To be clear, Appalachian stereotypes persist because people find them personally meaningful—*why* they do is the key to understanding the images' endurance. In Mountainville's tourist art market, artists act as both producer and consumer, selecting and reproducing images in their art. Examining the meanings artists associate with icons is an appropriate place to begin understanding their proliferation.

Artists find Appalachian icons meaningful in two distinct ways. Artists select certain icons to paint because they believe these icons will sell; there is economic incentive to produce them. Second, many artists make personal connections to local icons, and such emotional charges motivate them to paint these images. Many artists revealed the deep nostalgic feelings they have for historical buildings, landscapes and vistas, and local wildlife. Similar emotional effects are felt by tourists, whose resulting purchases help to reinforce the production of such icons. The following summarizes three central themes of the cultural values of nostalgia that gallery work references and promotes.

Hillbillies and Pioneer Mountain Culture

According to the content analysis of paintings in galleries, the largest body of paintings depicts elements of rural pioneer life in the mountains. Although these paintings do not produce images of "hillbillies" of the exaggerated cartoon type, they do suggest a romanticized portrayal of mountain life. For tourists, these paintings are manifestations of nearly two hundred years of media representations expressed through individual tastes and preferences. For the artists painting these cultural scenes, images of cabins, churches, barns, farmsteads, and so on act as icons conveying value and appreciation for life in the past. For example, one artist, Lyla, describes how she decides what to paint: "I live here. I drive down these roads. I see these things, and they disappear on me. I'm recording them as fast as I can, with my camera and my painting." For Lyla, capturing the material cultural landscape before it is gone, developed into rental communities, shopping centers, or roads, is a passionate motivation, one that also compels her to involvement in local zoning policy politics.

This pattern of value for the past and historical landscapes is repeated in another artist's work, reflected in his descriptions of how he selects his subjects. Luke even exaggerates distances he would go to paint a certain location that fits within his visual scheme. "If I find something that I really want to paint, a really nice covered bridge or a gristmill, I'll drive five hundred miles to paint it."

Another artist's personal values and connection to religion influence her subjects of choice. Denise says, "I love to paint churches, the little white frame churches . . . and I'm always scouting for those."

Mountains

The second-largest category of visual representations discerned by content analysis included paintings of landscapes, particularly mountains. As the pseudonym I've chosen for the town implies, Mountainville bases much of its touristic allure on the beauty of its undeveloped mountains. Visitors to the town experience buildings whose architectural styles reflect the slopes and contours of mountains. Joined with the vast number of paintings of mountains, these images serve as icons symbolizing and projecting the predominance of nature, perceived as untamed and boundless, in Mountainville—setting it apart as a consumable place of distinction.

Most artists in Mountainville who paint for a living offer images of mountains. Two artists in particular, Greg and Van, both of whom have successful, stable, and long-term businesses in Mountainville, display in their galleries hundreds of mountain scenes they have rendered over the course of twenty or thirty years. According to both artists, their paintings depict what they see every day. Greg explained, "I paint where I live . . . , and I paint my impressions of my surroundings." Van told me, "So I paint what I know, and growing up here in the mountains, I know the mountains . . . and if you paint what you know it's a better piece."

To paint what they know and what they feel most connected to in their natural environment is important to these artists. The mountain icon functions as a catalyst to convey personal meaning and experience with the local environment. Although Greg and Van have been painting similar mountain landscapes for years, their rendering of the scenes has changed as they have adjusted their palettes to include brighter and more popular colors. This reflects not only their attention to color trends in popular culture but also their own internalization of such trends.

Black Bears

In the body of images used in Mountainville, none is as singularly prolific as the icon of the black bear. Like images of the mountains, images of black bears symbolize nature and the untamable wilderness. This icon is often imbued with anthropomorphic features, exhibiting personality traits and human behaviors that art buyers may relate to. According to one artist who had a previous career as an official in the nearby national park, painting animals allows for a more engaging experience between viewer and subject—an experience facilitated by the way the artist portrays the subject. Building on her intimate knowledge of mountain wildlife, this artist endows her subjects with humanlike expressions. When asked why she paints animals so prolifically, Gertie responded: "I like to paint animals because you can get a personality and a character. Bears are what's pulling people into the area, so . . . that was another reason I decided to do a real bear." Gertie also understands the role of the black bear icon as an attraction that brings people into Mountainville. She realizes people are interested in seeing black bears, especially because of their assigned status as a symbol of both cuteness and wildness. Gertie's art concentrates on the former quality because she understands this appeals to some buyers, but several other Mountainville artists reproduce these icons in a naturalistic style void of any indication of anthropomorphism.

My study demonstrates the complicated role icons play in Mountainville's art market. They act as images of stigmatized culture and as representations of personal preference for nostalgia. Like the images of mountains, bears, and pioneer mountain life, depictions of local culture and place are trapped in the past and romanticized. Paintings portraying local scenes and people are free from evidence of daily life. Scenes do not contain contemporary automobiles, roadside trash, smog, dying forests, fancy cabins, park rangers, paved roads—all of which tourists experience during their visit to Mountainville. Moreover, these images ignore diversity and inclusion of people from various backgrounds, lifestyles, beliefs, ethnicities, and perspectives. Therefore, images contained in Mountainville art may not be regarded as authentic or true representations of the lived experiences of people associated with the Appalachian region.

Such representation thus limits an understanding of the region and its people. This limitation occurs because the tourism industry hinges on the creation of positive experiences. Paintings portraying poverty, social inequity, and urban and industrial Appalachia, for example, would certainly evoke different emotions in tourists—and those are images the tourism industry works to avoid. Misrepresenting Appalachia has been a key strategy in the pursuit of other economic activities of the region, like mining and resource extraction industries, and highway and land development, as well as in portrayals of community activists and resistance to oppression and inequality. Tourism adds to this misrepresentation as its market structures act with the compelling power of images to project and facilitate particular perceptions of and contrived interactions with Appalachian culture.

Still, these glamorized depictions of Appalachia are highly valued by both the people who paint them and those who purchase them. People express sincere emotional and personal connection to these depictions. Some artists describe a genuine passion for painting pioneer cabins. Tourists see in the paintings what motivates them to travel to Mountainville—beautiful landscapes, a perceivably different way of life. Images of mountains, bears, and pioneer mountain life have come to mean something significant to both viewers and artists. In this context of tourist paintings, that significance is related to assumptions about Appalachian culture in general. These icons function to assert cultural constructions of Appalachia. Because the Appalachian region has been sociohistorically constructed as a distinct cultural region in the public perception and because tourists have been influenced to expect an experience with this constructed culture, this body of artwork, and particularly paintings, functions to reinforce and legitimate preconceived cultural conceptions. In other words, Appalachia has been created as a pristine, undeveloped region, its culture stuck in the past, its poor, rural, simple folk tied to tradition and religion. Tourists are led to believe they can personally experience this culture. These icons portrayed in art convey messages characterizing the area as the tourism industry wants to promote it and as tourists want to see it. And the engagement of artists' visions, visitors' emotions, and the touristic experience certainly helps to facilitate sales.

Artists, like the tourists they paint for, live in a cultural context positioning them to consume icons of Appalachia. Even though these icons, like mountains, trees, cabins, barns, and black bears, might hold personal value to an artist, many artists depict such icons in artwork because the icons have evolved into normalized and appropriate representations signifying Appalachia. Artists may or may not be critical of such representations, but they are constrained by structural forces of the market to place icons in their paintings in order to sell them. The risk of business failure is too great for artists to offer alternative images. At the same time, artists evoke a degree of agency in the marketplace as they make choices among certain cultural images according to their preferences. These preferences can be based on many factors, including ensuring livelihood and expressing emotion. The point is that these icons are actively selected by artists and other image makers in the same way tourists choose which souvenir to purchase. Because artists create images for sale and because they are selective in the representations they choose, they are also consumers of cultural icons. As consumers, artists act out the creativity capacity inherent in the consumption process. Iconic stereotypes are perpetuated not because they accurately depict local place and people but because they are part of a body of symbols from which artists acting as consumers may select in order to signify what is perceived as "Appalachian" or what artists perceive as reflections of their own aesthetic and personal identities.

The goal of this project was to understand the meanings behind the persistence of icons among both producers (artists) and consumers (artists and tourists) in an effort to see the underlying structures enabling the continuation of stereotypes. The methodology used, content analysis, enabled me to identify local patterns of iconography and to connect those patterns to regional representations. Interviews, free listing, and surveys provided the opportunity for conversations with artists and tourists about the perceptions they have of icons. Interviews with artists also helped me understand the role icons play as economic strategies to sell paintings and support livelihood. Stereotypical icons persist because artists and tourists hold similar notions about Appalachian culture. Such notions are informed by a history of pop culture media representation, economic interests and capitalistic enterprise, and emotionalized experience of place. Although icons and stereotypes of Appalachia are widely known and reported (such as in the "Sign of the Times" section of the peer-reviewed *Appalachian Journal*), applying a systemic methodology to the study of these representations allows researchers to gain both a wider regional perspective and a view of the connections between individuals and society useful to explain the persistence of Appalachian stereotypes.

Notes

1. Mountainville is a pseudonym. All names in this study have been changed to protect the identity and livelihood of the project's participants. This is a common practice in anthropology as well as other social science research.

2. Per capita revenue from 2013 city sales tax was $3,922. For comparison, a nearby city with a larger manufacturing base economy and a population of twenty-seven thousand produced $7 million in sales tax, for a per capita of $259. These figures were reported by the County Economic Development Council and the city budget manager. I am grateful to K. R. Tallent for her assistance in obtaining this budget analysis and helping me make sense of it.

3. Philip Bell, "Content Analysis of Visual Images," in *Handbook of Visual Analysis,* ed. Theo van Leeuwen and Carey Jewitt (London: Sage, 2001), 10–34.

4. Most of Mountainville's paintings are produced in the style of realism. According to art history classifications, realism is the depiction of things as they would be seen in visible nature. Horst de la Croix, Richard Tansy, and Diane Kirkpatrick, *Gardner's Art through the Ages,* 9th ed. (New York: Harcourt Brace College, 1991).

5. By primary subject, I refer to the image that is a focal point, supported by other painted elements that form the context of the subject.

6. Paintings with nautical themes, mostly lighthouses, were primarily produced by one artist in this study. Although Mountainville is not a coastal locale, many tourists bought such paintings because of the religious connotation lighthouses hold for Christianity—a religion strongly associated with people in Appalachia.

7. Personality traits may be better communicated as emotions through abstract-styled art.

8. George Brosci, "Images and Icons," in *Encyclopedia of Appalachia*, ed. Rudy Abramson and Jean Haskell (Knoxville: University of Tennessee Press, 2006), 199–205.

9. Altina Waller, "Feuding in Appalachia: Evolution of a Cultural Stereotype," in *Appalachia in the Making: The Mountain South in the Nineteenth Century*, ed. Mary Beth Pudup, Dwight B. Billings, and Altina L. Waller (Chapel Hill: University of North Carolina Press, 1995), 347–76.

10. Dwight B. Billings and Kathleen M. Blee, *The Road to Poverty: The Making of Wealth and Hardship in Appalachia* (Cambridge: Cambridge University Press, 2000); Kathleen Blee and Dwight Billings, "Where 'Bloodshed Is a Pastime': Mountain Feuds and Appalachian Stereotyping," in *Confronting Appalachian Stereotypes: Back Talk from an American Region*, ed. Dwight B. Billings, Gurney Norman, and Katherine Ledford (Lexington: University Press of Kentucky, 1999), 119–37; Henry Shapiro, *Appalachia on Our Mind: The Southern Mountains and Mountaineers in the American Consciousness, 1870–1920* (Chapel Hill: University of North Carolina Press, 1978); Altina Waller, *Feud: Hatfields, McCoys, and Social Change in Appalachia, 1860–1900* (Chapel Hill: University of North Carolina Press, 1988); Waller, "Feuding in Appalachia."

11. J. W. Williamson, *Hillbillyland: What the Movies Did to the Mountains and What the Mountains Did to the Movies* (Chapel Hill: University of North Carolina Press, 1995).

12. Nina Silber, "'What Does America Need So Much as Americans?' Race and Northern Reconciliation with Southern Appalachia, 1870–1900," in *Appalachians and Race: The Mountain South from Slavery to Segregation*, ed. John Inscoe (Lexington: University Press of Kentucky, 2001), 245–58.

13. William Goodwell Frost used the phrase "our contemporary ancestors" in an 1899 article published in the *Atlantic Monthly*. As president of Berea College, Frost aimed to build financial support for the college as well as recruit white students. His representation of southern mountaineers as pure American stock appealed to Americans in a national context of immigrant flow and racial turmoil and resulted in the widely accepted yet inaccurate perception that Appalachia was homogeneously white. William Goodwell Frost, "Our Contemporary Ancestors in the Southern Mountains," *Atlantic Monthly* 83 (1899): 315–16.

14. Williamson, *Hillbillyland*, 252.

15. Dwight B. Billings, introduction to Billings, Norman, and Ledford, *Confronting Appalachian Stereotypes*, 3–20; Ronald D. Eller, foreword to Billings, Norman, and

Ledford, *Confronting Appalachian Stereotypes,* ix–xi; Stephen Fisher, ed., *Fighting Back in Appalachia: Traditions of Resistance and Change* (Philadelphia: Temple University Press, 1993); John Gaventa, *Power and Powerlessness: Quiescence and Rebellion in an Appalachian Valley* (Urbana: University of Illinois Press, 1980).

16. Anthony Harkins, "TV Depiction of Region," in *Encyclopedia of Appalachia,* ed. Rudy Abramson and Jean Haskell (Knoxville: University of Tennessee Press, 2006), 1746–48; Thomas Alan Holmes, "*The Waltons,*" in Abramson and Haskell, *Encyclopedia of Appalachia,* 1750; Hilton Smith, "Foxfire," in Abramson and Haskell, *Encyclopedia of Appalachia,* 1533–34.

17. Clara Hasorouck, "*Christy,*" in Abramson and Haskell, *Encyclopedia of Appalachia,* 1699–1700.

18. Marushka Svasek, *Anthropology, Art, and Cultural Production* (Ann Arbor, MI: Pluto, 2007), 12.

10

From the Coal Mine to the Prison Yard

The Human Cost of Appalachia's New Economy

Melissa Ooten and Jason Sawyer

The new prison economy in central Appalachia, which continues to be replicated across some of the country's poorest rural areas, builds upon a long history of profiteering in the region.[1] Much like the coal economy, it is built on exploitation not only of land but also of people, while offering little in terms of economic development. Repeatedly, new prisons have opened in poor rural counties in central Appalachia accompanied by the most ardent of prison boosters promising hundreds of jobs, abundant new industries, and a solution to long-term economic problems as they tout prisons as "recession-proof."[2] Yet while prison growth has rapidly expanded in the area over the past thirty years, economic vitality has not.[3] It is now all too clear that counties welcoming prisons have not experienced significant job growth, the sustained influx of other industries, or economic success of any kind. Multiple studies confirm the failure of prisons to stimulate economic growth, yet in areas with few other economic prospects, some community members, local officials, and prison boosters still tout them as worthy, unproblematic routes to regional growth and vitality.

In subregions of central Appalachia where coal once singularly dominated the economy, companies destroyed, and continue to destroy, the land through strip mining and mountaintop removal, with disastrous ecological and economic consequences. Furthermore, mining companies have historically provided miners with as little as possible in wages and health care while exposing them to innumerable hazards. Mining jobs have decreased since the 1980s, in some areas by as much as 82 percent, although much of the reduction is due to fewer workers being required rather than a decline in industry activity.[4] By the late twentieth century, as central Appalachia struggled with deep structural unemployment, prison promoters and politicians recommended prisons as the answer to the region's compounding economic problems.

Yet, when viewed from theoretical perspectives on power as well as in the comparative context of the larger US prison system, an economic strategy based on prisons leads to new avenues of exploitation, as the very survival of the prison economy rests on imprisoning ever-increasing numbers of people. As Huling notes, "The use of prisons as money-makers for struggling rural communities has become a major force driving criminal justice policy toward mass incarceration of the urban poor."[5] For example, Virginia showed in the 1990s that policies to lengthen prison sentences, establish mandatory minimum sentences, and abolish parole must accompany prison building in order to fill new prisons, particularly when crime rates are falling, as they have been since the 1980s.[6] Potent histories and interlocking systems of discrimination, institutionalized racism, and structural unemployment ensure that those in prison continue to be overwhelmingly people of color.

In terms of isolation, exploitation, limited economic prospects, and high unemployment numbers, the urban communities of color that most of these prisoners call home share many qualities with Appalachia. White notes ways in which both white Appalachia and urban communities of color have been conceptualized as internal, exploited colonies. Both face geographic isolation and exploited labor markets.[7] But the continual use of white privilege to thwart class alliances across racial and ethnic boundaries means that if anyone benefits from the prison economy, it will be white communities. If the prison economy creates jobs, those jobs will overwhelmingly be held by white men, and since inmates are figured into the population of the area in which their prison is located, it will be white communities that benefit from greater government resources and political clout since prisoners, for all official purposes, now reside in rural, white-majority areas.[8]

In short, the prison economy represents the most exploitative system of supposed economic gain yet to enter Appalachia. Appalachians are promised jobs and economic revitalization for their communities, yet few locals ever work at these prisons.[9] Counties expend enormous resources to attract prisons, yet more than one has faced bankruptcy as it becomes clear that prisons cannot solve the generations-old structural economic problems of the area.[10] Some scholars of Appalachia have described the region's status as that of a "colony" because of the history of resource extraction, which primarily benefits outsiders while causing great human and environmental damage to the region itself.[11] This extraction of resources continues with prisons, given their reliance on extracting and imprisoning people of color from urban centers, further fracturing those communities while literally depopulating them. Even if the new prison economy offered economic prosperity—and it does not—surely no moral economy could be sustained, as the very system of prison growth in Appalachia implicates whole communities in furthering a supposed economic growth strategy based on generating an ever-growing racialized prison population at a time of historically low crime.[12]

As Eller states, repeatedly employed local community development strategies have "done little to correct the structural problems of land abuse, political corruption, economic shortsightedness, and the loss of community and culture" in Appalachia, and the prison strategy is no different.[13] Although Appalachia is often described as isolated, the region's very link to globalization and widespread deindustrialization have forced towns and communities to broadly seek new strategies for economic vitality.[14] As both Alexander and Gilmore note, these issues of globalization and deindustrialization have implications for black urban communities wherein imprisonment becomes the solution for inadequate educational systems, mass unemployment, and poverty.[15]

Technological Power, Institutional Oppression, and Exploitation

Several theories help us better understand the converging factors of race, class, globalization, and the expanding prison system. A comprehensive investigation of the rising prison industry would be incomplete without Michel Foucault's research related to power, discipline, social control, and the modern prison. Foucault's study of the historical roots of the modern prison and its implications for public and private life as well as social institutions centers on the dominant cultural shifts that have led to a new technological power present in many of today's institutions.[16] This view of technical power within institutions is analogous to that espoused by critical race theorists and black feminists who have used the image of "the school to prison pipeline" to problematize ways in which urban students of color are too often funneled out of schools and into the criminal justice system.[17]

Critical theory also informs our work as it focuses on multiple sources of oppression, domination, and power.[18] Its forerunners emphasized the fundamental emancipatory goal "to liberate human beings from the circumstances that enslave them," and critical theorists extend their analysis to the oppressive structures within institutions, patterns of organizational behavior, and culture within capitalist societies.[19] A critical theoretical framework locates social problems and their effects within modern institutional systems by revealing the foundation of oppressive practices and structures.[20] As it relates to this work, critical theory makes clear how prison building and incarceration function as problematic ways to address poverty, structural unemployment, and community disinvestment by politicians and government officials from both urban communities of color and rural, white communities in Appalachia.

Critical race theory also undergirds this study. Critical race theorists assert that racism thrives as a dominant norm in contemporary society.[21] These theorists compel us to question the very notion of "objectivity" as they actively challenge the neutrality of legal doctrine and practices.[22] Michelle Alexander's critique of the current prison system as "the new Jim Crow," due to its analogous restriction of African Americans' rights within the segregationist South, stands as a powerful example of this analysis.[23] Just as our study does, this theory frames racism as a systemic phenomenon found within institutions, policies, and economic systems which, in the case of prisons, means that disproportionate numbers of young men of color will be incarcerated due to the ways in which racism structures systems of surveillance and crime in American society.[24]

Finally, neoliberalism, an advanced stage of global capitalism that arranges institutions, social structures, and organizational practices along market lines, also frames our study.[25] Increasingly, local, state, and federal governments are transferring their roles to for-profit entities, thereby reorienting social, political, economic, and cultural institutional values and practices to corporate ones.[26] Wacquant characterizes neoliberalism in relation to the prison industry as "a violation of the rules of civil democracy" due to its inherently oppressive nature.[27] Creating a political and economic dynamic whereby corporations incentivize incarceration fuels mass incarceration, which some have termed the "prison-industrial complex"; prisons need ever-growing numbers of prisoners in order to profit under a corporate model.[28]

Rural Colonization, Structural Racism, and Economic Fallacy

While most prisoners come from urban communities, most prisons are now located in rural areas.[29] Between 1991 and 2001, officials built 245 prisons in rural counties and small towns, averaging a new prison in a rural community every fifteen days for more than ten years.[30] In that same decade, one-third of all rural prison construction took place in four of the most economically depressed regions of the country, including central Appalachia.[31] Currently, fourteen state and federal prisons are located in central Appalachia, more than half built since 1990, in addition to a number of private prisons. Yet another federal prison is currently planned for Letcher County, Kentucky, which would be the sixth federal prison to open in central Appalachia since 1992.[32]

While prisons have come to central Appalachia in force, the enormous growth in prisons across the past three decades is certainly not unique to the area. The United States, which contains 5 percent of the world's population, now incarcerates 25 percent of the world's prisoners.[33] Incarceration rates have ballooned from around 300,000 in the 1970s to over 2.3 million in 2012.[34]

The fact that most prisons are now built in rural areas signals how those areas have been particularly affected by national and global economic forces. According to Yanarella and Blankenship, "As the forces of top-down globalization have conspired with the processes of deindustrialization and economic restructuring, rural towns and communities have become involved in business renewal and industrial recruitment programs designed to bring new businesses and good-paying jobs to their inhabitants."[35] Gilmore writes: "Rural economies . . . are integrated into broader economic flows, via transnational social division of labor and global consumption regimes. Resource depletion, mechanization of agricultural labor processes, and closure of manufacturing and other employment establishments can devastate rural economies that lack flexibility due to their tendency to be dominated by monopolies or oligopolies."[36] Thus it is not central Appalachia's isolation but rather its very economic connectedness and interdependency with national and global markets that has led to many of its current economic struggles.

Eller, for example, notes that Appalachian economies have long been tied to the economies of the nation and that economic problems in Appalachia are those of the nation. By the 1990s, Eller shows, Appalachia's economy declined as significant decreases in employment rates in coal mining and manufacturing were accompanied by the additional loss of tobacco farms in the region.[37] Communities in the region, as throughout the United States, felt the loss of manufacturing jobs as these were permanently relocated overseas. And in many rural communities, officials tried to fill the gap with prisons.

But do prisons boost local economies? In an interview related to the possible siting of a new federal prison in eastern Kentucky, Judge Executive Jim Ward of Letcher County describes the county's unemployment rate as "skyrocketing" and notes that a new prison would bring four hundred jobs with good benefits to the county.[38] These are arguments prison boosters often make. Yet there is little to no evidence that prisons boost local economies in either the short or long term.

Mosher, Hooks, and Wood studied all prisons built in the United States since 1960 to better understand their impact on employment growth. In rural counties, in terms of both income per capita and total earnings, counties without a prison experienced faster economic growth. The team found that in nonmetropolitan counties, "there is no evidence that prisons have had a positive [economic] impact." In faster-growing rural counties, they found no evidence of prisons making a noticeable impact on employment. In slower-growing counties, "prisons appeared to do more harm than good; new prisons in these counties actually impeded private sector and total employment growth."[39] In an earlier study, Hooks, Mosher, Rotolo, and Lobao analyzed data on every rural county in the United States, those with and without prisons, between 1969 and 1994. They found "no evidence that prison expansion has stimulated economic growth. In fact, we provide evidence that prison construction has impeded economic growth in rural counties that have been growing at a slow pace."[40]

Since new prisons clearly do bring hundreds of jobs to economically depressed areas, what explains the lack of job growth? Mosher, Hooks, and Wood note the near impossibility of locally based companies winning prison service contracts when competing against national firms that regularly work with prisons. Additionally, rural prison jobs are often highly desired by those already in the prison system who have seniority in terms of job placement when new prisons open.[41]

Additionally, prison employment, particularly in state and federal prisons, often requires conditions that many residents of central Appalachia cannot meet. Applicants must pass drug tests and extensive background checks for federal prison jobs. Yet Ronald Eller has described the use of prescription narcotics in the area as an "epidemic."[42] Applicants also must be younger than thirty-eight per federal pension requirements and pass a series of meticulous interviews and physical exams. Employment is also highly stratified by gender, with most of the jobs going to men. Female workers regularly report harassment from both coworkers and inmates. Additionally, high school diplomas are required, and local community members receive no preference in the hiring process.[43]

Ryerson reports that even when counties attempt to close the gap between prison jobs' requirements and local residents' qualifications, the results have been poor. She writes that prior to the opening of the high-security United States Penitentiary (USP) Big Sandy in Martin County, Kentucky, Big Sandy Community and Technical College began a program specifically designed to prepare local residents for prison jobs.[44] In 2009, the program's coordinator, Mike Dixon, reported that while the initiative has graduated 250 students in over a decade, no more than 10 to 15 have acquired jobs at Big Sandy. If they want to work in prisons, graduates must leave the area to work at lower-security state prisons or private prisons, which typically have less stringent employment requirements.[45] Thus, although the program may have trained area community members to work in prisons, that did not translate into their employment at local prisons.

A few hundred miles to the southeast in Inez, Kentucky, the employment statistics are similar. Blaine Phillips, judge executive of McCreary County, Kentucky, told Ryerson that after five years of operation, the high-security USP McCreary does not employ more than twenty-five to thirty local people, despite having more than three hundred employees in total.[46] Furthermore, promises of great economic gain notwithstanding, McCreary County still has the lowest per capita income of any county in Kentucky, with nearly one-third of its residents living below the poverty line.[47]

Ryerson shows that most new prison employees do not live in the county where the new prison is sited. Instead, they prefer to commute from the nearest sizable town.[48] Moreover, nearby area residents will be competing with those who live more than an hour away, as commutes of fifty to sixty miles are common in rural areas.[49] Although the county that houses the prison has expended large sums of money and resources to attract a prison, new employees tend not to buy real estate in the county, patronize the county's businesses, or enroll their children in the county's schools. Instead, the county permanently reduces its property tax base as land for the prison transfers from private to governmental ownership.[50] Also, prisons create few linkages to local economies in terms of attracting more industry. While prisons may successfully attract chain stores, these stores often trigger a replacement effect that pushes out locally owned businesses.

There's also the problem of prison work itself. According to Huling, "Prisoners themselves may also displace low-wage workers in struggling rural areas."[51] It is common for prisoners to perform work projects for local governments, churches, hospitals, and libraries. Furthermore, all states run prison industries that may pit local residents against prisoners in competition for work. Companies ranging from Boeing to Starbucks use prison labor; the practice allows them to pay rates much lower than minimum wage and eliminates concerns about unionization or labor shortages.[52] In areas that already face significant long-term, structural economic depression, captive laborers employed for mere pennies per hour further hinder employment opportunities for local residents.

Furthermore, although promoters claim the prison industry is environmentally clean, it has a history of noncompliance with environmental controls. Several prisons in central Appalachia sit atop former mountaintop removal sites. USP Big Sandy, built at a cost of over $170 million, the most expensive prison to date at the time of construction, literally sank into the former mining site on which it was built; it opened a year later in 2003.[53]

Yet local officials and residents alike often continue to welcome prisons. As Gilmore points out, "For towns with unemployment that has stayed above 25% during the longest economic expansion in US history, a single new job is a benefit."[54] Prisons, however, still often make less than desirable neighbors. Due to the difficulty areas like central Appalachia face in attracting other industries and partially due to their reputation as prison towns, counties all too often lobby for more prisons, creating a "one-company town" reminiscent of the mining and lumber towns of the past.[55] Huling relates how this tendency "to 'cluster' prisons in distinct rural areas has created dozens of rural penal colonies where prisons dominate the community's economic, social, political, and cultural landscape."[56] Far from prison boosters' claims that prisons will operate in virtually "invisible" ways, much evidence concludes that the prison industry will infuse all aspects of life in rural communities as it becomes the dominant industry.[57]

The fact that in areas like central Appalachia white guards will be policing primarily inmates of color must also be more closely analyzed. Most of the counties housing state and federal prisons in Appalachia have white populations of over 90 percent. As Huling notes, "Racial hatred behind and beyond prison walls is another deeply troubling consequence of the increasing dependence of rural communities on prisons."[58] While we do not suggest that white rural communities are necessarily more racist than white suburban or urban communities, such racial segregation means that those who work most closely with the prisoners may have little to no understanding of prisoners' cultural backgrounds and histories, reinforcing racial biases and stereotypes. For example, white guards have often been too quick to label behavior as gang related when it's not. And guards' racism has been duly noted: in the mid-1990s, reports emerged in six different states of white guards wearing mock KKK regalia to antagonize inmates of color.[59] Regardless of the community, the opportunity for individual acts of racism by white guards against inmates of color remains high while institutionalized racism continues to structure every aspect of the prison system.

In terms of its economic vitality, the prison industry has actually been proven to be anything but recession proof. Some counties are already in debt for millions of dollars when they first open a new prison due to the outlay of expenses necessary to attract and build it.[60] County and state officials throughout the country are now finding how financially unfeasible it is to imprison millions of people per year.

One reason for soaring prison costs is the increased reliance on solitary confinement, often termed *segregation.* The term is apt, given its linkages to Jim Crow laws and the nation's long history of criminalizing black bodies and communities for everything from being unemployed to attempting to be served at whites-only facilities. Segregation clearly symbolizes the problem of institutionalized racism that lies at the center of the prison-industrial complex as it represents the very literal segregation of people of color from society by placing them in prison facilities and then further isolating them within those facilities under inhumane conditions. The United States holds more prisoners in solitary confinement than any other democratic nation.[61] In Virginia's super-maximum facility, Red Onion State Prison, 505 of its 745 inmates were held in solitary confinement for twenty-three hours per day as of October 2011. Legal and medical experts alike have long noted the negative effects of prolonged solitary confinement.[62]

Entities ranging from Human Rights Watch to the United Nations have condemned the US prison system's reliance on solitary confinement and its prison abuses in general.[63] Additionally, local communities and prisoners themselves have organized to demand better treatment and address some continuing concerns. On May 22, 2012, forty-five prisoners at Red Onion launched a hunger strike. Prisoners cited beatings by guards and attacks by dogs as reasons for their protest. The hunger strikers' ten demands, which were not met, ranged from "an end to torture in the form of indefinite segregation" to adequate medical care, including a special note on access to decent toothpaste.[64] Economic arguments rather than humanitarian concerns may prove more likely to persuade officials to end the practice of solitary confinement—it is simply too expensive to maintain. Mississippi's notorious super-maximum facility, Parchman, has begun to employ new strategies to address problems of both violence and expense, and these changes have resulted not only in decreased violence but the closure of one entire isolation unit, amounting to an annual savings of $5 million, as many prisoners have successfully moved into the general prison population elsewhere.[65]

Local community organizations in central Appalachia have sponsored initiatives to provide inmates with better access to their families. In Whitesburg, Kentucky, community radio station WMMT 88.7 has aired the weekly one-hour program *Calls from Home* for over a decade. On Monday nights, family and friends of inmates at area high-security prisons call in to leave messages for inmates, who are not always able to phone home because of the expense or limited permitted call times. Inmates buy and share radios in order to listen to the show. This work is particularly important given how few families of inmates can visit due to the great distance between inmates' homes and the prison, the lack of financial resources many families of prisoners experience, and the frequency with which these high-security prisons go on "lock down" and allow no visitors.

The negative effects of the Appalachian prison-industrial complex emerge as logical extensions of analyses of critical race theory, neoliberalism, and critical theory. The preponderance of practical and theoretical evidence bears witness that the existing prison system is maladaptive to prisoners, local economies, and communities and an example of an oppressive system of systematic exploitation and colonization. Critiquing economic and social injustice within a critical theoretical framework means examining the ramifications of institutional behavior across systems. The Appalachian prison system as it is currently conducted has complex social implications across local and global contexts.

US attorney general Eric Holder has stated the problem succinctly: "Too many Americans go to too many prisons for far too long, and for no truly good law enforcement reason."[66] Leaders from across the political spectrum are supporting sentencing reform to lessen states' burdens of prison expense.

Yet given the extraordinarily high number of prisoners in America and the fact that they are disproportionally people of color, prison abolitionists insist that only a complete dismantling of the present incarceration system will bring about justice. Abolitionists like Angela Y. Davis argue that Americans must engage with "the ideological work that the prison performs," making it everyone's responsibility to solve America's most pressing societal problems, particularly those produced by poverty, "racism and, increasingly, global capitalism," rather than relying on the prison-industrial complex to be the solution.[67]

All communities must consider what a sustainable, just, moral economy for their area would look like and advocate for it. A prison economy in Appalachia will not only fail to sustain the area economically, it will also fail to provide residents with a robust moral economy that they can be proud to participate in, develop, and grow. Not only do prisons fail to provide economic prosperity, they work to further institutionalize racism as they break apart urban communities of color. Looking forward, economic development in Appalachia must empower the community without causing harm to other communities, as the prison-industrial economy surely does. Preeminent Appalachian historian Ronald Eller has eloquently shown that in Appalachia, "the land [has] always shaped human relationships and personal identity. It [has] always defined cultural meaning."[68] Due to this reality, if the region and its people are to prosper, they must actively reject the prison-industrial complex in favor of linking human relationships, personal identity, and culture to a just economy that works to recognize, respect, and reaffirm the humanity of all peoples.

Notes

1. Sylvia Ryerson, "Speak Your Piece: Prison Progress," February 20, 2013, DailyYonder.com http://www.dailyyonder.com/speak-your-piece-prison-progress/2013/02/12/5651 (accessed February 13, 2014).

2. Ernest Yanarella and Susan Blankenship, "Big House on the Rural Landscape: Prison Recruitment as a Policy Tool of Local Economic Development," *Journal of Appalachian Studies* 12, no. 2 (2006): 111; Tracy Huling, "Building a Prison Economy in Rural America," in *From Invisible Punishment: The Collateral Consequences of Mass Imprisonment*, ed. Marc Mauer and Meda Chesney-Lind (New York: New Press, 2002), 4.

3. Ryerson, "Speak Your Piece."

4. Sylvia Ryerson, "'Prison Progress: Neocolonialism as a Relocation Project in

'Post-racial' America,' an Appalachian Case; or, Listening to the Canaries in the Coal Mine" (undergraduate honors thesis, Wesleyan University, 2010).

5. Huling, "Building a Prison Economy in Rural America," 206.

6. Craig Timberg, "At Va's Toughest Prison, Tight Controls," *Washington Post,* April 18, 1999.

7. Julie Anne White, "The Hollow and the Ghetto: Space, Race, and the Politics of Poverty," *Politics & Gender* (2007): 273. Although in these communities, unlike in Appalachia, deliberate government policies created racially segregated ghettos.

8. Federal Bureau of Prisons, *FY 2014 Congressional Budget,* http://www.justice .gov/sites/default/files/jmd/legacy/2014/06/23/bop-bf-justification.pdf (accessed October 14, 2015).

9. Ryerson, "Speak Your Piece."

10. Clayton Mosher, Gregory Hooks, and Peter B. Wood, "Don't Built It Here: The Hype versus the Reality of Prisons and Local Employment," in *Prison Profiteers: Who Makes Money from Mass Incarceration,* ed. Tara Herivel and Paul Wright (New York: New Press, 2007); Ryerson, "Speak Your Piece."

11. Henry Caudill, *Night Comes to the Cumberland* (Boston: Little, Brown, 1962).

12. Michelle Alexander, *The New Jim Crow: Mass Incarceration in the Age of Colorblindness* (New York: New Press, 2010), 93; Stephen Richards, James Austin, and Richard S. Jones, "Thinking about Prison Release and Budget Crises in the Blue Grass State," *Critical Criminology* 12, no. 3 (2004): 245; Ruth Wilson Gilmore, *Golden Gulag: Prisons, Surplus, Crisis, and Opposition in Globalizing California* (Berkeley: University of California Press, 2007), 7.

13. Ronald Eller, *Uneven Ground: Appalachia since 1945* (Lexington: University Press of Kentucky, 2008), 3.

14. Yanarella and Blankenship, "Big House on the Rural Landscape," 111.

15. Gilmore, *Golden Gulag,* 57; Alexander, *The New Jim Crow,* 219.

16. Michel Foucault, *Discipline and Punish: The Birth of the Prison* (New York: Random House, 1977).

17. Patricia Hill Collins, *Another Kind of Public Education: Race, the Media, and New Democratic Possibilities* (Boston: Beacon, 2009).

18. George Ritzer, *Modern Sociological Theory* (New York: McGraw-Hill, 2007).

19. Max Horkheimer, *Critical Theory* (New York: Seabury, 1982), 244; Loretta Pyles, *Progressive Community Organizing: A Critical Approach for a Globalizing World* (New York: Routledge, 2009).

20. Donna Baines, "Everyday Practices of Race, Class, and Gender," *Journal of Progressive Human Services* 11 (2001): 5–27; Robert Mulally, *The New Structural Social Work* (New York: Oxford University Press, 2006).

21. Richard Delgado and Jean Stefancic, *Critical Race Theory: An Introduction* (New York: New York University Press, 2012).

22. Martin Ruck, Anita Harris, Michelle Fine, and Nick Freudenberg, "Youth Expe-

riences of Surveillance: A Cross-National Analysis," in *Globalizing the Streets: Cross Cultural Perspectives on Youth, Social Control, and Empowerment,* ed. Michael Flynn and David Brotherton (New York: Columbia University Press, 2008).

23. Alexander, *The New Jim Crow.*

24. Collins, *Another Kind of Public Education;* Rose Brewer and Nancy Heitzeg, "The Racialization of Crime and Punishment: Criminal Justice, Color-blind Racism, and the Political Economy of the Prison Industrial Complex," *American Behavioral Scientist* 51 (2008): 625–44.

25. Colleen Lundy, *Social Work, Social Justice, and Human Rights* (Toronto: University of Toronto Press, 2011).

26. Lynn Nybell, Jeffry Shook, and Janet Finn, "Introduction and Conceptual Framework," in *Childhood, Youth and Social Work in Transformation,* ed. Lynn Nybell, Jeffry Shook, and Janet Finn (New York: Columbia University Press, 2009).

27. Loic Wacquant, "Crafting the Neo-liberal State: Workfare, Prisonfare, and Social Insecurity," *Sociological Forum* 25 (2010): 197–220.

28. Younhee Kim and Byron E. Price, "Revisiting Prison Privatization: An Examination of the Magnitude of Prison Privatization," *Administration and Society* 46 (2014): 255–75.

29. Huling, "Building a Prison Economy in Rural America," 199.

30. Mosher, Hooks, and Wood, "Don't Built It Here," 90. They consider a rural prison one located in a rural community or town not considered a "metropolitan area," which is defined as "a central city of at least 50,000 people or an urbanized area consisting of 50,000 people or more."

31. The three other areas are the west Texas plains, south central Georgia, and the Mississippi Delta. Ryerson, "Speak Your Piece."

32. Katie Roach, "Plans Still Underway to Bring Federal Prison to Letcher Co.," *WYMT Mountain News* (Whitesburg, KY), April 16, 2013; Ryerson, "Speak Your Piece."

33. Tara Herivel, introduction to Herivel and Wright, *Prison Profiteers,* ix.

34. Lauren Glaze and Erinn Herberman, *Correctional Populations in the United States, 2012,* Bureau of Justice Statistics, December 19, 2013, http://www.bjs.gov/content/pub/press/cpus12pr.cfm (accessed January 3, 2014).

35. Yanarella and Blankenship, "Big House on the Rural Landscape," 111.

36. Gilmore, *Golden Gulag,* 64.

37. Eller, *Uneven Ground,* 221, 231.

38. Roach, "Plans Still Underway."

39. Mosher, Hooks, and Wood, "Don't Built It Here," 92, 93.

40. Gregory Hooks, Clayton Mosher, Thomas Rotola, and Linda Lobao, "The Prison Industry: Carceral Expansion and Employment in U.S. Counties, 1969–1994," *Social Science Quarterly* 85, no. 1 (2004): 37–57.

41. Mosher, Hooks, and Wood, "Don't Built It Here," 94.

42. Eller, *Uneven Ground,* 243.

43. Ryerson, "Speak Your Piece."

44. Ibid. USP Big Sandy opened in 2003. Currently, 35.7 percent of Martin County residents live below the poverty line.

45. Ibid.

46. Ibid.

47. U.S. Census, 2010, http://www.census.gov/2010census/ (accessed October 14, 2014).

48. Ryerson, "Speak Your Piece."

49. Huling, "Building a Prison Economy in Rural America," 201.

50. Ryerson, "Speak Your Piece."

51. Huling, "Building a Prison Economy in Rural America," 202.

52. Mosher, Hooks, and Wood, "Don't Build It Here," 95.

53. Ryerson, "Prison Progress," 193.

54. Gilmore, *Golden Gulag,* 176.

55. Huling, "Building a Prison Economy in Rural America," 205.

56. Ibid., 206.

57. Ibid., 199.

58. Ibid., 208.

59. Ibid.

60. Ibid., 204.

61. Erica Goode, "Prisons Rethink Isolation, Saving Moving, Lives, and Sanity," *New York Times,* March 10, 2012.

62. Anita Kumar, "Va. Prisons' Use of Solitary Confinement Is Scrutinized," *Washington Post,* January 7, 2011.

63. Goode, "Prisons Rethink Isolation," reports that Juan Mendez, the United Nation's special rapporteur on torture and abuse for the UN Human Rights Council, called for a ban on solitary confinement and specifically singled out the United States for its reliance on the system.

64. Mary Ratcliff, "Prisoners at Virginia's Red Onion State Prison on Hunger Strike," *San Francisco Bay View,* May 27, 2012.

65. Goode, "Prisons Rethink Isolation."

66. "Prison Reform: An Unlikely Alliance of Left and Right," *Economist,* August 17, 2013.

67. Angela Y. Davis, *Are Prisons Obsolete?* (Toronto: Seven Stories, 2003), 16.

68. Eller, *Uneven Ground,* 255.

11

Walking the Fence Line of The Crooked Road

Engaging in the Marketplace of Tourism while Empowering a Place-Based Civic Commons

Anita Puckett

Critical to the remapping of "Appalachia" as a region must be an examination of how residents and various groups and institutions constitute and reconstitute their relationship to contemporary transglobal economies. Not long ago, corporate capitalism relied on the physical need to dominate and control a specific territory in order to survive and produce capital. In so doing, companies ushered in changes often in conflict with local valuations of "place." Now, the dominant corporate strategy for producing capital expects mobility of all elements of production, including labor and land, such that production simply moves to a new location when profit variables become problematic.[1] The result is that "global capitalism in the present era is highly destructive of place."[2] The fallout from this dynamic system is the destruction of communities and of the lives of the people who live in them. Certainly, coalfield Appalachia and areas affected by hydraulic natural gas fracking constitute frontline examples of the application of this neoliberal ideology.

Yet transglobal economics *is* the dominant economy everywhere, and its hegemonic handmaiden, neoliberalism, is its ideology. Neoliberalism has multiple meanings and theoretical formulations, but as used here, it is "an ideology that values market exchange as 'an ethic in itself, capable of act-ing as a guide to all human action and substituting for all previously held ethical beliefs.'"[3] In this paradigm, anything and everything that exists in tangible or intangible form (for example, mined coal, storytelling events, attitudes and beliefs, and the idea of Appalachia itself) can be marketed and sold or acquired for some set price. People are often treated simply as elements that contribute to getting "things" to market. Contemporary Appalachia cannot escape from this transglobal neoliberal economy, despite well-developed systems of barter and reciprocity in many areas of the region. Appalachian residents need money to survive. So how can locales construct a viable monetary economy and, perhaps more basically, provide enough environmental, social, and political capital to construct livable and valued lives?[4] And how can they do so in a manner that reproduces core cultural processes, including sacred and expressive ones? Ones that give their lives value and sustain them?

The purpose of this chapter is to address these questions by exploring the theoretical and practical implications of an emerging model of trans-global economics observed during a Montgomery County, Virginia, multi-venue traditional music festival in March 2014. The festival suggested a way to construct a balance between neoliberal economics, with its emphasis on commodification of everything for market transactions, and Appalachian community cultural life, with its focus on the reproduction of meaning sys-tems that invest in the network of family, kin, ancestors, and place relations as crucial to what it means to be human. My goal is to apply the concept of commodification, or the transformation of goods and services into saleable products, to examine the potential for alternatives to the neoliberal dilemma of an either/or schema that pits local socioeconomies and environmental sustainability against global corporate jobs.[5] This bifurcated approach, which is very popular in corporation and federal government publicity, commonly results in community tensions that undermine community sustainability through factionalism. In this discussion, however, I assert that these polar-ized points of view distract from the fundamental need to create a regional socioeconomy that both promotes ecologically viable, democratically sus-taining livelihoods *for* its citizens and provides enough monetary capital *to* its citizens to achieve a certain economic "quality of life" within the domi-nant neoliberal transglobal economies.[6] This chapter first identifies differ-ent levels of neoliberal integration across multiple performers, audiences, and venues in Montgomery County and then analyzes questions of "value" underlying the cultural commodification of regional music under neoliber-alism. Finally, I apply the concept of "registers" from linguistic anthropol-ogy to formulate a model for communicating and privileging the artistic creativity and political decision making of local Appalachian communities within this neoliberal context.

The Crooked Road

The Crooked Road: Virginia's Heritage Music Trail (TCR) originated with traditional southwest Virginia music aficionado Joe Wilson in 2002. He, in collaboration with Todd Christenson, currently the executive director of the Southwest Virginia Heritage Commission, conceived the idea of a driving tour along two-lane roads that linked key "traditional music" sites in southwest Virginia. The original goal was to "empower the people along The Crooked Road—to make it their road" and not, as some have said, to be like Disneyland.[7] Wilson, Christenson, and others worked with the Vir-ginia Tourism Corporation to turn TCR into a state-recognized tourism and economic development organization in 2004.[8]

The result is a successful tourism initiative with an international repu-tation and reach that has created a set of pathways throughout southwest Virginia indicated on tourism maps, websites, road signs, venue banners, and "Wayside" kiosks. The venues themselves are identified either as "major venues," meaning sites that exist specifically for performance or recognition of traditional music, or as "affiliates." Among the major sites are such well-known venues as the Carter Family Fold, the Blue Ridge Institute & Museum, the Floyd Country Store, the Old Fiddlers Convention, and the Ralph Stanley Museum.[9] Contrastively, affiliated venues "present high-quality traditional music and more in a family friendly setting" and include restaurants, local festivals, farmers' markets, regular music jams, and other informal gather-ings.[10] There are currently over sixty sites on these TCR "side roads" where more informal performances or festivals occur, usually with no entrance fees.

With TCR's success in partnering with state and federal agencies, how-ever, came an underlying tension: the original vision to "empower" and foster ownership of the music and its cultural traditions as an inalienable posses-sion of a place versus the potential for economic growth through tourism, wherein visitors "take away" cultural experiences as alienable commodities or transitory memories.[11] In fact, the purpose of TCR, as listed on its non-profit organization application and appearing on its website until 2014, is

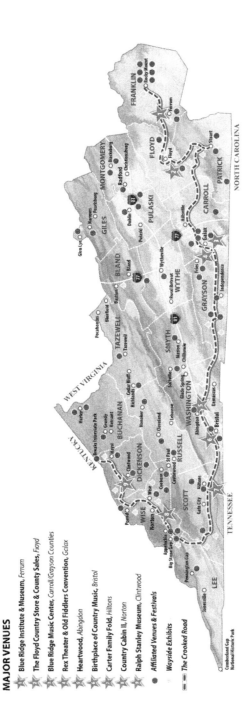

MAJOR VENUES

☆ Blue Ridge Institute & Museum, *Ferrum*

☆ The Floyd Country Store & County Sales, *Floyd*

☆ Blue Ridge Music Center, *Carroll/Grayson Counties*

☆ Rex Theater & Old Fiddlers Convention, *Galax*

☆ Heartwood, *Abingdon*

☆ Birthplace of Country Music, *Bristol*

☆ Carter Family Fold, *Hiltons*

☆ Country Cabin II, *Norton*

☆ Ralph Stanley Museum, *Clintwood*

● Affiliated Venues & Festivals

○ Wayside Exhibits

– – – The Crooked Road

Map 11.1. The Crooked Road road map with venues

"to generate tourism and economic development in the Appalachian region of Southwestern Virginia."[12]

This tension between TCR's local and global economic orientations became more complicated as the organization began to earn national and international recognition through the support of local, state, and federal governmental agencies. Most public officials supported a neoliberal perspective toward tourism development: to bring monetary capital to the region.[13] Indeed, TCR appears to have had a significant economic impact. According to the 2008 Crooked Road Economic Impact, tourist spending on accommodation increased by 232 percent in Galax City from 2004 to 2007 and by 90 percent from 2000 to 2007 in Floyd County. Direct spending in the region from visitation attributable to the TCR is estimated at $12.9 million out of a total economic impact estimated at $23 million per year.[14]

Yet, investigation of how this impact is actually benefiting TCR locales reveals a more complex picture than is suggested by these generalized, and now old, data.[15] Qualitative data from Floyd and Montgomery County venues indicate that visitors or tourists do spend money in the area, but it is, with some exceptions, commonly at chain restaurants and hotels, and thus does not benefit locally owned businesses significantly.[16] Counties, however, receive more in food and luxury taxes, regardless of who owns the businesses, and their administrators are therefore often very interested in having TCR venues.[17] Most of the time, TCR musicians are paid nothing or close to nothing; they rely on donations—if these are collected at all.[18] Many performers and others (such as luthiers and venue owners) report that they are involved because of family traditions, love of performing the music itself, the close interpersonal relationships created among performers, affinity to the people and places that produce the music, and a sense of affective or spiritual diffusion into a timeless dimension of creative expression.[19]

Performances at affiliated venues (see the case study discussed below) are often peripheral to and constructed differently than the "main stage" performances at major venues, which exhibit timed sets, require raised stages and amplification of acoustic instruments, and feature songs visitors expect to hear. Such tunes may include dance music, which often is expected to be accompanied by highly polished, nearly professional, clogging, flat footing, or square dancing. In contrast, at affiliated venues, performers fluidly appear in meeting halls, farmers' market stalls, small-business lobbies, or restaurant corners in a flow of co-constructed music that changes according to who is present at the time and what their status is relative to the other musicians present. Currently, then, TCR is attempting to meet the expectations of multiple investors and stakeholders, not only at various locales and counties across the region but also across socioeconomic sectors and sociopolitical levels of institutional power. This gives it the capacity to create what Reid and Taylor identify as a "civic commons" in which citizens become empowered to reclaim socioeconomic and sociopolitical power at the grassroots local or regional level rather than in the international sphere of corporate decision making.[20]

Indeed, the original vision of the creators of TCR is still very much alive, as the current website suggests—the organization's mission statement is no longer restricted to promoting tourism—and as initiatives to integrate traditional music education in K-12 schools in some counties support.[21] Yet the tensions between tourism-oriented displays of "heritage music" and place-based, noncommodified, and culturally sustaining music performances have not yet been resolved.[22] TCR is currently walking a fence line, and it would be all too easy to fall off. Potentially the tourism component, with its infusion of cash and outside funding, might be lost, or conversely, the local cultural practices that nurture noncommodified music might be destroyed in favor of cultural commodification for tourism markets. In both cases, southwest Virginia communities are likely to suffer, either through cultural disintegration or economic adversity.

Planning the Montgomery County Crooked Road Festival, 2014

The Montgomery County Crooked Road Festival, held March 19–23, 2014, offers an interesting insight into how the socioeconomic fence straddling of TCR can be crafted into a civic commons of significant empowerment to the region it serves. The countywide endeavor involved nine county venues plus Virginia Tech's new Center for the Arts (hereafter the center) for a total of ten different county events occurring over four days. The festival offered an unusual opportunity to enjoy different music styles, community valuations of local performers, and reproductions of local cultural identities through the actual performances themselves—all within a remarkably short time frame. Similarities and differences in their local cultural meanings were therefore far more obvious than they would have been if performed throughout a year.

The center partnered with TCR to create the festival. Plans developed during summer 2013 when a number of interested parties met to develop a marketing grant proposal (ultimately successful) for the Virginia Tourism Corporation: Montgomery County, Christiansburg, and Town of Blacksburg tourism directors; directors of the two museums in the county; TCR administrators; director and staff of the center; and other invested Virginia Tech faculty, including myself as a consultant.[23] Emerging from this planning session was a division of festival organizing labor, with the center director overseeing Virginia Tech activities and the executive director of the Montgomery Tourism Development Council organizing off-campus county events. These organizational meetings were crucial to successfully launching the festival because stakeholders who normally don't talk to each other, except casually, were actively working together to pull off a significant coordinated countywide set of events. Despite ideological differences, the collaboration was convivial and productive, promising development of a civic commons that could, indeed, offer a model for TCR and Appalachian tourism more generally.

The ten festival events were located in different geographical sectors of the county, chosen according to specific historical and economic contexts that give each its own sense of identity. Having full county representation was paramount to county organizers' goals; having events at venues that had been designated TCR affiliates was not. TCR was agreeable to this plan as long as traditional music was being celebrated (see table 11.1).

Performances were different in terms of their purposes, outcomes, how they unfolded, and their value to the immediate audience and the community where they were located. All events were open to tourists, but most, with the two museum venues as exceptions, were targeted toward the communities in which they took place, as performed by specific local communities of practice such as a church congregation, or musicians.[24] This county-internal variation therefore constructed an overarching mosaic of intersecting but local semiotic processes for constructing how the venues related to neoliberal-constituted tourism markets, if at all. Critical to understanding these processes is appreciating how intangible noncommodities can become commodities.

Processes of Commodification

Definitions of commodities vary but generally involve objects that are exchanged under some need or want using a standardized medium of exchange, that is, money. "A commodity is defined as a socially desirable

Table 11.1. The Crooked Road Festival, March 19–23, 2014, venues and events

Countywide venues

Venue	Event	Date	Location	Time	Setting	Attendance
Montgomery Museum and Lewis Miller Art Center	Virginia heritage music instrument exhibit / student art exhibition: music of The Crooked Road / John Hollandsworth—instrument-making demonstration	Wednesday, March 19	Christiansburg, Virginia	11:00 a.m.–3:00 p.m.	Montgomery Museum and Lewis Miller Art Center	About 60; generally older, but about 20 younger with children; 6 Virginia Tech (VT) students + professor
	Olin Gardner—instrument-making demonstration	Friday, March 21	Christiansburg, Virginia	11:00 a.m.–3:00 p.m.	Montgomery Museum and Lewis Miller Art Center	About 40; mostly older, but about 10 children with parents
Prices Fork Elementary School	Open house with old-time music and square dance with caller	Wednesday, March 19	Prices Fork, Virginia	6:00 p.m.: open house; 6:30 p.m.: community/school history presentation; 7:00–about 8:30 p.m.: music	General-purpose room with stage in school; portable chairs; a few collapsible tables for oral history recruitment & displays	About 80; about 30 were older, 10 20+ year-old visitors from New England; about 15 elementary school children with parents; 8 VT students + professor
St. Luke and Odd Fellows Hall Museum	The New Town Connection exhibit	Thursday–Saturday, March 20–22	Blacksburg, Virginia	Noon–5:00 p.m., Thursday–Friday; noon–4:00 p.m., Saturday	Meeting hall of early 20th-century African American fraternal organization	About 20–25, mostly older, with a few VT students and younger faculty + professor; no African Americans reported

Shawsville Middle School	Eastern Montgomery County gospel music program with Nancy Smith and Friends and the Eastern Montgomery County Community Choir	Saturday, March 22	Shawsville, Virginia	1:00–3:00 p.m.	Auditorium of a middle school; seats about 400; has stage	About 120 of various ages and races, representing Pentecostal, Methodist, and Baptist churches in the area; about 6 VT students + brief visit of professor
St. Paul's African Methodist Episcopal Church	Oral history of St. Paul's African Methodist Episcopal Church by Jacquelyn Eaves / St. Paul's Choir / First Baptist Church (Clay Street) Choir / Alexis Johnson / Michael Herndon and Lynette Wilcox / Enlightened Gospel Choir / Ada Sherman	Saturday, March 22	Blacksburg, Virginia	2:00–3:00 p.m.	Small, active church; seats about 300	Mixed-race audience of various ages; about 4 VT students + professor
Main St. Baptist Church	Traditional music concert / Olin Gardner and Friends / the Blackberries / the Gravel Road / Mike Mitchell	Saturday, March 22	Christiansburg, Virginia	6:00–8:00 p.m.	Sanctuary of the main Baptist church in Christiansburg, now vacant and for sale; seats about 500; has dais	About 80 of various ages; about 20 teenage attendees who were friends or relatives of young performers; 4 VT students + professor; 1 African American

Venue	Event	Date	Location	Time	Setting	Atendance
Meadowbrook Center	An evening of beans and banjos	Saturday, March 22	Shawsville, Virginia	6:00–8:00 p.m.	Meeting room of center, which was a former nursing home; no stage; holds about 100–120; comfort food served in side room	About 120–130, mostly older; about 30 of parental age with children
Barn on private property (Phil Louer's barn)	Square dance with the Indian Run String Band and caller Phil Louer	Sunday, March 23	Riner, Virginia	4:00–7:00 p.m.	Wooden barn of about 5,000 square feet; used only for events, no animals boarded or fodder stored	About 60; various ages ranging from 30 to 75; about 10 young children with parents; about 8 VT students + professor
Holiday Inn	Jam session for centrally involved TCR musicians	Friday–Saturday, March 21–22	Blacksburg, Virginia	11:00 p.m.–2:00 a.m.	Meeting room at Holiday Inn	About 10–15 musicians; 2–5 observers

Center for the Arts venues

Event	Date	Location	Time	Attendance[a]	Cost[b]
Olin Gardner, John Hollandsworth, and Mac Trayhham—instrument-making demonstration / the Virginia Luthiers—instrument display	Thursday, March 20	Lobby area	6:30–7:30 p.m.	250; pre-concert event	Less than $800
Mountain fling / Mac and Jenny Trayhham / Wayne Henderson and the Virginia Luthiers	Thursday, March 20	Performance hall; state-of-the-art performance stage; seats about 1,000	8:00–10:00 p.m.	707; 38 under 18	Tickets $45 with VT student discounts; Henderson was paid several thousand $; others paid under $1,000

Event	Date	Venue	Time	Attendance[a]	Cost[b]
Pete Reiniger, Smithsonian folkways recordings—presentation	Friday, March 21	Lobby area	6:45–7:30 p.m.	63; 5 under 18; pre-concert event	Free; costs covered by the Smithsonian
No Strings Attached / the Seldom Scene	Friday, March 21	Performance hall	8:00–10:00 p.m.	748; 35 under 18	Tickets $35–$45; VT student discounts; the band was paid several thousand $
Clogging workshop with Phil Louer and Jon Barton / square dance with Giles Mt. String Band and callers Ginger Wagner and Phil Louer	Saturday, March 22	Greater lobby area	2:00–5:00 p.m.	46; 5 under 18	Free; performers were paid less than $800
Crankies performance by Anna Roberts-Gevalt and Elizabeth LaPrelle with Montgomery County Elementary School students (Workshops at local elementary schools also held Monday, March 17–Wednesday, March 19 during school hours)	Saturday, March 22	Performed in a center "Cube"	7:00–7:30 p.m.	150; 29 under 18; pre-performance event 307 total; nearly all under 18 (teachers only adults)	Free; demonstrators were paid less than $800 Free to schools; demonstrators were paid less than $800
Indian Run String Band / Hoorah Cloggers / Rickie Simpkins Quartet	Saturday, March 22	Performance hall	8:00–10:00 p.m.	604; 35 under 18	Tickets $35–$45; VT student discount

Note on Center for the Arts venues: All events were at the same venue, the Moss Arts Center on the Virginia Tech Campus, Blacksburg, Virginia.

[a] Attendance figures provided by Ruth Waalkes, executive director and associate provost, Center for the Arts, Virginia Tech, January 5, 2015.

[b] Costs provided by Ruth Waalkes, January 5, 2015.

thing with a use-value and an exchange-value," according to economic anthropologist C. A. Gregory.[25] That is, the buyer perceives something to be of use, and he or she is willing to pay a certain price for it. Under the tenets of neoliberalism, everything, not merely objects, is marketable, however. This reformulation of the meaning of both markets and commodities as conceived during the nineteenth and twentieth centuries has resulted in theoretical shifts in definition and focus in order to accommodate marketing intangibles such as various types of "experiences" or other affective-based entities, such as traditional music performances, leading to issues of how to determine what their exchange value is or should be.[26]

In assessing these nebulous forms of commodities, Kockelman argues, issues of exchange or market value as well as use value are significant, but the meaning or affective "value" of the relationship between producer, product, and consumer must also be considered.[27] Neoliberalism wants this relationship to be standardized for a given commodity, but this expectation may not always be possible. For example, a tourist's experience of a "traditional" flat-footing performance, such as occurs every Friday night at the Floyd Country Store, a TCR major venue, has a certain use value: say, the acquisition of symbolic capital. One can communicate to friends or colleagues one's experiences on a "special vacation trip," complete with selfies, descriptions of flat-footing attempts, and sampling of local food.[28] The performance has an exchange value: the $5 admission fee, the cost of transportation to and from the store, the food, gifts, or tourist items one buys while there, and any extra cash donations one might make for the musicians performing outside the store in one of the side venues.

What must also be considered, however, is an intangible value given to the relationship between use and exchange values, that is, the emotive response. Although different bands perform at the Floyd jamboree each week, the event is in a sense standardized; tourists can expect more or less the same set of experiences every Friday night. They can attend with the expectation that they will come away with similar feelings every time. Therefore, when the emotive response is one that can be predicted as commonly occurring for most tourists, then the performance or display can be considered fully commodified. In the case of the Floyd jamboree, the "value" of the event for many tourists and out-of-county visitors is commonly reported to be one of feeling entertained, of being transported to a "simpler" time, of being welcomed into a strange and different community, and of being in a place where "real American culture" is celebrated.[29]

The Festival Events and Levels of Neoliberal Integration

The information presented in tables 11.2–11.4 for the Montgomery County TCR Festival offers different configurations in which use value, exchange value, and value relations are in various inchoate states of development with respect to conforming to neoliberal definitions of market commodities. Events are arranged according to three different types of relationships: minimal to no commodification present; partial commodification present; and public sphere events.

MINIMAL TO NO COMMODIFICATION

Venue hosts in the first category (see table 11.2) volunteered events that were already occurring in their communities, modified only slightly to accommodate the festival. Community venue organizers simply consulted event hosts for the purpose of dedicating one of their events to the festival. None charged an entrance fee. A characteristic of the Shawsville and Ellison events was that most members of the audience knew the performers as kin, neighbors, or fellow churchgoers. The performers, whether at the gospel sing or the Beans and Banjos event, played their music *with* the audience, not *to* the audience. Tunes at all events were part of an expected repertoire. Therefore, the function of the events was to reproduce local identity as an inalienable right of habitation of place. While visitors were certainly accepted and treated kindly, the communications and broader meanings of the audience-musicians' performance signaled mutual possession—the event was *theirs* and the value of the event was one of belonging to both a place and a community.

The third venue in this category, a barn on private land featuring a barn dance, reproduced an event that occurs as scheduled by the property owner. Attendees, except for Virginia Tech students present under my direction, were musicians and dancers who lived from five to about fifty miles away. The co-construction of identity was therefore rooted in knowledge of and positive affect (or "love" as participants often said) for the music and traditional dancing rather than a celebration of a community identity based on living in the same locale or community. And everyone was expected to dance, interacting with the musicians through co-construction of a performance rather than strictly through verbal communication. Therefore, interactional bonding was more on a personal, few-on-few basis, and the sense of community was one based on common practices, not on kinship or place. Nevertheless, the actual performance was, as one participant stated, *ours,* meaning possessed by those on and off the stage who were co-

Table 11.2. Events with minimal to no commodification present

Venue	Targeted audience	Type of monetary payment by attendees	Basis for value	Band/performers' fee	Comments
Meadowbrook Center	Local community; established community event	None	Various individual valuations of family/kin/ancestors/place interrelationships	None asked, but less than $500 given by TCR/Montgomery Tourism Council via sponsors' contributions	Reproduced inalienable relations to "place"; skill of performers need not be at commercial level; money went to support the Meadowbrook Center
Shawsville Elementary School	Local community & community Christian church membership; church choirs established, but a joint "gospel sing" was a new event	None	Various individual and group valuations of church communities as well as family/kin/ancestors/place interrelationships	None asked, but less than $500 given by TCR/Montgomery Tourism Council via sponsors' contributions	Reproduced inalienable relations to "place" via local church membership; skill level of performers need not be at commercial level; money went to various churches
Phil Lauer's barn	Square dancers/cloggers/flatfooter dances in area; visitors who had learned of the event through media coverage or word of mouth were welcome; callers "taught" square dancing at one point	None	Intensive bonding among musicians and dancers from affective feelings for music and "place" as defined by region rather than a specific locale; activities co-constructed their music identities through playing and dancing together	None asked, but less than $500 given by TCR/Montgomery Tourism Council via sponsors' contributions	Reproduced a diffuse sense of "place" and "identity" via dancing and playing of dance music; skill level of musicians at semicommercial level, but dancers' skills could be elementary; money went to pay for event costs, such as porta-potty and food
Holiday Inn	Fellow traditional music (old-time) musicians who were part of the jam	None	Intensive bonding among musicians from strong affective feelings for traditional music, the region in which it occurs, and the co-construction of their music identity through playing together	Donations at the door suggested, but few visitors, so very little collected	Considered core and almost sacred events by musicians deeply committed to TCR and/or the aesthetic/cultural "value" of this music; performed for themselves, not for an audience; skill level high according to their criteria, not commercial market criteria

constructing the performance. However, the event had mixed meanings in terms of ownership and potential alienability for commodification, should it be marketed: the property owner controlled the setting, location, order of performances and events (the late-night potluck, for example), but all the participants owned the performance as something that was *theirs*. "Place" was therefore a more diffuse concept, applying to a broader geographical area rather than a specific physical location.

Similarly, the fourth event, at the Blacksburg Holiday Inn, was reported to be a late-night jam attended only by a few (ten or so) semiprofessional and professional traditional and bluegrass musicians who were good friends and devotees of traditional music. Here, location was determined by ease of access, size, and availability; community location did not matter. The event was not well advertised; guests were not encouraged, although they were not turned away, and a donation amount of $10 was suggested if they attended. This event also was *theirs* and it was a (re)production of personal identity among those who had earned the right to "belong" to the group. These performances were not marketable.

For all performances in this category, the conditions for commodification were semiotically absent, that is, meanings or distinctions between use value, exchange value, and affective value were not defined. Instead, participants reproduced nonsalable conditions of relating one to another in a place, although "place" was defined differently in different venues. What was potentially conforming to commodification relations, however, was the marketing of the events through various media, such as public service announcements, posters, flyers, and newspaper notifications. These semiotic "signs" represented displaced circulations of information about the potential use value directed almost entirely to potential visitors and tourists. Nontourists, that is, locals, knew of the events by word of mouth, postings at the Meadowbrook Community Center or businesses in their immediate locale, or a regional old-time music followers' electronic listserv. The media marketing activities therefore served as an interface, a potential conduit to the tourism marketplace, where region and place are irrelevant except as commodities purchased by consumers.

PARTIAL COMMODIFICATION

The second tier of venues (see table 11.3) all exhibited some degree of market formation by construction of performative frames that are readily amenable to commodification. These three venues—a school and two

Table 11.3. **Events with semicommodification present**

Venue	Targeted audience	Type of monetary payment by attendees	Basis for value	Band/performers' fee	Comments
Main St. Baptist Church	Local community and visitors and tourists; a designed performance; not preexisting except that individual bands play at available venues in the area; alienable relationships between most of audience and bands	None	Various individual valuations of the performances of the four bands; one band was made up of teenagers, so family/friend valuations for them more kinship based	None asked, but less than $500 given by TCR/Montgomery Tourism Council via sponsors' contributions; paid to performers	The event most crafted for tourists of the festival in terms of assembling bands, unusual setting, and organizers' emphasis on skill of performers; commodification through targeted audience's "valuation" of bands' skill as a commodity and their alienable relation to the performers
Prices Fork Elementary School	Local community and anyone interested in traditional dance music; alienable relationship among over half of the audience, who knew little to nothing about the band or the music; some there to support Prices Fork community and place-based family/kin relations	None	Various individual and group valuations of music and square dancing as an "experience" and learned about or as a reproduction of community heritage, depending on cultural and community orientation of audience member	None asked, but less than $800 given by TCR/Montgomery Tourism Council via sponsors' contributions; paid to performers	A staged performance in which the skill and talent of the band was on display, for which it expected payment; audience composition and band "valuation" criteria introduced issues of exchange value and use value
St. Paul's African Methodist Episcopal Church	Church members and African Americans in the area plus visitors and tourists	None	Church members and other Christians valued the event in terms of its religious artistry and conformity to expected religious message and affect; visitors valued it individually according to their aesthetic standards of black religious spirituals and affect created by performers and audience in the church sanctuary	None asked, but less than $500 given by TCR/Montgomery Tourism Council via sponsors' contributions; distributed to churches whose members performed	Reproduced a strong sense of inalienable identity and spiritual "community of saints" for church members and other Christians who affirm similar beliefs and religious traditions; visitors introduced alienability and exchange value and use value vis-à-vis their assessment of the quality of the performance

churches—were all organized by the county tourism director or by a host recruited by her. Consequently, they were community artifacts built upon preexisting resources and contacts but not preexisting events. None charged an admission fee, but different constituents of the event received small payments from donations obtained from community sponsors.[30]

One such event, at an African American church in Blacksburg, was a gospel and spiritual sing performed by church members and other talented singers from the county. It was organized by a church member who worked with the minister to host a tribute to the history of black forms of worship in Montgomery County through describing the rise of this specific church. The audience was mixed, both racially and in terms of church members or visitors. The church was packed. After TCR executive director Jack Hinshelwood's introductory remarks, the minister and other church elders gave a talk on this history; then the musical performance followed. Members of the congregation and others familiar with this form of Christian worship sometimes stood and engaged in call-and-response, hand raisings, and other appropriate forms of religious interaction with the music. Singers were applauded at the end of their numbers by nearly all, but the overarching affect of the event was spiritual, and its affective "value" was clearly one of congregants, but not necessarily visitors, celebrating a noncommodifiable relationship with God.

The other two events conformed to more standardized old-time music performances in that bands stood on a stage and played to an audience who applauded at the end of a song or, in the case of the Prices Fork event, square or slowed danced to the music.

For these types of venues, steps toward participation in a commodity-based market are salient, particularly from the perspective of audience/performer relations. Although members of each event's audience conformed to the types of inalienable relations present in the first category, discussed above, a significant percentage of each was constituted by "visitors" who were "sampling" "Appalachian" (or "black") culture through performances of traditional music. The events were structured to target such audiences and, even if visitors were few, as in the Main Street Baptist church venue, they were the ones to whom the organizers and hosts intended to appeal. Consequently, the organizers themselves were fostering a nascent commodity relationship between audience and performers.

The payment of these groups is more complicated than just a straightforward check for labor and services—which would indeed define the events as commodity based. Two of the three group organizers were not particularly interested in any remuneration, but took it when the county tourism director offered. The leader of the Prices Fork Elementary band, however, made clear that his band was to be paid. His arguments for payment were linked to observing that the center's major performer, Wayne Henderson, was receiving several thousand dollars whereas his band was originally expected to play for nothing. Issues of center versus TCR resources and organizational structure were not relevant; issues of prestige and performative competency, however, were. The payment amount was too small to be considered truly adequate for the services of five band members and a caller. Instead, the bandleader wanted his group and himself recognized as equals in terms of status within the circle of professional performers that included Henderson. In requiring payment, he and his band separated themselves from the co-constructing of a place-based identity, as revealed in the first type of events, redefining themselves as a professional entity, a commodity, on the market for hire, if only on a part-time basis.

Commodification could be introduced into all three events relatively easily by charging admission, by changing the event location to more tourist-appealing venues than an elementary school, a small African American church, and a vacant but large Protestant church, and by offering the events on a regular schedule so tourists and visitors could sample them at known and predictable times. In addition, the Baptist church set of performances would need to be more standardized in terms of what kinds of music and what types of audience participation would be needed to evoke a more consistent emotive response from the audience. The other two events, however, were already rather scripted and would require few alterations to achieve the desired affective outcome.

PUBLIC SPHERE EVENTS

Events classified in this last category (see table 11.4) stood out because of their public setting. Both occurred at nonprofit museum venues, which are open to the public at regular times during the week. They are locations funded and sustained by private foundations and donations, with minimal funding from county or town government. Therefore, both represented sites where neoliberal economics, with its emphasis on privatizing and marketing public resources, is strictly limited by the organizations' by-laws and mission.[31] The main purpose of each event was to provide the public with music or narrative presentations that elaborated on local or areal traditional music

Table 11.4. Public sphere events

Venue	Targeted audience	Type of monetary payment by attendees	Basis for value	Band/performers' fee	Comments
Montgomery Museum and Lewis Miller Art Center	Local or regional visitors who might be interested in traditional music in the Montgomery County area; tourists from anywhere	None	Various individual, family, or group valuations according to how the arrangement of the various artifacts created meaning for them; valuations also directed by the narrations of the luthiers at their demonstrations, by the spontaneous jams at the events, and by the talk among the visitors in the small exhibit room	None asked, but less than $500 given by TCR/Montgomery Tourism Council via sponsors' contributions	Offered multilayered valuation of local music "heritage" vis-á-vis multimodal means of communicating meaning (objects, old house, talk, demonstration, nonverbal affect, and music); civic space created as a result where attendees could potentially develop common civic goals and identities
St. Luke and Odd Fellows Hall	Local or regional visitors who might be interested in African American history and cultural life in the Blacksburg area; tourists from anywhere; while one band performed on Friday afternoon, the four-day open house was primarily a museum exhibit venue, not a performance venue	None	Various individual, family, or group valuations according to how the arrangement of the various artifacts created meaning for them; valuations also directed by the narrations of the museum curators when present, by the music performed on Friday afternoon by a semicommercial local old-time band, the spontaneous playing of the banjo on loan by a visitor, and by the talk among the visitors in the small exhibit room	None asked, but less than $500 given by TCR/Montgomery Tourism Council via sponsors' contributions	Offered multilayered valuation of local music "heritage" vis-á-vis multimodal means of communicating meaning (objects, old building, talk, playing of banjo, nonverbal affect, and music); civic space created as a result where attendees could potentially develop common civic goals and identities; in this case, however, the exhibits and building's focus on African American cultural history without the performance of local African American traditional music created confusion among primarily white visitors when old-time band music was performed

history and artistic excellence as embedded within an exhibit that already signified that history and artistry. These sites were therefore multilayered semiotically before they became festival venues. However, by virtue of the venues being museums, that is, sites of material object display, the meanings signified by the preexisting exhibits were open to individual interpretation, with few contextual constraints limiting or directing a visitor's understanding. That is, the kinds of inalienable relations created by events in the first tier are ipso facto impossible to create in these museums. Instead they create opportunities for congregations of visitors to develop new or reconstituted value relations. They then become loci for expressions of civil society, or places where government and markets, with their commodity transactions, are kept at bay or counterbalanced by the formation of citizen groups that intentionally or unintentionally promote the common good for areas larger than the immediate communities celebrated in the first tier of venues.[32] In short, they are focal points for the construction and demonstration of community building where various publics can visit as citizens to celebrate civic values, in this case, traditional local music.

Registers and Construction of a Civic Commons

The different types of relationships constructed by festival events at venue locations offer insights into how TCR and traditional music communities and communities of practice can build a civic commons that both accommodates the need for commodity-based tourism markets and simultaneously protects and perpetuates the performance of traditional local music as a core cultural practice and expected set of forms. These practices serve major functions as well, empowering local people, assigning and reproducing place-based identities, and permitting residents to engage in ecologically sustaining relationships that will allow them to continue to live on land that is infused with narratives of family, kin, ancestors, and place. To bring the seemingly disparate socioeconomic paradigms into one common model, however, is daunting, requiring a different lens than is commonly used to protect cultural "assets."[33] Perhaps useful is the term *register* as it is used in linguistic anthropology.

"Register" is a constellation of verbal and nonverbal signs that construct a way of talking that, in turn, consistently points to, or indexes, certain kinds of human or human/nonhuman relationships.[34] Among these relationships are, in general terms, informality versus formality, intimacy versus distance, reason versus emotion, politeness versus impoliteness, authority versus sub-servience, maleness versus femaleness, and land stewardship versus exploita-tion. We all adjust the way we talk (word choice, phrasing, intonation, syntax, and various bodily gestures and ways of placing our bodies) according to our perceived relationship to others. When these adjustments are patterned and regularized, they can be called "registers."[35] Successful use of registers has the potential to create positive relationships across a spectrum of possible rela-tionships. For example, talking to a religious cleric usually requires speech that is more formal, with little to no cursing and, commonly, reference to a sacred text or a deity. Conversely, talk with friends in a bar may involve cursing, off-color jokes, and gossip. The summation of registers over which people have mastery gives them a wide range of possible communications with broad sectors of society in ways that assist significantly in empowering them to engage in democratic governance, civil society, and preservation of what they consider sacred or highly valuable.

Each of the three types of socioeconomic configurations represented by the festival events can metaphorically be considered a register, capturing how close or distant the event performances were to either tourism market exchanges of commodities or inalienable residents' reproductions of non-commodified and highly valued cultural art forms. They therefore constitute choices in how a local group of event organizers, hosts, and participants can relate to neoliberal economic ideology. They can fully embrace it, partially embrace it, using many different strategies or approaches, or decide not to take it into consideration, according to their goals and desired outcomes for their music events.

Using this approach by applying the concept of register to different pat-terns of relating to market economies can then circumvent problems that arise in existing binary classifications such as "insider/outsider," "been heres/come heres," "money/heritage," "on the grid/off the grid," and "for TCR/against TCR." Instead, conscious recognition that multiple ways of relating to multiple economic structures are possible within one locale or region per-mits strategic decision making as to how and to what degree citizens want or need to engage in the continuum of socioeconomic possibilities, from the most globalized and market focused (that is, neoliberal) to the most local-ized, nonmonetary, and noncommodified means of constructing a livelihood.

Construction of a civic commons based on recognition of different socio-economic registers could potentially occur at different geographical levels:

community, county, or the entire TCR region. This chapter has viewed the potential for recognizing and valuing these registers through the lens of commodification of traditional music. The potential application of these registers, however, for consciously getting constituencies to actually talk or communicate about their concerns across a range of economic issues is one of their strengths. One major outcome in drawing constituencies into discussions under the concept of register is that the outcomes can potentially empower residents. As offered in this chapter, recognizing different forms of knowledge and experience in economic decision making can inform what music configurations and performance structures communities want to keep, change, or discourage, but also allow space for communicating *why* these discussions have value within different sites of oversight, review, program administration, and performance. Thus, communities' interfacing with a market-based, neoliberally dominated, global economic system that forces standardization of meanings to market the music commodities tourists expect would then become a more democratically empowered set of decisions, rather than ones based on immediate opportunity, emotional rush to the acquisition of money for daily living or capital accumulation, or being forced completely into an economy that reduces a major source of performers' identity, their music, to an atavism, to something from a bygone era that functions only as a commodity. And, if such commodification were to happen, and current cultural trends suggest it might, then it would contribute to the erasure of "Appalachia" more generally as a viable, livable region, one that tourists would no longer visit to experience "heritage" music and the culture that creates it because they would no longer exist.

TCR held a regionwide Mountains of Music Homecoming Festival June 12–20, 2015, to celebrate "heritage" music in southwest Virginia, and is planning another one for June 2016.[36] As TCR's first effort to incorporate all venues and counties included in its orbit, this festival's structure was based on the Montgomery County Crooked Road Festival discussed here. How it related to transglobal markets under neoliberal economic ideology and whether it created a rigorous model for a civic commons continue to be matters of ongoing planning and further discussion with TCR administration and, at local levels, the various counties' tourism committees, councils, and directors. In so doing, we have potentially contributed to a new vision of how "Appalachia" can continue to exist as a grounded, viable, place-based region while still engaging in the construction of a lively monetary economy to sustain it.

Notes

1. David Harvey, *A Brief History of Neoliberalism* (New York: Oxford University Press, 2005).

2. Barbara Ellen Smith, "The Place of Appalachia," *Journal of Appalachian Studies* 8, no. 1 (2002): 43.

3. P. Treanor, *Neoliberalism: Origins, Theory, Definition*, 2014, http://web.inter.nl.net/users/Paul.Treanor/neoliberalism.html, quoted in Tejaswini Ganti, "Neoliberalism," *Annual Review of Anthropology*, ed. Donald Brenneis and Karen B. Strier (Palo Alto, CA: Annual Reviews, 2015), 91.

4. Cornelia Butler Flora and Jan L. Flora, *Rural Communities: Legacy and Change*, 4th ed. (Boulder, CO: Westview, 2012); also see the concept of "durable architectonics of livability" in Herbert Reid and Betsy Taylor, *Recovering the Commons: Democracy, Place, and Global Justice* (Urbana: University of Illinois Press, 2010), 9.

5. Rebecca R. Scott, *Removing Mountains: Extracting Nature and Identity in the Appalachian Coalfields* (Minneapolis: University of Minnesota Press, 2010).

6. Stephen L. Fisher and Barbara Ellen Smith, "Introduction: Placing Appalachia," in *Transforming Places: Lessons from Appalachia*, ed. Stephen L. Fisher and Barbara Ellen Smith (Urbana: University of Illinois Press, 2012), 1–15.

7. Appalachian Voices, "The Crooked Road," *Appalachian Voices*, July 6, 2007, http://appvoices.org/2007/07/06/2980/ (accessed January 2, 2015); Ryan Chaney, "Straightening the Crooked Road," *Ethnography* 14 (2013): 387–411.

8. Appalachian Voices, "The Crooked Road."

9. The Crooked Road, "Major Venues on the Crooked Road," *The Crooked Road*, 2014, /www.myswva.org/tcr/venues/major (accessed January 2, 2015).

10. The Crooked Road, "Affiliated Venues and Festivals," *The Crooked Road*, 2014, https://www.myswva.org/tcr/venues/affiliated (accessed January 2, 2015).

11. Chaney, "Straightening the Crooked Road."

12. Virginia Freedom of Information Advisory Council, "Memorandum to Jack Hinshelwood, Executive Director, the Crooked Road: *Virginia's Heritage Music Trail*" (Richmond: Commonwealth of Virginia), advisory opinion AO-07-12, December 19, 2012, http://foiacouncil.dls.virginia.gov/ops/12/AO_07_12.htm (accessed January 3, 2015).

13. See "Crooked Road, Internet Access" (Bristol, VA: WCYB.com), October 19, 2012, http://www.wcyb.com/news/politics/va-9-debate/6-Crooked-Road-internet-access/17061536 (accessed January 3, 2015).

14. Sonja Ingram, "The Crooked Road to Improving Local Economies," *The Revivalist: Word from the Appalachian South*, November 21, 2015, http://therevivalist.info/the-crooked-road-local-economies (accessed January 3, 2015).

15. TCR received a $10,000 Appalachian Regional Commission federal grant facilitated by Virginia senator Mark Warner in 2013 to conduct a financial impact analysis that would update these figures. See Allie Robinson Gibson, "More Than

$2M in ARC Grants Headed for SWVA," *Bristol Herald Courier,* December 9, 2013, http://www.tricities.com/news/local/article_d01e5c4a-5efe-11e3-8d3b-0019bb30f31a .html?mode=jqm (accessed January 3, 2015). This report is not yet completed, however.

16. Lisa Bleakley, Montgomery County, Virginia, tourism director, personal communication, June 10, 2014, stated that the Commonwealth of Virginia defines a "tourist" as someone who travels more than fifty miles to visit a site; visitors are those who don't live in the immediate area. See also Anita Puckett, "Final Report: Cultural Impact and Development of 'The Crooked Road: Virginia's Heritage Music Trail' in Montgomery and Giles Counties, Virginia," *Appalachian Teaching Project,* May 30, 2014, http:// www.etsu.edu/cass/projects/vt/ATP2013_VT_Final_Report_revised.pdf (accessed January 3, 2015).

17. Bleakley, personal communication.

18. Chaney, "Straightening the Crooked Road."

19. Puckett, "Final Report"; Anita Puckett, "Proposal for: Development of Wayside Kiosks for Virginia's Heritage Music Trail in Montgomery and Giles Counties, Virginia: Cultural and Economic Implications," *Appalachian Teaching Project,* June 30, 2014, http:// www.etsu.edu/cass/projects/vt/2014_ATP_VA_Proposal.pdf (accessed January 3, 2015).

20. Reid and Taylor, *Recovering the Commons,* 25, identify a "civic commons" as the social space in which the "social webs of everyday practices," also linked to the natural relations in which they are inalienably embedded, can become empowered so that participants "contest, ratify, or celebrate the forms and decisions through which [the] social and ecological order is reproduced—a space with political, cultural, and social dimensions."

21. The Crooked Road, *Traditional Music Education,* 2014, https://www.myswva .org/tcr/tmep (accessed January 1, 2015).

22. See Chaney, "Straightening the Crooked Road."

23. As a linguistic anthropologist who conducts ethnographic research in Appalachia, I have had the opportunity to network among many different constituencies in Montgomery County over the twenty years I have been employed by Virginia Tech, located in Montgomery County, Virginia.

24. In speaking of "community of practice," I have simplified Wenger, McDermott, and Snyder's definition to mean a group of people who share similar interests in a craft or profession to the point that they consciously recognize they are co-members in a type of community. See Etienne Wenger, Richard McDermott, and William M. Snyder, *Cultivating Communities of Practice* (Boston: Harvard Business Review Press, 2002).

25. C. A. Gregory, *Gifts and Commodities* (New York: Academic, 1982), 10.

26. Paul Kockelman, "A Semiotic Ontology of the Commodity," *Journal of Linguistic Anthropology* 16, no. 1 (2006): 76–102.

27. Ibid., 79–81.

28. Pierre Bourdieu, *Distinction: A Social Critique of the Judgement of Taste* (Boston: Harvard University Press, 1984).

29. Emily Satterwhite, "'That's What They're All Singing About': Appalachian Heritage, Celtic Pride, and American Nationalism at the 2003 Smithsonian Folklife Festival," *Appalachian Journal* 32, no. 3 (2005): 325. Claims made about tourists' or visitors' responses are based on anecdotal data I've collected over the last decade in visits to the jamboree and should be considered as illustrative rather than analytically rigorous. In addition, however, some local residents have also reported that they now avoid the Friday jamboree because it is "too touristy" and no longer represents how they value *their* music.

30. Bleakley, personal communication. Money came from solicited donations from county businesspeople and individuals contacted by the country tourism director or myself.

31. Harvey, *A Brief History of Neoliberalism,* 65.

32. Flora and Flora, *Rural Communities,* 15–16.

33. Civic Practices Network, "A Profile of HandMade in America," *Topics,* n.d., http://www.cpn.org/topics/work/handmade.html (accessed January 3, 2015), notes, for example, that Becky Andersen, founder and former executive director of HandMade in America, applied a model that is binary, keeping the "sacred" cultural elements off the market and apart from tourists while marketing "profane" elements to tourists. The Appalachian Regional Commission's approach, on the other hand, is to market everything possible, supposedly without destroying the resources that produce the commodities marketed. See Appalachian Regional Commission, *Asset Based Development,* 2014, http://www.arc.gov/abd (accessed January 3, 2015).

34. Asif Agha, *Language and Social Relations* (New York: Cambridge University Press, 2007), 145–89.

35. A register is not identical to "dialect" or "speech variety" because among the factors determining it are nonverbal cues or levels in diction or lexicon, and because every speaker uses more than one register, depending on event and context.

36. The Crooked Road, "Mountains of Music Homecoming," *Mountains of Music Homecoming,* 2014, http://mtnsofmusic.com/ (accessed January 1, 2015).

Part 4

Engagement

12

"No One's Ever Talked to Us Before"

Participatory Approaches and Economic Development in
Rural Appalachian Communities

Tim Ezzell

"No one's ever been here," the woman remarked, adding, "no one's ever talked to us before."[1] This simple statement, made in a West Virginia community center, is indicative of the state of policy research in Appalachia and in rural communities across the nation. Increasingly, over the past half century, policy research related to economic and community development has become dominated by quantitative and econometric research approaches. While ethnographers, sociologists, and other social scientists have long used qualitative and participatory approaches to better understand Appalachian culture and traditions, few have applied these methods to economic development efforts. Most research related to Appalachian economic and business development consists of sweeping regional studies derived from "robust" quantitative data sets and analyses. While these studies have contributed much to the understanding of the regional economy, they often ignore the experiences of small rural communities. Such communities, with few residents and modest economic activity, often fall between the cracks of these studies, leaving their issues unrecognized and their residents feeling forgotten and unheard.[2]

This chapter explores methodological approaches to bringing these "unheard voices" to the fore of economic development planning in rural

Appalachia. Between 2010 and 2012, researchers from the University of Tennessee (UT) conducted an assessment of economic development strategies for the Appalachian Regional Commission (ARC). The study, designed to compare communities coping with economic distress, represented an important effort by the agency to explore development challenges at the local level. It also presented an opportunity for the UT research team to introduce participatory and qualitative approaches into the field of economic development research. In doing so, however, the UT team created a new challenge—conducting research that gave voice to local residents and accurately portrayed their experiences and successes while satisfying the needs of agency leaders for empirical data capable of withstanding the scrutiny of regional and national decision makers. The resulting report, *Strategies for Economic Improvement in Appalachia's Distressed Rural Counties,* largely accomplished these goals.[3] Its success can be attributed to the use of a hybrid research approach that combined econometric, qualitative, and participatory research techniques. This approach, discussed on the following pages, brought "forgotten" communities to the forefront of policy discussions and created a new model for developing and promoting rural development policies and practices.

Project Background

The project began in August 2009 when the ARC issued a request for proposals (RFP) "to evaluate economic growth in Appalachia's distressed rural counties, analyze and compare strategies for economic development in these counties, and identify factors that led to success as well as factors that inhibited or constrained growth." The stated goal of the proposed project was to "present practical methods and analytical tools that, when coupled with case study examples, can help identify potential sources of regional economic growth in distressed rural counties." The completed research, the RFP stated, would be used to "provide valuable insights and methodology for local economic development practitioners that can be used to analyze growth prospects in other counties and regions." To accomplish these goals, ARC requested a cohort study comparing similar distressed and nondistressed counties. This comparison would evaluate several factors, including spatial influences and the role of cultural and natural assets as well as the impact of social, political, and institutional circumstances. The project was also to determine the impact of ARC investments, such as infrastructure and road improvements, tourism initiatives, or workforce development programs.[4]

The project goals and guidelines set forth in the 2009 RFP presented special challenges and suggested a dichotomous research approach. On the one hand, the agency appeared to suggest a traditional econometric study. The RFP, for example, called for the empirical testing of growth theories and suggested using regression analysis, a statistical tool used to evaluate relationships between multiple variables. The proposal call also referenced prior ARC studies with strong quantitative elements, including *Sources of Regional Growth in Non-metro Appalachia.*[5] At the same time, however, important elements of the proposed study—topics like political trends, quality of life factors, or asset impacts—called for qualitative tools. In addition, UT researchers feared that a quantitative approach could not accurately record conditions in these rural communities. Such communities often lack complete data sets and their residents, with few resources and little voice, often fall below the traditional data collection radar.

The use of qualitative tools appeared to be necessary, but their employment raised important issues related to the perceived validity of descriptive data in the national policy community. Policy decisions at all levels of government are increasingly dominated by positivist researchers from the hard sciences. Positivists contend that objective scientific research is possible, even within the social sciences, and provable using logical and mathematical approaches. The study that is the focus of this chapter is not the first instance in which a locally based qualitative approach to Appalachian research encountered difficulties with positivist policy science. In the late 1970s, a collaborative team led by the Highlander Research and Education Center (New Market, Tennessee) and Appalachian State University (Boone, North Carolina) organized to study the problem of absentee landownership in Appalachia. A precursor to contemporary action research methods, the Appalachian Landownership Taskforce was funded by the Appalachian Regional Commission to blend citizen-driven qualitative data collection with statistical analysis to describe changing landownership patterns in the region. The research organizers relied on local citizen-based groups to collect qualitative data to contextualize broader research findings. Yet the citizen-based qualitative work accomplished was subject to immediate government criticism after the eighteen-hundred-page report's submission in 1981; findings from citizens' data collection, for example, were relabeled as merely a "reflection of local opinion" when they contradicted government data sources.[6] In the present, this "reemergent scientism," promoted by the National Research Council through the scientifically based research movement and "evidence-based" analysis, has permeated political decision making and, in the process, delegated qualitative research to a diminished or even heretical status. Decried as "scholarship, not science," qualitative research is dismissed for lacking the objectivity and randomization associated with "value-free" science. While some researchers have criticized this emphasis as "dogmatic" and "narrow," its accepted status would likely make a highly qualitative approach suspect and, as a result, unfundable.[7]

In an effort to address these concerns, the UT research team proposed a hybrid research approach: using both qualitative and quantitative methods combined the credibility of a quantitative strategy with the rich detail and context descriptive sources provide. Yet this approach, while promising, also carried some risks. Mixed-method experimentalism has been criticized as presuming "methodological hierarchy in which quantitative methods are at the top and qualitative methods are relegated to a largely auxiliary role." Such approaches, critics argue, "divide inquiry into a dichotomous framework: exploration (qualitative) versus confirmation (quantitative)." In many cases, this secondary descriptive role "excludes stakeholders from dialogue" and decreases the likelihood that previously silenced voices will be heard."[8]

In light of these criticisms, the UT team developed a balanced approach that placed considerable emphasis on qualitative case studies and incorporated significant and substantive participatory efforts. The final UT methodology included the following components:

- *Economic analysis*—Team members identified industry clusters and their regional multiplier effects.
- *Demographic analysis*—Research staff analyzed established community data sets, including census data, public health statistics, and school test scores.
- *Stakeholder survey*—UT researchers conducted a survey of stakeholders in case study communities to assess local assets, obstacles, and other factors.
- *Site visits*—Members of the UT research team conducted site visits to each case study community to observe local conditions and review development efforts. During site visits, researchers conducted interviews with local officials and facilitated focus groups with community stakeholders.

While this approach included many strong qualitative and participatory activities, it also included a significant and visible quantitative element. The process was strengthened by the survey and demographic analyses, which also included quantitative characteristics. As a result, this mixed methodology met the threshold of credibility necessary for project acceptance.[9]

Cohort Selection

The UT team's first major task was to select five pairs of case study counties from among the 420 counties in the ARC region. These pairs would be distributed among the five ARC subregions, one pair (a distressed county and a formerly distressed cohort) from each subregion. As planned, the researchers utilized a two-tier approach incorporating both quantitative and qualitative elements. First, the team identified formerly distressed counties by noting the twenty-three most significantly improved counties in the ARC region since 1960 using the ARC's economic status index. Team economists then performed a statistical matching process to identify potential distressed cohorts.

Final cohort pairs were then selected from these candidates using a qualitative matrix. County pairings were scored according to a number of characteristics, including proximity, area, population, interstate access, and ARC highway investments. Highest-scoring pairs were included in the study. In implementing this strategy, the team encountered issues in two subregions. In the northern subregion, a lack of distressed counties led researchers to select Morgan County, Ohio—a county on the border of the north central subregion, as the distressed cohort. In the central subregion, researchers experienced the opposite problem—a lack of nondistressed counties. In this case, the team selected Pike County, Kentucky—a high-performing at-risk community—as the nondistressed cohort.

The ten counties that emerged as the final cohort pairings are shown in table 12.1.

Table 12.1. Cohort pairings

Subregion	Distressed cohort	Formerly distressed cohort
North	Morgan County, OH	Greene County, PA
North central	Calhoun County, WV	Pendleton County, WV
Central	Bell County, KY	Pike County, KY
South central	Johnson County, TN	Avery County, NC
South	Noxubee County, MS	Lawrence County, AL

In general, the mixed cohort selection process worked well: selected communities presented a range of regional issues, including fracking, globalization, race relations, welfare reform, substance abuse, and the coal transition. Interestingly, all five distressed counties were located west of their non-distressed cohorts. While this trend may be coincidental, it might also be indicative of the influence of East Coast urban areas' policy decisions and their impact on economic growth.[10]

Economic and Demographic Analysis

After selection of the cohort communities, economists on the research team conducted an economic analysis of all ten case studies. Using regression analysis tools, researchers evaluated a number of factors, including industry clusters, location, educational attainment, employment data, and local business counts. The results of this analysis revealed few surprises. Communities located near urban areas or along major highways tend to perform better than those in remote areas. Areas overly dependent on extractive resources, like coal or shale gas, risk diminished manufacturing competitiveness. Perhaps the most important finding of the analysis was the identification of several high-skill and high-tech growth economic sectors that might potentially be attracted by the region's labor, infrastructure, market access, and cultural amenities.[11]

Concurrent with the economic analysis, the qualitative research staff conducted an analysis of demographic statistics and other data sets. As with the economic analysis, many results were predictable. Most distressed counties, for example, were characterized by declining populations and aging residents. These early profiles, however, did yield some interesting surprises. Morgan County, Ohio, for example, boasted high school test scores more typical of an affluent suburb than a distressed Appalachian community. Likewise, Pendleton County, West Virginia, displayed impressive health outcomes while Noxubee County, Mississippi, exhibited alarming indicators of poor sexual health. These outlying statistics raised important questions and became the subject of further qualitative inquiry.[12]

Stakeholder Survey

Although these analyses revealed significant data about the region, it is important to note the information that was not included. The statistics alone revealed little about actual development issues at the local level or the human impact of development policies: to determine these, qualitative research was needed. For the UT team, the first step in the qualitative process was the development, distribution, and analysis of a community survey. The UT survey had three goals. First, it would assess a wide range of local assets and conditions. Second, many of the results would be expressed quantitatively, thus strengthening the viability of the final study among policy makers. Finally, the process would provide preliminary community-specific data to establish a basis for subsequent site visit discussions.

Past ARC research reports often limited engagement to "the usual suspects"—elected officials, economic development directors, or development district staff. While these stakeholders have valuable knowledge, they also have a significant personal or professional interest in study outcomes. In order to reduce the impact of this conflict and expand local engagement, the UT research team elected to survey a broad range of stakeholders including business owners, educators, health-care providers, nonprofits, and other government workers. Participants were asked about a range of subjects, including local services, infrastructure, youth retention, substance abuse, and social capital. Survey forms included an area for additional comments and also featured a number of open-ended questions designed to ascertain local perceptions, assets, and barriers.[13]

Given the limits on Internet access in some rural areas, the research team elected to distribute surveys via mail. One thousand surveys were distributed, one hundred for each study community. Just over one-fourth of the surveys were returned. Among the survey findings were the following:

- Both distressed and nondistressed communities saw tourism as their strongest growth opportunity.
- Despite opportunities in high-tech or high-skill sectors, stakeholders were generally pessimistic about high-tech and alternative energy sectors.
- Workforce development and substance abuse programs were identified as service areas in most need of improvement.
- Homelessness and animal welfare were also identified as significant areas of concern.
- Planning and zoning were rated among the worst-performing public services.
- Residents in most counties expressed pride and satisfaction in

their community. A notable exception was Noxubee County, Mississippi, where no one expressed strong pride in their community and 30 percent of respondents were neither proud nor satisfied.[14]

The open-ended questions also yielded important—at times compelling—results. The short-answer questions related to local perceptions, assets, and needs seemed to capsulize local conditions while creating a moving portrait of the entire Appalachian region. The UT research team created "word cloud" charts to visually convey these results. In these graphic images, the size of the word or phrase increases with the frequency of use. UT researchers created word clouds at the community and regional level for each of these three questions: "What are three words that describe your county?" "What is your county best known for?" and "What are three problems in your county that need to be solved?" The resulting images became some of the most widely discussed outcomes from the research. Particularly moving were the three regionwide word clouds. Together, they portray the contradictions that define Appalachia—a region of abundance and beauty and yet a place of privation and hardship.[15]

Also telling were the comments provided by survey participants. Over one-third of the participants left comments, some of them extensive. The comments covered numerous topics, but a handful of themes prevailed. Leadership, for example, was a concern among many counties. One respondent from Avery County wrote, "Our commissioners are stuck. As a very rural area they are caught between fiscal responsibility, an older population, and not knowing what to do." From Pike County: "Local city leaders make decisions with very little input from the community. When they take input, it only takes one or two voices to influence their decisions. Mostly they make decisions with very little thought or debate."

Welfare reform and substance abuse were other common causes for concern. A Bell County resident wrote, "A serious local issue is the fact that many residents would rather draw government funds. Very hard to find workers that are drug free." According to a respondent from Calhoun County: "Many are content to not work and live off government assistance, because that is what their family has always done. This leads to a poor, over populated community."

Survey participants also expressed concerns related to race relations and racial perceptions. Interestingly, these concerns were not limited to the racially diverse areas of the Deep South. Residents of overwhelmingly white counties in central Appalachia noted problems in their communities as well. Wrote one Noxubee County resident, "This county is a holdover from the 1960s where blacks still believe they are being mistreated or are consumed with 'payback.' Though there are some leaders who are reaching out to other factions, to a large degree the effort is not successful." From Johnson County: "People in this town do not want to move forward. They do not like outside people. There is a need to run fair elections. Government craziness. We only want white people in the area." "Very little racial diversity here," noted a writer from Calhoun County. "More cultural awareness would improve the community."

Overall, the survey was well received, with some participants even expressing gratitude for being asked to participate. Given the length and complexity of the survey, this response suggested that residents in these communities wanted to be heard and engaged in the research process.[16]

Site Visits and Focus Groups

These suspicions were confirmed during community site visits. For members of the UT team, site visits were from the outset an integral element of the research approach. Appalachian communities are often complex organisms with wide-ranging issues and resources. Political and social contexts are often impossible to understand without visiting the communities and talking directly with local stakeholders. Some barriers, such as road conditions, imagability, or livability can sometimes only be fully appreciated firsthand. Research team members confirmed this early in their first visit when, shortly after crossing the county line in Pendleton County, West Virginia, they encountered a flashing road sign warning of steep road grades and stating, "Trucks Must Stop." Immediately, the team recognized that access was likely a barrier to the county's development. A few days later, the team found another, less formal portent just after crossing the line into Calhoun County, West Virginia. A skeletal deer carcass on the road shoulder was a visual indicator the researchers were entering a remote community with limited services. These experiences conveyed the realities of these communities in a way no spreadsheet, database, or phone call could ever accomplish.

Logistical and budgetary considerations were significant factors in the development of the site visit methodology. Given the diverse range of the communities involved and the emphasis placed on the cohort comparisons, the team felt it was better to conduct ten brief but intensive site visits rather than fewer extended trips. From the outset, the team understood the risks associated with this approach. First impressions can be misleading and could lead to distorted results. Team members tried to correct for this through the pre-visit survey and by including a broad range of stakeholders in site visit activities. Visits were arranged weeks in advance through discussions with local officials. Focus group participants were recruited through local contacts and survey responses.

All ten one-day site visits followed a similar agenda. The site visit team would arrive early for morning discussions with local officials. This group usually included the lead elected official, such as a county executive, the economic development director, the local chamber of commerce director, planning officials, commissioners, or other key figures. This morning meeting served multiple purposes. First, it introduced the site team to the community and established a foundation for the day's visit. It also gave local officials an opportunity to talk about their efforts and share their perspectives. Finally, the morning session gave researchers a chance to introduce themselves to local leaders, establish an equitable relationship, and assure officials that the project was not an attempt to pass judgment or undermine local authority.

Focus groups were conducted in the afternoon and were usually held in a public meeting room or community center. These sessions typically included a wide range of local stakeholders: business owners, educators, nonprofit leaders, activists, health-care providers, extension staff, and ministers. The goal of these meetings was to build upon prior research and better understand the survey results and the discussions with local leaders. The diverse nature of this group provided multiple local perspectives and sometimes led to lively discussions. In order to encourage a free and open dialogue, anonymity was promised to group members. Comments were transcribed on paper but were not recorded, as electronic recording sometimes deters participation. While comments were incorporated in the final report, none were ascribed to any particular participant.

In between the two meetings, members of the site visit team conducted an observation survey of the community. They visited sites, evaluated establishments, and made note of conditions. Researchers evaluated infrastructure, assessed downtown activity, and made note of scenic and historic resources. In many cases, community members or officials showed the team an important site or facility, such as vacant industrial space or an ARC highway or other investment. Team members also dropped in on the local visitor's center, when available, talking with docents and collecting brochures, guides, and other promotional materials. Conditions were documented with photographs and summarized in writing immediately following each visit.

Local reactions to the site visits were generally positive and, in some cases, downright enthusiastic. Site visit teams were well received in most communities, although local officials sometimes expressed concerns. In most cases, these misgivings focused on their county's selection as a case study. This was particularly true of distressed counties, where officials felt they were being singled out for special scrutiny. In other cases, officials wondered if they were under consideration for new funding or special opportunities. In either event, these perceptions were soon laid to rest by a summary of the cohort selection methodology, which made it clear that participant counties were selected based on empirical factors and not because of personalities or politics. The team's association with a recognized regional institution also helped allay concerns about participation. Team members reinforced this association by using school logos, colors, and presentation templates.

While local officials were generally pleased to discuss their issues and development efforts, focus group participants were often excited to have the opportunity to talk about their communities. A common sentiment among the focus groups was that these communities and their residents had been "forgotten" by the nation and were endowed with little or no voice in the policy decisions that helped determine their destiny. Given the opportunity to be heard, participants spoke openly and forthrightly about the challenges facing rural communities. During the first site visit, in fact, one participant pointedly enjoined the research team, "Please don't sugarcoat the results." Many participants expressed gratitude for being asked to participate and some asked researchers to conduct additional visits.[17]

Information gathered during the site visits proved invaluable to the research team. Local stakeholders, particularly focus group participants, disclosed important findings that might not have been uncovered through traditional evidence-based research approaches. Discussions, for example, revealed the unintended consequences of some popular development strategies. While agglomeration, growth center, and supply chain strategies often work well in attracting employers, the energy and time costs associated with these long commutes impact a number of important areas, including family incomes, nutrition, and family stress. Stakeholders also talked about their concerns related to shale-gas fracking and expressed frustration with the current welfare system. Researchers also garnered important information related to awareness and perceptions of the ARC. Many stakeholders, for example, were unaware of ARC programs and opportunities. Others recognized the agency's contributions but felt it was often detached from the region's poorest communities. Lastly, the team found disparate views of local development districts (LDDs). While most considered their LDD a vital partner in development efforts, a few communities felt their LDD was unresponsive or overly politicized.

In some cases, the study finding contradicted or questioned the validity of hard data sets. On paper, for example, Pendleton County, West Virginia, appears to be a stable community far removed from past economic distress. In reality, researchers found a community facing economic uncertainty. Recent economic progress was largely attributed to a small military facility—a complex threatened with closure. The complex skewed the economic data, creating an illusion of economic parity. In Avery County, North Carolina, the research team encountered a similar situation. That community was characterized by significant income disparities between affluent retirees and a large number of low-wage, low-skill workers. These statistics were further distorted by a large immigrant population, many of whom were undocumented and probably underreported. In both cases, qualitative field research revealed the flaws inherent in remote quantitative studies and demonstrated the value of local participation through site visits.[18]

Report Findings and Recommendations

The research team identified best practices in eleven subject areas, ranging from downtown redevelopment to youth retention and small-business development. The UT team also developed several recommendations to help promote local growth, including the following:

- The ARC should evaluate the existing LDD network and develop improved performance standards.
- Local and county governments should form strong partnerships with academic institutions.
- Communities and agencies at all levels of government should make rural broadband access a priority.

- Communities should develop youth leadership programs.
- Small counties should consider shared government services.
- The ARC should assist counties with the redevelopment of vacant industrial sites.
- Small counties should focus on strategies that grow local jobs through entrepreneurship, education and training, and the leveraging of local assets.
- As infrastructure improves, more resources should be devoted to education, leadership development, and entrepreneurship programs.
- Communities should expand the use of social media networks.
- Counties and agencies should do more to promote racial diversity and tolerance.
- Communities should devote additional resources to hospitality training.[19]

It was important that the recommendations be accessible to both governments and the communities the project was intended to serve. All too often, policy reports go largely unread beyond the executive summary. This is particularly true among practitioners in the field—those who actually apply policy changes. This trend then raises the question: Do people not read the report because they are not interested, because they lack the time, or because the reports are not accessible to a lay audience? One of the problems, the team suggested, was that the new "scientific" approach was so laden with technical language that, while valuable to policy makers and other academic researchers, it was of little use to local audiences. In an effort to reverse this trend, the UT team utilized the qualitative data to engage the reader and present findings in a narrative form. They accomplished this in a number of ways. Word clouds and site visit photos, for example, were used to engage readers and draw them into the report text. Quotes gleaned from survey comments and focus groups were placed in "bubbles" and incorporated into the text to further illustrate project findings. Charts and graphics were also used to increase reader appeal. Authors avoided the use of academic jargon to make the report accessible to lay readers. Technical material, such as detailed econometric findings, was retained but placed in an appendix.

Reaction to the report was generally positive. Participating communities were, for the most part, pleased with the results, calling the community profiles truthful and fair. The public response was also favorable, particularly among practitioners, who found the research "very relevant" and "enlightening." Many felt the study confirmed local issues and conditions and planned to use the research to support local funding proposals and project ideas. Yet, while the report was largely embraced by economic and community development professionals in the field, it was less popular in some academic circles. Some traditional economists were critical of the research and particularly of the site visit components, which they found anecdotal and lacking objectivity. For its part, the ARC embraced the report and promoted it through social media. The organization also implemented policy changes based on report findings, such as requiring development districts to devote more ARC resources to addressing issues in distressed counties.

Lessons Learned

The balanced mixed-methods approach developed by the UT research team proved to be an effective and equitable model for assessing development opportunities and barriers facing distressed rural communities. This approach, which supplemented traditional quantitative research with extensive qualitative and participatory elements, offered several significant advantages. It essentially combined the best of both worlds: the perceived reliability and relative objectivity of a quantitative study with the rich descriptive and narrative characteristics of qualitative research. The perceived validity of the study among policy makers was further strengthened by including replicable and countable activities, such as the systematic cohort selection process and an extensive community survey. In achieving this acceptance, the study achieved vital goals—to give voice to community research in the policy evaluation process and to accurately portray the wide range of opportunities, barriers, and impacts that exist in many Appalachian communities.

While the study achieved wide acceptance by the study communities and practitioners in the field, it faced criticism from some so-called scientific researchers who felt it lacked objectivity. Yet, despite this resistance, the research confirmed that distressed rural communities cannot be fully or accurately portrayed within the columns of a spreadsheet. These communities, and the people within them, are far too complex for these distant assessments. Those seeking simple answers to Appalachian poverty, such as a list of quick and inexpensive solutions to deeply rooted ills, were also likely disappointed. The study demonstrated that there are no silver bullet solutions to local hardships. Solutions will require significant time, continued investments, equitable partnerships, and sustained engagement. Talking with people in these communities, and listening to their voices, is surely an important and necessary step in this process.

Notes

1. Pendleton County focus group, Franklin, WV, November 15, 2010, University of Tennessee Community Partnership Center, Knoxville.

2. While participatory approaches are uncommon in economic development research, they are used for community development studies. See Susan E. Keefe, *Participatory Development in Appalachia: Cultural Identity, Community, and Sustainability* (Knoxville: University of Tennessee Press, 2009).

3. Tim Ezzell, Dayton Lambert, and Eric Ogle, *Strategies for Economic Improvement in Appalachia's Distressed Rural Counties: An Analysis of Ten Distressed and Formerly Distressed Appalachian Counties* (Washington, DC: Appalachian Regional Commission, 2012).

4. David Carrier, "Request for Proposals: Evaluation of Strategies for Economic Improvement in Appalachia's Distressed Rural Counties," July 2009, 1–3, Appalachian Regional Commission, Washington, DC.

5. Economic Development Research Group, Inc., Regional Technology Strategies, Inc., and MIT Dept. of Urban Studies and Planning, *Sources of Regional Growth in Non-metro Appalachia* (Washington, DC: Appalachian Regional Commission, 2007).

6. Shaunna L. Scott, "Discovering What the People Knew: The 1979 Appalachian Land Ownership Study," *Action Research* 7, no. 2 (2009): 185–205.

7. J. A. Maxwell, "Reemergent Scientism, Postmodernism, and Dialogue across Differences," *Qualitative Inquiry* 10 (2004): 35–41; Norman K. Denzin and Yvonna S. Lincoln, *The Sage Handbook of Qualitative Research,* 3rd ed. (Thousand Oaks, CA: Sage, 2005), 9.

8. K. R. Howe, "A Critique of Experimentalism," *Qualitative Inquiry* 10 (2004): 42–61; Denzin and Lincoln, *Sage Handbook of Qualitative Research*, 9–10.

9. Ezzell, Lambert, and Ogle, *Strategies for Economic Improvement*, 22–32.

10. Ibid., 28–29, 206.

11. Ibid., 210–14.

12. Ibid., 147, 171, 173.

13. Ibid., 29–30.

14. Ibid., 146–82.

15. Ibid., 10–12.

16. University of Tennessee Community Partnership Center, "2010 ARC Community Survey," Knoxville, Appalachian Regional Commission, Washington, DC.

17. Ezzell, Lambert, and Ogle, *Strategies for Economic Improvement,* 25.

18. Ibid., 61, 105–6.

19. Ibid., 184.

13

Strength in Numbers

The Federation of Appalachian Housing Enterprises

Diane N. Loeffler and Jim King

As we revisit Appalachia, it is important to continually appraise what sets the region apart from other parts of the United States, and it is equally important to understand how the region can be, paraphrasing Eller, a bellwether for broader change.[1] Highlighting the innovation within the region can help to reframe dialogue and to shape perception. Rather than character-ize Appalachia as "underprivileged" or "quaint," we should consider that, while persistent poverty and significant distinct challenges remain, there is a great deal to learn from innovation within the region.[2] The Federation of Appalachian Housing Enterprises (Fahe) is an excellent touchstone for such discussion and dialogue. A one-of-a-kind, member-driven, nonprofit community development financial institution (CDFI) with fifty-six member organizations across six states and 178 Appalachian counties, Fahe offers an exciting and important approach to community development within the region. This chapter discusses Fahe's history and growth and examines the organization's intentional organization toward innovation, development, and sustainability. The concept of social capital is introduced and discussed as a key driver of Fahe's success; strong social capital enhances access to politi-cal, financial, and human capital, and this in turn supports local economic development.

This chapter examines the issues of housing and regional sustainability from the theoretical perspective of social capital and in the context of work-ing within the opportunity structures of regional policy networks. Social capital, while a somewhat elastic and difficult concept to define, is broadly constructed as the "norms and networks that enable people to act collectively."[3] We examine Fahe's ability to create and utilize social capital at the bonding, bridging, and linking level and will further explore how this capital then leverages other capital that is important for successful community development work. We examine the organization's capacity to bend and to grow and to face adversity. Ultimately, this chapter provides an excellent case study of one organization's ability to access and leverage resources to continue to provide opportunities to nonprofit organizations that are committed to core values of affordable housing and community development within the region. This study of Fahe offers one example of progressive, innovative, and "outside the box" strategies for community and economic development.

History

To fully understand Fahe's accomplishments and uniqueness, it is important to first review the organization's history and philosophical beginnings. The Federation of Appalachian Housing Enterprises, Inc., Fahe was established in Berea, Kentucky, in 1980 in response to the call for support and development of safe and affordable housing within the central Appalachian region. The Commission on Religion in Appalachia (CORA), its subsidiary, the Human/Economic Appalachian Development Corporation (HEAD), and the Housing Assistance Council (HAC) spearheaded the development of a membership network that could bring together the different voices and small nonprofit organizations that had developed out of the War on Poverty and were now working to provide housing and related services. The intent was to address the affordable housing crisis in the central Appalachian counties of Virginia, West Virginia, Tennessee, Kentucky, and North Carolina. Concurrent with the proliferation of small nonprofits and community development corporations, "a number of federally and state funded revolving loan funds were created," though these often focused on urban growth and development.[4] Fahe's role, as identified by the original stakeholders (HEAD, HAC, CORA) was to create a resource wherein those interested in creating change and fighting poverty could come together to learn, challenge one another, work cooperatively, and seek support. Fahe has deep roots in the social justice tradition and has always maintained, at its core, a commitment to the communities in which it works. That much of what Fahe does is relational is very intentional.

For over thirty years, Fahe has been committed to community development and housing and has worked to meet the changing needs of the communities served by member organizations. Fahe has transformed itself from a small and very specific organization focused on the development of single-family homes to a much larger and more far-reaching association. In 1985 Fahe made its first mortgage loan, had twelve members, and had a relatively small impact in the region as a whole. Success, in the early years, was measured through outputs—through the number of houses built/rehabilitated and the number of families served. Policy shifts motivated change— for example, in the mid-1980s Fahe established its own revolving loan fund in response to member organization needs for access to capital during the Reagan administration, when interest rates skyrocketed and funding for housing and community development saw a sharp decline.

As the organization developed heightened influence at the federal level, Fahe was a leading voice in national discussion related to the passage of the Reigle Community Development and Regulatory Improvement Act (1994), which created the Community Development Financial Institution Fund and certified CDFIs. While much of the national dialogue related to community development financing was still inherently urban, Fahe ensured that rural community development—and central Appalachia specifically—was not forgotten in this discussion. Then CEO Dave Lollis testified before Congress and was present when the legislation was signed. In 1995 Fahe became the region's only CDFI. This allowed Fahe to enhance its lending capacity and to better support member organizations in their community-level development. For twenty years Fahe has been one of the few large, rural CDFIs and is arguably the only one serving the central Appalachian region.

Thus, Fahe continued to grow through the 1980s and 1990s. By the early 2000s, Fahe (through its member organizations) was "producing about 2000 units per year and . . . was originating about $5 million of financing."[5] This output was "small compared to the needs of Central Appalachia: an estimated 100,000 units of housing were either physically substandard or overcrowded, and 17% of homeowners and 33% of all renters in the region were cost burdened by their housing."[6] Fahe therefore faced a new challenge—to transform itself into an organization with a broader impact in the region. Perhaps at its inception Fahe did not intend to become a "bank"—yet the needs of the underserved communities where member organizations worked were best met by the CDFI model. And at the organizational level, Fahe was used to stepping outside the box, responding to members' needs and making large-scale changes. The early 2000s were a time of intentional growth and diversification, creating new ways for the organization to finance community development within the region.

Today, Fahe operates with a mission to "lead a network of Appalachian organizations to sustainable growth and measurable impact through collective voice and to provide access to capital that creates housing and promotes community development."[7] Fahe provides mortgage and community lending, consulting, loan servicing, capital development, and membership services within the Appalachian region. As of the end of the 2014 fiscal year Fahe had $209 million of loans and assets under management and was instrumental in the creation of $470 million in direct investments to member organizations and communities. Collectively, Fahe's member organizations have financed over eighty-five thousand units of housing and have, in the past ten years, increased their total assets to over $800 million. Funding for these efforts continues to come from federal, state, and local grants and contracts, private donations (from individuals and corporations), and private foundations. There is no one wellspring of backing for the work Fahe is doing; support is leveraged from myriad sources and no possibility is left unexplored in the search for funding to advance housing and economic development in the region.

This continued growth is important. Within the central Appalachian region, the quality, affordability, and availability of housing stock continue to be social issues that are often overlooked. While the region has higher than average rates of homeownership, these rates include substandard properties and mobile homes. Fahe estimates that over one hundred thousand households in the region live in substandard units and that over seven hundred thousand households are "cost burdened"—paying over 30 percent of their income for housing that is often substandard. Opportunities for affordable and adequate rental units are scarce, and households often sacrifice safety/adequacy for affordability.[8] Fahe's work—and that of its member organizations—in housing and economic development is critical as it creates opportunities for local organizations to address community-specific housing and development needs.

A willingness to take risks has created a unique organizational culture that ensures Fahe's longevity, which in turn ensures that the organization will continue to effect change in local communities. By embracing what Crutchfield and Grant identify as "practices for high impact non-profits," Fahe has become an organization that will continue to fight the injustices of poverty and inequality within the central Appalachian region.[9] A willingness to meld lessons learned from the private sector with innovations in nonprofit management and development is important in Fahe's development and continued success.

We maintain that the organization's success is due to its emphasis on creating and maintaining strong social capital—within the membership and broader communities as well as within the political context. By its nature, the member-driven organizational structure allows for the development of "trusting relationships, mutual understanding and shared action."[10] Emphasizing shared values and cooperative action, Fahe is able to provide its member organizations with access to resources that enhance each member's ability to create economic development and social change. Stated otherwise, this rich social capital yields access to physical capital, financial capital, human capital, and political capital.

Defining Key Terms

The concept of social capital was first broached in the Progressive Era—Hanifan's discussion of rural settlement and community schools characterized social capital as "those tangible substances [that] count for most in the daily lives of people."[11] The concept lost momentum, however, and was not revived until the late twentieth century, when work by Coleman and Putnam brought the idea back into the academic and popular lexicon.[12] Thus, much of the conceptual work related to defining and understanding social capital comes from the 1990s and early 2000s. Today, there is broad support for the utility—and necessity—of social capital as elemental to the enhancement of and access to other forms of capital. Krishna and Uphoff posit that social capital is an important component of successful economic development and sustainability. Cohen and Prusak view the concept as helpful in understanding effective organizational development and growth.[13] While other forms of capital—for example, financial capital or physical capital—are easily quantifiable and measurable, social capital is a bit more abstract. Still, it has distinct value as a form of developmental leverage and is often what allows for entree to other kinds of capital. The very idea of social capital is somewhat intuitive—when trust, shared value, and reciprocity exist, relationships flourish and grow. One can employ that trust to access or leverage resources that may not be available without that underlying network or support.[14] Social capital is frequently viewed as broken down into different levels—often referred to as *bonding, bridging,* and *linking.* Bonding social capital refers to the connections that are created within groups—wherein there is shared agency, common purpose, and so on. Bridging social capital then refers to the connections cultivated between groups—wherein there may be fewer shared qualities or norms, yet relationships are mutually beneficial and broaden each constituent's knowledge/understanding and access to shared resources. Linking social capital refers to more linear linkages between individuals—or organizations—and institutions or those in positions of power.

Estes and Green and Haines provide frameworks for understanding social capital as essential for community development.[15] Social capital is the conduit through which individuals—and organizations—can enable cooperative action and generate opportunity (political capital) or resources (financial capital, physical capital, human capital).[16]

Fahe's Theory of Change and Social Capital

How then, does this relate to Fahe? As stated earlier, Fahe has, from its beginning, nurtured relationships between organizations. Without labeling this as intentional social capital development, the organization has taken to heart the idea of "strength in numbers" and has worked to ensure that reciprocal and trusting relationships are cultivated and maintained. Through these relationships, Fahe has strengthened its position in the region (and in the nation) and has been able to continue to grow and to meet the needs of member organizations and their communities. As figure 13.1 shows, the organizational theory of change posits that history and context shape core drivers and assumptions, which then shape an organization's key functions, creating short- and midterm outcomes that lead to long-term and lasting change.

Fahe's work respects and values the history of the organization and its member groups. Acknowledging that at its inception Fahe was created by and for members as a way for people to share knowledge and experience and that the expertise was to be used to effect change locally within the Appalachian region provides solid footing for the organization. This commitment to local community development is important.

Fahe's respect for member organizations is a paramount reason the organization is able to engender trust and reciprocity—the building blocks of social capital. Fahe recognizes the uniqueness of each member organization and each community in which members work. In an effort to ensure that

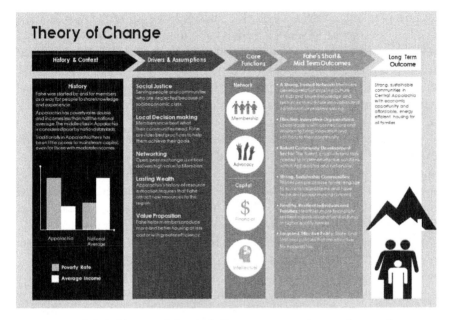

Figure 13.1. Fahe's "theory of change," illustrating organizational commitment to social capital

all members have a voice and remain connected, Fahe's members meet in state caucuses four times each year. By continuing to create opportunities for members from each state to come together and discuss important state-level challenges and opportunities, Fahe nurtures local voices and local decision making. Prospective members must demonstrate their commitment to the core values that shape Fahe's work and must be ready to contribute to the expertise and knowledge of the membership. New members are voted on by the state-level caucuses and then recommended to the board of directors. This process ensures that there is local leadership within the membership.

As Fahe has grown over the last thirty years, there has been ample opportunity to grow outside of the region and to move beyond the membership model. Thus, Fahe's administrative team has, over the years, had to experiment with different avenues for growth and development. While recognizing that change and innovation are essential for sustainability, Fahe has made choices that always come back to its core organizational principles. For example, Fahe now operates both capital and consulting branches that can, according to organizational bylaws, do business outside of the Appalachian region. The revenue generated from these efforts is folded back into Fahe's funds that are used within the region. This business platform helps Fahe to solidify its position as an anchor institution in the region. The development of the capital and consulting branches has allowed Fahe to honor its organizational history and has created opportunity to strengthen the delivery of services within the region.

These new branches open prospects for Fahe to hire key personnel with expertise in lending, capital development, organizational management, and technology. This growth has been intentional and transparent, allowing members to understand how the development will enhance their own opportunity to do good work within their communities. The changes and the way they were handled underscore the commitment to trust and the shared values—elemental to Fahe's membership model—that are the basis for the advancement of bonding social capital between members. Moreover, Fahe's reputation as an organization of integrity and principle aided development of the capital and consulting branches as the organization employed the strength of bridging social capital to open doors for contracts and opportunities.

An excellent example of how Fahe's theory of change generates and utilizes social capital is the development of the Berea performance compacts (BPC). Inherent in the development of the BPCs is a commitment to Fahe's key drivers and assumptions. In 2006 Fahe challenged members to articulate the strengths and weaknesses of their organizational structure. They were then asked to consider how what they do best could be done more effectively, on a broader scale, and with less duplication. Answers to these questions led to the development of BPCs, to scale up Fahe's work and to enhance and redefine collaboration between members. In order for Fahe to move forward on a BPC, it had to meet three criteria: (1) the compact had to be focused on services relevant to the majority of members' work, (2) a natural leader for the compact had to emerge—the organization(s) that would be leading the effort must have the expertise and infrastructure to develop the compact and to work with the broader membership, and (3) the services identified had to be marketable to Fahe and non-Fahe members in the region.

The development of the compacts was member-driven and focused on needs that were important to the region's continued provision of affordable housing and related services. Rather than going outside of the network of members, Fahe sought expertise from within—building on the success and knowledge already found within the membership. Four compacts are highlighted here: loan servicing (led by Fahe), multi-family housing development (led by Community Housing Partners of Virginia), a secondary mortgage compact (led by Fahe), and the newest compact, which focuses on green energy and is led by Fahe, Community Housing Partners, and Peoples' Self Help Housing of Kentucky. Each compact was created with the idea of leveraging capital—human, financial, political, and social—to continue to confront the affordable housing crisis within the region.

The idea of the BPCs had strong roots in the organization's early years, when service providers were coming together, sharing expertise, and responding to the changing landscape of service provision and access to resources for community development. This time, however, the scale was much larger. The BPCs could not exist if member organizations did not share common values and goals and if there was not a strong basis of trust and mutual understanding. This underlying network of support allowed for the broader development and collaboration exhibited by the BPCs.

Loan Servicing

Fahe serves as the lead organization in the loan servicing compact. This is intuitive; Fahe has the staff expertise and the necessary infrastructure to do so. Members of this compact pay a fee to Fahe and Fahe takes on their loan servicing. Initial results of this compact show that members who participate reduce their servicing costs by almost 30 percent when they use Fahe's services. Additionally, delinquency rates and revenue collected are improved. Utilizing Fahe's expertise (human capital) in this area, members can redirect their own staff talent and expertise toward mission-driven work and can trust that their loan servicing will be done with fidelity and respect for the organizations and individuals served. This is much less daunting than "outsourcing" loan servicing to an entity outside Fahe's network that may not have the same common understanding of the challenges associated with loan servicing within the broader central Appalachian region. At the time of writing, Fahe had twenty-two loan servicing contracts and was responsible for over forty-eight hundred loans. While hard data is scarce, there is an understanding among nonprofit lenders and community development professionals that much of the region is "underbanked" and that the access to financial capital and resources that is often taken for granted in urban communities is not available in rural areas. Thus, Fahe's role to help provide these services is very necessary.

Multi-family Housing Development

The development of multi-family housing requires expertise in construction, management, and financing that diverges from many members' expertise in single-family housing. However, there is a great need in the region for affordable multi-family housing (including but not limited to senior housing and mixed-income housing units). Community Housing Partners brings expertise to the table and leads the multi-family compact. Partners in the compact are able to draw on that expertise to create multi-family projects in their own communities. Fahe leverages Low Income Housing Tax Credit and Affordable Housing Trust Fund dollars to support these projects. Through this collaboration, multi-family units have been successfully built in communities served by members who could not have created projects on this scale on their own. To date, Fahe has been instrumental in creating 416 units of affordable multi-family housing using $61 million in Fahe-financed funds.

An excellent example of this compact's success is the Boodry project in Morehead, Kentucky, which involved a Fahe member (Frontier Housing), the city, Fahe, and the compact leader, Community Housing Partnership. Fahe syndicated and financed the project with tax credits; Community Housing Partners provided the design, construction, and property management; and the member provided local project management and construction. Each player employed its own strengths and expertise to develop a much-needed affordable housing complex in Rowan County, Kentucky. Tax credit projects require expertise and knowledge that are often outside a member organization's scope. Thus, Fahe can provide expertise needed to use this complicated program and can help to navigate the challenges associated with the development. This multi-family housing project shows the importance of social capital development at the bonding level—between Fahe member groups that committed to working together and with Fahe—at the bridging level—between the Rowan County member and the local government—and at the linking level—between Fahe and the stakeholders involved with the tax credit programs at the national level. Without long-standing and well-nurtured relationships, the project would not have been successful.

Because homeownership rates are high in the region and affordable rental housing is scarce, it is important for Fahe's member groups to continue to utilize available resources and funding to creatively address the multifamily rental housing needs within their communities. Central Appalachia is characterized as a "high-need" region where rental housing is all too often substandard and old.[17] Federal programs such as the Low Income Housing Tax Credit are competitive. For small nonprofits to compete for this funding, expertise such as that developed by Fahe is paramount to success.

Just Choice Lending

The third BPC discussed is the Just Choice Lending performance compact, for which Fahe serves as the lead organization. Again, this indicates Fahe's depth of staff and expertise in the mortgage-financing sector. Fahe, unique in that it is the only regional financial intermediary in central Appalachia, was able to create Just Choice Lending, a consumer mortgage company housed within Fahe's Berea offices. Through Just Choice, members can access secondary mortgage market products not otherwise accessible. Within the Just Choice compact, Fahe has been instrumental in keeping the federal USDA Rural 502 Loan Program alive. In 2008 the 502 program, which is one of the main sources of mortgage financing for low-income rural households, was slated for dramatic cuts and possible elimination. Fahe utilized its strength in numbers to successfully call on members of Congress to save the program. Fahe's economy of scale (the size of the membership, assets held by the membership, geographic distribution of members among congressional districts, and so on) was influential in this process. Further, Fahe took a risk by stepping up to become a demonstration site for the packaging of 502 loans—proving to the federal government that the program could be done in a cost-effective and efficient way. From 2010 to 2012 alone, Fahe closed $26 million in section 502 loans through Just Choice. Since 2007 this compact has originated 995 loans totaling $77 million. This series of successes could not have happened without the strong social capital that has been created over time.

Green Energy

The Green Energy BPC is the newest of the four compacts. For five years now, Fahe and member organizations have been invested in exploring how to advance the design and delivery of residential homes improved by sustainable housing interventions. Inherent in this project is the belief that sustainable and "green" energy sources should not be reserved for the privileged; rather, it makes sense to find ways to maximize energy efficiency in homes for lower-income citizens so that cost savings can be realized. For many low-income households, utilities are unaffordable. Particularly during times of extreme weather (whether hotter than usual summers or longer cold spells during the winter), families are forced to make difficult choices. The American Gas Association reports that low-income households are often forced to choose *either* home heating or necessities such as groceries and prescription drugs.[18] Given the region's high poverty and preponderance of poor housing stock, coupled with limited/decreasing assistance available for energy-related needs, bringing energy efficiency to low-income central Appalachian households is vital. Fahe's research, collaboration, and exploration confirmed that improving energy performance of single-family residences increases livelihood and stability for low- to middle-income families through a cost savings of at least 5 percent over five years. Fahe estimates this to be a savings of $4,500. Further, energy efficiency can enhance a home's value. Using members' technical expertise, Fahe was able to come up with ways that energy efficiency could be improved without substantially increasing construction costs for members.

By focusing on energy performance as the guiding value of this compact, Fahe has identified and piloted interventions for the delivery of energy-efficient homes that meet a "green" standard, thus allowing for specific "PowerSaver" mortgage financing. Through these innovations, Fahe is incentivizing the production and increased affordability of energy-efficient housing in central Appalachia. In the past three years, over two thousand units of housing have been provided through the green compact. This success would not have been possible without a willingness to take risks and to learn from member organizations. Further, this compact is an excellent example of one driven by core organizational values related to social justice and value proposition.

In the rural communities served by Fahe, individual organizations often play many roles—from land development to housing counseling (and everything in between). In creating the BPCs, Fahe has leveraged the expertise and knowledge of members, allowing growth and development on a larger scale. Because this has been done within the organization's framework for change and has taken into consideration the core drivers and assumptions of social justice, local decision making, networking, lasting wealth, and value proposition, members have been supportive and open to this newer collaborative model.

Much of what Fahe does coalesces around the concept of building effective networks. From the state caucuses to the BPCs, Fahe creates opportunities for members to come together to learn from one another and to work collaboratively to produce solutions to regional challenges. This peer exchange generates shared norms and trust, enhances reciprocity, and creates opportunities for human, financial, and physical capital development among members. Fahe members act as economic drivers in communities by providing opportunities for asset accumulation (through ownership), employment opportunities, and community access to capital and financing for community development projects (such as homeless shelters and senior housing).

Over the course of thirty years, Fahe has grown and changed to meet the needs of members and communities, but it has stayed true to its fundamental drivers and assumptions that guide core functions and organizational outcomes. In creating an organizational culture that balances measured risk and change with long-term commitment to affordable housing in the region, Fahe has become a key player at the local, state, and national levels. Because of a long-standing commitment to relationships and local communities, Fahe's model has been successful within the region, where the values of local decision making and respect for regional culture are important. By generating and maintaining strong social capital that bonds, bridges, and links members, communities, and political players, Fahe has enhanced access to other forms of capital (human, financial, and political) necessary for community development.

This discussion is but a beginning, as it does not touch on other key forms of capital—such as cultural and environmental—yet it provides a short overview of one organization's ability to "increase scale of impact" through the development of strong social capital.

It seems fitting, in many ways, to close with thoughts from Hanifan, who introduced the term *social capital* to the broader social science community through his work of community building in rural West Virginia. Through his work we are reminded that "in community building as in business organization and expansion there must be an accumulation of capital before constructive work can be done."[19] Our discussion of Fahe demonstrates this well. Fahe has enhanced opportunities and services within the central Appalachian region. These efforts could not have been

successful without intentional emphasis on the cultivation and maintenance of social capital.

Notes

1. Ronald Eller, *Uneven Ground: Appalachia since 1945* (Lexington: University Press of Kentucky, 2008), 2.

2. Michael Harrington, *The Other America* (New York: Touchstone, 1962), 4.

3. Michael Woolcock and Deepa Narayan, "Social Capital: Implications for Development Theory and Research," *World Bank Research Observer* 31, no. 1 (2000): 225.

4. Lehn Benjamin, Julia Sass Rubin, and Sean Zielenbach, "Community Development Financial Institutions: Current Issues and Future Prospects," 3, *Federal Reserve Office of Community Affairs,* 2007, http://www.federalreserve .gov/communityaffairs/national/CA_Conf_SusCommDev/pdf/zeilenbachsean.pdf (accessed April 1, 2014).

5. Alan Okagaki, "Federation of Appalachian Housing Enterprises: A Case Study," 2, *Fahe,* 2011, http://www.fahe.org/wpcontent/uploads/AlanOkagakiReport-FINAL .pdf, 2 (accessed April 1, 2014).

6. Ibid., 6.

7. Fahe, Inc., *Annual Report* (Berea, KY: Fahe, 2011), 19.

8. Mark Mather, "Housing and Community Patterns in Appalachia," *Population Reference Bureau,* 2004, http://www.prb.org/pdf04/housingcommutingappalachia.pdf (accessed April 2, 2014).

9. Leslie Crutchfield and Heather McLeod Grant, *Forces for Good: The Six Practices of High-Impact Nonprofits* (San Francisco: Jossey Bass, 2012), 3.

10. Diane Loeffler et al., "Social Capital for Social Work: Towards a Definition and Conceptual Framework," *Social Development Issues* 26, nos. 2-3 (2004): 25.

11. Lyda Hanifan, "The Rural School Community Centre," *Annals of the American Academy of Political and Social Sciences* 67 (1916): 130.

12. James Coleman, "Social Capital in the Creation of Human Capital," *American Journal of Sociology* 94 (1988): 95–120; Robert Putnam, "Bowling Alone: America's Declining Social Capital," *Journal of Democracy* 6, no. 1 (1995): 65–78.

13. Anirudh Krishna and Norman Uphoff, *Mapping and Measuring Social Capital: A Conceptual and Empirical Study of Collective Action for Conserving and Developing Watersheds in Rajastahan, India* (Washington, DC: World Bank, 1999); Don Cohen and Laurence Prusak, *In Good Company: How Social Capital Makes Organizations Work* (Boston: Harvard Business School Press, 2001).

14. Loeffler et al., "Social Capital for Social Work," 22.

15. Richard Estes, "Social Capital: A New Concept or Old Wine in New Bottles?" (paper presented at the University of Kentucky College of Social Work, Lexington, April

15, 2003); Gary Green and Anna Haines, *Asset Building and Community Development* (Los Angeles: Sage, 2012).

16. Loeffler et al., "Social Capital for Social Work," 22.

17. Rapoza Associates, "The Low Income Housing Tax Credit: Overcoming Barriers to Affordable Housing in Rural America," 2004, http://ruralhousingcoalition.org/wp-content/uploads/2013/08/rapozaRuralLihtcRpt+CaseStudiesFinal1.pdf (accessed July 2, 2014).

18. American Gas Association, "The Increasing Burden of Energy Costs on Low-Income Consumers," September 26, 2007, http://www.aga.org/Kc/analyses-and-statistics/studies/demand/Documents/EA0709-Increasing-Burden-Energy-Costs-Low-Income-Customers.pdf (accessed July 23, 2014).

19. Hanifan, "The Rural School Community Centre," 130.

14

When Collaboration Leads to Action

Collecting and Making History in a Deep South State

Mark Wilson

After centuries of perceiving the relationship between higher education and the public as that of service provider and client or patron, some colleges and universities are beginning to relate to the public in ways that acknowledge the power of citizens' lived experiences, focusing as much on lending technical expertise to communities as co-creating the community's capacity to solve the problems that ail them. This shift in emphasis, however slight in some institutional contexts, seems to embody what Appalachian communities have known all along: the problems communities face are not all technical in nature; many of them are relational, and issues of power are always at the core. Conceptualizing university-community collaborations and interactions in the framework of democracy, democratic citizenship, and the public good levels the playing field, disorients the ivory tower, and creates local capacity for success.

The National Task Force on Civic Learning and Democratic Engagement's report *The Crucible Moment: College Learning and Democracy's Future* is the best, most recent articulation of this shift. "Two-year and four-year colleges and universities offer an intellectual and public commons where it is possible not only to theorize about what education and democratic citizenship might require in a diverse society," the report states, "but also to rehearse that citizenship daily in the fertile, roiling context of pedagogic inquiry and hands-on experiences."[1] The report identifies notable models and examples of university-community engagement that embody democratic practices and teaching and urgently calls educators and administrators to action. This chapter offers a comparative perspective on the dual contexts of community and institutional engagement in Appalachia. By reporting on the process of building support for outreach and applied student learning as *integral* to community development work, my goal is to highlight how engaged pedagogy can reflect back on the institutional cultures of higher education in Appalachia.

Eleven years before the release of the *Crucible Moment* report, the Appalachian Regional Commission (ARC) and faculty from centers for Appalachian studies across the region launched the Appalachian Teaching Project (ATP), whose first meeting was held in the fall of 2001. ATP is a small consortium of colleges whose faculty offer classes characterized by assignments that weave students and communities into productive relationships with each other. The consortium is intentionally mixed, composed of small liberal arts colleges, regional comprehensive schools, community colleges, and research universities, as a way of democratizing traditional collaborative work, which usually segregates colleges by size and mission. ATP's success in building relationships in the region among faculty, institutions, nonprofit organizations, and local citizens is a story worth telling and repeating.

This chapter is the narrative of Auburn University's recent participation in the ATP and the productive relationship begun and maintained between its College of Liberal Arts and the Tuskegee Human and Civil Rights Multicultural Center (THCRMC). The ongoing collaboration has yielded measurable results and outcomes for both students and the center, but it has created something much more: a focus on local assets that can be used for education, economic development, and the further progression of a sense of place among residents of Macon County.

The Beginning of a Cooperative Relationship

Auburn University was established in 1856 as the East Alabama Male College, and in 1872, under the Morrill Act, the school became the first land-grant college in the South and was renamed the Agricultural and Mechanical College of Alabama. In 1899 the name was changed to Alabama Polytechnic Institute, and then in 1969 changed again to its present name. Over twenty-five thousand students are enrolled in the university's thirteen colleges and schools. African American graduate student Harold Franklin broke the color barrier in 1964 as a result of a federal court order, but even fifty years later the black student enrollment is still below 8 percent of the total student body, in a state where African Americans make up over a quarter of the total population.

As a land-grant college, Auburn University fulfills its public mission through the statewide Alabama Cooperative Extension System, but equally important are nonextension faculty and staff. In 2001, the faculty revised the *Faculty Handbook* to include a chapter on outreach, defining the term as the "function of applying academic expertise to the direct benefit of external audiences in support of university and unit missions." The handbook distinguishes outreach from "service," and through these revisions, Auburn became one of the first universities in the United States to describe the conditions by which an endeavor may be regarded as outreach scholarship. Auburn University is most known for the College of Architecture, Design, and Construction's Rural Studio, a program based in rural Hale County that develops its students as "citizen architects." The College of Liberal Arts developed an initiative and interdisciplinary minor in community and engagement in 2009, seeking to foster greater faculty and student collaboration with citizens, and the minor can be seen as a direct outgrowth of the culture of outreach and engagement that has grown over the past several decades.

The Tuskegee Human and Civil Rights Multicultural Center is located in neighboring Macon County, Alabama. Citizens, led by civil rights attorney Fred Gray, established the center in 1997 to serve as a permanent memorial to the victims and survivors of the infamous Tuskegee syphilis experiment.[2] The center, located in a former bank building downtown, opened its first exhibit in 2001. Permanent exhibits tell the story of Macon County from prehistory through the civil rights era. Although the center has only one full-time employee, it serves as a visitor's center and local educational resource for the community.[3]

Twenty miles of highway separate Auburn and Tuskegee, but geography is not the only factor in the distance between them. Auburn's residents are 75 percent Caucasian; Tuskegee's are 96 percent African American. Auburn's median household income is $37,590; Tuskegee's is $25,804. Of the thirty-seven counties in the Alabama ARC region, Macon is designated as one of six economically distressed counties, a result of high unemployment and persistent poverty. Tuskegee University, founded in 1881 under the leadership of Booker T. Washington, has an enrollment of 3,156 students. Faculty at Auburn University and Tuskegee University collaborate on various projects and programs, but the need for consistent, long-term collaborative opportunities remains.

The Appalachian Teaching Project asks students and citizens to answer the following question through course work and action projects: How can we build a sustainable future for Appalachian communities? The question assumes an asset-based model for community development, and the asset under continual development by the Tuskegee Human and Civil Rights Multicultural Center is the shared history of the three cultures that inhabit Macon County—Native American, European American, and African American. Museums and cultural centers have tourism potential, but they also serve as catalysts of the pride and community building necessary for long-term community health and economic growth.

The first conversation regarding ATP took place at the THCRMC in 2011 and explored whether the opportunity might be a platform for collaboration that would result in mutually beneficial and collaboratively developed outcomes for ATP, Auburn students, and THCRMC. Oftentimes university-led projects begin with a question designed to reveal answers regarding the body of technical knowledge that exists with the academy. Community engagement projects, on the other hand, answer questions that the community is asking. The question on the mind of the director of the THCRMC was how the upcoming fiftieth anniversary of the integration of Tuskegee High School—the result of a court case that affected the entire state of Alabama and received national attention—might be properly commemorated for the public in the year 2013. The partners could not have predicted how a small, semester-long project would reach a national audience and have so many community and institutional outcomes. Although neither the Auburn University ATP faculty coordinator nor the THCRMC staff knew exactly how to organize the project in its entirety, they committed to taking small steps, the first of which was understanding the importance of the history to Tuskegee and identifying individuals who remembered the integration of the high school.

Public School Integration in Macon County

In May 1964, newspapers from around the nation reported on the graduation of three students from Macon County High School in the small town of Notasulga, Alabama. "Three Negro youths—first of their race in Alabama to be graduated from an integrated high school—now have diplomas," read the *Spartanburg Herald-Journal*.[4] The *Tuscaloosa News* added the adjective "proud" to describe the graduates, who received diplomas "in a quiet informal ceremony," noting that the entire student body—including three black underclassmen—witnessed the presentation.[5] When principal Dan Clements handed Willie Wyatt Jr., Anthony Lee, and Robert Judkins their diplomas in the school's auditorium, it signaled a historic event in the segregated South.

Wyatt, Lee, and Judkins were three of thirteen students chosen in September 1963 by black leaders in Macon County to end the separate-but-equal status of public education in Tuskegee. Historian Robert Norrell, in his award-winning account of the civil rights movement in Tuskegee, details the events of the 1963–1964 school year, beginning with Governor George Wallace's executive order to close schools in defiance of federal district judge Frank Johnson's injunction to the Macon County Board of Education to desegregate Tuskegee High School.[6] When the newly integrated high school reopened one week later, two hundred state troopers surrounded the building, a dramatic indication that white citizens would be forced to decide how they would respond.

Their decision was to completely withdraw their children from the school. Judge Johnson then ordered the black cohort of students, now reduced from thirteen to twelve students, to attend Shorter High School and Macon County High School in Notasulga, six students to each, in February 1964. Notasulga mayor James Rea, Dallas County sheriff Jim Clark, and a number of other whites met the students' bus in front of the school, prepared to prevent them from entering on the stated grounds that additional students would create overcrowded conditions and compromise student safety in the event of fire. Vernon Merritt, a white freelance photographer there to document the historic event, ignited the assembled crowd with his presence on the bus. *Time* magazine reported the scene in detail: "When the bus arrived, [Clark] leaped aboard, armed with a billy and an electric cattle prod. He jammed the billy in Merritt's belly, and he applied the prod to the photographer's neck. With the aid of a deputy, he threw Merritt off the bus, there prodded him some more as he lay on the ground."[7]

Nonetheless, the six students became students at Macon County High School, but whites once again departed, either to a newly organized private academy or to a public school outside Macon County. Macon County High School was severely damaged by arson in April 1964, so the six students completed their school year in the auditorium, where the principal delivered diplomas to Wyatt, Lee, and Judkins in lieu of a public graduation ceremony.

We rediscovered the details of Willie Wyatt Jr.'s experience in the fall of 2011. Wyatt lives in Stone Mountain, Georgia, so students Marian Royston and Blake Evans and I arranged to meet him halfway, holding the interview in a room at the Newnan Public Library in Georgia. The details of his experience were fascinating, especially for the two students, born long after the integration of their own high schools in Alabama. Wyatt explained how he had come to be chosen as one of the students to spearhead school integration. The organizers of integration were not looking for the brightest students but rather those who were "somewhere in the middle." His parents had told him he would be a named litigant in the lawsuit and would integrate Tuskegee High School, but the reality of the situation did not hit him until he found himself in Judge Frank M. Johnson's federal courtroom in Montgomery—the same courtroom where Rosa Parks and Martin Luther King Jr. spent a considerable amount of time.[8]

Wyatt recalled in detail the spring semester at Macon County High School in Notasulga. After the departure of all the whites, an arsonist destroyed the main part of the school. The gym became the temporary classroom. "And then on the last day of school," Wyatt said, the principal "came and said, 'This is the last day of school for you,' and then he handed us diplomas, for [Anthony] Lee, [Robert] Judkins, and myself . . . so that was my graduation from high school." (Anthony Lee, whom we had interviewed days earlier, recalled that the African American Tuskegee Institute High School included the six Macon County High School students' photographs in that school's yearbook. Lee continues to meet for class reunions with students from the institute.)[9]

As we drove back to Auburn after the interview with Wyatt, we reflected on what we had learned about the events of 1963 and 1964. One unsettling aspect was that the school year had seemed to end without much closure for the three seniors who graduated from Macon County High School, celebrating their achievement surrounded by a building in ashes and memories of the flight of the student body. Neither Wyatt nor Lee had been back to Macon County High School, now Notasulga High School, since that spring. Few local people remembered the events of 1964, and few, if any, current high school students had heard of them. Wyatt and Lee (Judkins was now deceased) deserved closure and recognition. They deserved a graduation ceremony.

When the Past Teaches the Present

On January 29, 2012, nearly two months after Auburn students presented findings on the integration of Macon County schools to their peers from fourteen other institutions at the Appalachian Teaching Project Symposium in Washington, DC, I wrote Dr. Jacqueline Brooks, superintendent of education for Macon County Public Schools. "I've been working with AU students on an oral history project. . . . I think we have an opportunity to do something meaningful and important."[10] Dr. Brooks and Notasulga High School principal Brelinda Sullen agreed that we should invite Wyatt and Lee to walk across the stage in the spring graduation ceremony with the class of 2012.

On the morning of May 23, 2012, Wyatt and Lee spoke to the senior class after the morning graduation practice. They told the forty-eight-year-old story of integration, which students had never heard. Wyatt recalled, "Mayor Rea decided on his order that six more students would create an overcrowded situation, so as a result . . . he said 'Driver, turn around and take them back.'" Wyatt went on to tell the students what his school experience had been like, with all the whites gone. "It was a task; it was lonely. . . . But at the same time, we knew this is what we needed to do, and our parents were behind us. We were foolish enough not to think about how dangerous the situation could be." Wyatt encouraged students to "set your goals and set your mind to it."[11]

After the talk with seniors, Wyatt and Lee participated in a press conference and public session at THCRMC. Attorney Fred Gray began the press conference by noting the historic significance of the event. "The contribution of these young men and their parents . . . resulted in accomplishing many of the things we now enjoy and take for granted, and we don't even realize how it all came about." Gray recognized all the "young ladies and young men who were courageous enough to want a quality education and lay their lives on the line in order to get it," and he discussed the court case and its statewide significance.[12]

The audience then heard for the first time a sound recording from the collection of ABC news correspondent Paul Good, who was on the scene for the attempted integration of Macon County High School and captured the horrific beating of photographer Vernon Merritt. Next Wyatt and Lee discussed their experiences, and audience members—black and white— reflected on the period and its significance for their lives. Tuskegee mayor Omar Neal presented Wyatt and Lee with a special recognition from the city.

Later that night, Wyatt and Lee participated in the graduation ceremony alongside the other thirty-six graduates of Notasulga High School. Wyatt joked about the irony of wearing a white graduation gown in Notasulga, a town known in 1964 for significant Ku Klux Klan activity. Wyatt and Lee marched with the class, proudly accepted commendations from school officials, and received the recognition they had not forty-eight years earlier. The *Opelika-Auburn News* published a front-page article that was quickly picked up by the Associated Press and reprinted in newspapers across the country. The headline read, "Righting an Old Wrong," and the large photograph captured Wyatt speaking while Lee looked on, both in their caps and gowns. "We weren't conscious what we were doing would then make history today," Lee told the reporter. "We were just trying to get a good, basic education."[13]

The 2012 graduation ceremony stood as a high point in the community-university collaboration between the College of Liberal Arts and the THCRMC, but the project continued over the next year through planning for a commemorative event to be held near the date of the fiftieth anniversary of integration. In August 2013, project coordinators convened a symposium that featured several people—black and white—who had been students at the time. Wilma Jones Scott, one of the original thirteen students who integrated the school, spoke about how her parents empowered her to believe she could do anything she wanted to do. She recalled her father's calming presence outside the bus when she ripped apart the executive order, given to her by a state trooper, that stated Governor George Wallace had closed Tuskegee High School.[14]

The symposium included white students from the period whose lives had also been affected by that tumultuous year. Rebecca Wadsworth Sickles was excited about her junior year in high school in the summer of 1963. Her mother and several other members of the community were determined that integration could be accomplished successfully and smoothly, and Mrs. Wadsworth accompanied Rebecca to school that first day in September. They were shocked to find state troopers in helmets, some on horseback, and her mother was quite angry that Governor Wallace had closed the school. Mrs. Wadsworth asked a trooper to deliver a stern message to the governor that the school should be reopened. Rebecca's parents disagreed with whites in the community who refused to allow their children to attend school with the black students. They did not support plans to build an all-white private school. Rebecca moved to Alexander City to complete high school, living with her aunt and uncle. After the Klan erected a burning cross on her parents' lawn, the entire family moved from Tuskegee.

The August gathering allowed black and white former students to meet for the very first time, something they would have done in 1963 if the community had successfully integrated the schools. Peggy Wallace Kennedy, the daughter of Governor George Wallace, spoke to attendees in the lunchroom of the school now located where integration first took place. She discussed how her father used race as a political tool, and she reflected on her own personal journey of overcoming his legacy of racism with a message of racial healing. Several attendees remarked that the event provided a much-needed public opportunity to discuss the events that had shaped their lives and future of Tuskegee. C-Span recorded the first three hours of the event, and they remain available online, a significant asset for educators, the public, and the community. The voices of local people needed to be heard, and the story received the national attention it deserves.

The Ecology of Engagement

Sustained, productive community-university relationships cannot be captured by simple flowcharts of activity or road maps to success, since relationships are always changing based on circumstances. But relationships do reveal habits and principles that shape and deliver outcomes, and the following three are evident in the project described above: (1) reflection and feedback for shared learning, (2) identifying self-interests of additional collaborators, and (3) focusing on outcomes as well as outputs.

Students' involvement in ATP projects at Auburn University is part of the Introduction to Community and Civic Engagement course. Structured opportunities for reflection during project meetings allow students to respond to three important prompts that are often used by service-learning practitioners: What, So What, and Now What. What have we experienced or discovered? So what does it mean in the context of our course content and other lived experiences? Now what do we do as a result of what we've learned? Constant communication with community collaborators allows everyone participating in the project to experience the same type of reflection and support one another's individual discoveries and resulting next steps. The danger as well as the strength of reflection—if taken seriously—is that it assumes a level of flexibility in project management and project outputs.

The ecology of engagement acknowledges that universities and communities are not monolithic entities but dynamic organisms made up of units and cells of like-minded self-interests, and project organizers are always seeking collaborators who share some facet of a project's or relationship's signifying aspects. In this project, for example, a critical opportunity for expanding the collaboration came during planning for the fiftieth anniversary of Tuskegee High School integration. Two AU offices with missions in diversity and outreach joined the event as cosponsors, which provided additional leverage for the Office of Communications and Marketing to respond positively to an invitation to announce and report on the event. A student minoring in community and civic engagement assisted with the development of a successful grant application to the Alabama Humanities Foundation, and the additional exposure of the event throughout that organization's network increased the visibility of the project and its local sponsors.

An institutional approach to engagement often focuses on *outputs*—deliverables that meet a need and satisfy consumer expectations—but an ecology of engagement suggests the identification of *outcomes,* a description of the type of change or changes in relationships sought. In the project described above, the outcome is a flourishing relationship between a local nonprofit organization, its staff and volunteers, and a small unit within a large university that exists twenty miles down the road. Outcomes are dependent on well-designed outputs, but the reverse is not necessarily the case. A university-community project can be designed and executed without necessarily existing in the context of a long-term relationship that has transformative power for both entities. We aim for transformation rather than transactions.

In practice, the ecology of engagement is more closely aligned with the work of community organizing rather than traditional academic work, and the project/relationship described above resonates with what pioneers of educational and social change Myles Horton and Paulo Freire call experimenting *with* people, not *on* people. The purpose of academic work seen from a traditional university approach is the publication of new, generalizable knowledge and solutions that can be implemented by clients and consumers. The community organizing purpose of research is to increase the possibility of working more effectively *together.* "We needed to know what was happening in the economic, social, and cultural realm where we were working," Horton and Freire write, reflecting on decades of experience in Appalachia, "but we didn't come in and make a lecture on it or write a book about it. We used this knowledge to have insights out of which we asked questions and led discussions."[15] The ecology of engagement depends on traditional academic research for strategic facts, contextualization of issues, and more, but it always places priority on the processes that develop power in and among project participants to effect positive change.

An Unexpected Contribution to Auburn University's Story of Integration

Open-ended, flexible, outcomes-based relationships that break down walls between students, faculty, administrators, community leaders, and active citizens often result in positive, unpredictable opportunities that occur in the ecology of engagement. Interviews with Willie Wyatt Jr., Anthony Lee, and others that began the collaboration that included the 2012 graduation ceremony and the historic 2013 symposium contributed to Auburn University's reflection on its own commitment to become more racially and ethnically diverse as an institution. It was not known before the interviews that Lee and Wyatt both enrolled in Auburn University in the fall of 1964 after their tumultuous year in Macon County. (Graduate student Harold Franklin, represented by attorney Fred Gray, had begun classes at Auburn in January 1964 without opposition.) Wyatt recalled that he wanted to go to a state school, and since AU was only nineteen miles from home, it made sense. The university could not provide housing, so he and Lee boarded with a local African American business owner until the next quarter, when Auburn provided a room, albeit one outside of the general population.

Wyatt recalled that students from the North, who "weren't in touch with southern ways," would ask him to play ping-pong, but in the middle of a game it was not uncommon for a male student outside the group of players to announce that the game was over, crushing the ball with his foot. At football games, state troopers would surround Wyatt in the stands, ensuring his safety. After his freshman year, he transferred to Tuskegee University to ease his father's worries, and he graduated in 1969.[16]

Anthony Lee became the first African American to begin and complete an undergraduate career at Auburn when he graduated with a degree in history in 1969. Lee tried to join a fraternity but was denied, and because of the housing situation, he spent most of his nonclass time with civil rights organizations and churches in the community. Lee recalls just one progressive white student who befriended him; most Auburn students considered him invisible. He is quite proud of the fact that he achieved a milestone in the institution's history.[17]

Neither Wyatt nor Lee had set foot on Auburn University's campus since the 1960s until October 1, 2013. Faculty and students greeted them with a standing ovation, eager to hear their reflections. Also attending were Ralph and Jean Foster, a local African American couple who provided housing to the young students during the first quarter when Auburn did not offer dormitory space. "If anybody gets credit for helping Auburn along where it should have been at that time, that's the Fosters," Wyatt said, a reminder that countless people unknown to history are responsible for social movements and civic life.[18] Before the ATP project, the same could be said for Wyatt and Lee, since no one at Auburn University had knowledge of their contribution to integration.

Wyatt recalled the loneliness of student life; he and Lee were not invited to study sessions or other events. Lee remembered one white student whose only goal in a math class was to earn a higher grade than the lone black student—although Lee's recollection is that he passed and the other student did not. Throughout the hardships, there were some encouraging moments, including the swimming instructor who encouraged Lee not to drop his class, despite the fact that Anthony, who still cannot swim, wondered whether he would wind up drowning at the bottom of the pool. "[The instructor] said, 'You are not going to quit my class. I don't want you to quit my class,'" Lee said. "To me, that was a welcome."[19]

In January 2014, Auburn University invited Willie Wyatt Jr. and Anthony Lee to participate in a panel and luncheon as honored guests to commemorate the fiftieth anniversary of integration. They joined Dr. Harold Franklin, who became the face of integration in 1964, and Dr. Samuel Pettijohn, the school's first African American graduate in 1967, who had transferred from Tuskegee University in his junior year. Before 2011, Wyatt and Lee were unknown to Auburn University, but as a result of the Appalachian Teaching Project and the collaboration with the Tuskegee Human and Civil Rights Multicultural Center, they have spoken to campus audiences twice. They have finally received the recognition they deserve.

What began as an ordinary community-university project to locate and interview students and citizens about their memories of desegregation became a series of notable events in the life of a community and university—the high school graduation ceremony that included honorees Willie Wyatt Jr. and Anthony Lee; the symposium that brought back residents for reflection and discussion of integration and provided a national audience through C-Span; the return of Wyatt and Lee to Auburn University—for the first time in fifty years—and institutional recognition of their involvement in integration. Although each of these events attracted the attention of the Auburn University community, the last one had a disorienting factor—students, faculty, and staff were filled with awe and pride that Wyatt and Lee had been invited back to campus to share their stories, yet they were dismayed that a half century had passed without any institutional knowledge, memory, or recognition of their contributions to integration. When asked by an audience member how he felt about Auburn University's progress in integration, Anthony Lee pointed out that since the audience was overwhelmingly white, he thought there was plenty of work yet to be done.

Additional ATP project teams since 2011 have worked on other Macon County topics in collaboration with THCRMC. The 2012 team researched, created, and tested educational programs on the life of Isaac Scott Hathaway, an important but not well-known African American ceramics artist who taught at Tuskegee University, Alabama State University, and, ironically, as a summer extension course instructor at Auburn (then Alabama Polytechnic Institute) in 1947, seventeen years before integration. The 2013 team, building on the work of past teams, developed and tested a one-day Macon County History and Culture Camp, held at THCRMC, and the 2014 team developed a public humanities series of programs, including a theatrical production telling the story of Tuskegee High School integration based on memories contributed by citizens from the period. Since 2011, twenty students have participated in ATP projects, and additional students have worked on projects in Macon County as a result of the relationship that ATP catalyzed between the College of Liberal Arts and THCRMC.

The goal of such work, however, is not just to produce projects and outcomes that can be easily measured. The goal is a relationship among institutions, organizations, university faculty, staff, and students that challenges traditional understandings of power and partnership. "At every level, educational institutions have enormous power that operates invisibly to shape identities, assumptions, and ways of looking at the world," write Harry Boyte and Blase Scarnati in the recently published anthology *Civic Studies: Approaches to the Emerging Field.*[20] Recognizing that power—visible or hidden—exists in all human and institutional relationships is the most important step toward uncovering common ground for action in community-university collaborations. In a Deep South state with a history of racial antagonism and mistrust, situated in a context of higher education increasingly affected by external threats of increased consumer demands and cuts in public funding, the kind of change we seek will only happen over time. But for the citizens, students, and faculty whose lives have been educated and enriched by the projects described in this chapter, it is time well spent.

Notes

1. National Task Force on Civic Learning and Democratic Engagement, *A Crucible Moment: College Learning and Democracy's Future* (Washington, DC, 2012), 2.

2. The United States Public Health Service performed a study of the natural history of syphilis in black men, without their informed consent, from 1932 to 1972.

3. For more information on the Tuskegee Human and Civil Rights Multicultural Center, visit www.tuskegeecenter.org.

4. "3 Negroes Get Diplomas in Notasulga," *Spartanburg Herald-Journal,* May 23, 1964.

5. "Three Negroes Graduated from Macon County High," *Tuscaloosa News,* May 22, 1964.

6. Robert J. Norrell, *Reaping the Whirlwind: The Civil Rights Movement in Tuskegee* (New York: Vintage Books, 1986).

7. "Reporting: Trouble in Notasulga," *Time,* February 14, 1964.

8. Interview with Willie Wyatt Jr., September 20, 2011, transcript in author's possession.

9. Ibid.; interview with Anthony Lee, September 16, 2011, transcript in author's possession.

10. E-mail from Mark Wilson to Jacqueline Brooks, January 30, 2012.

11. Audio recording of session, in author's possession.

12. Ibid.

13. "Righting an Old Wrong," *Opelika-Auburn News,* May 24, 2012.

14. www.c-span.org/video/?314498-1/50th-anniversary-tuskegee-public-high-schol-integration&start=3270 (accessed February 12, 2015).

15. Myles Horton and Paulo Freire, *We Make the Road By Walking: Conversations on Education and Social Change,* ed. Brenda Bell, John Gaventa, and John Peters (Philadelphia: Temple University Press, 1990), 149.

16. Interview with Wyatt.

17. Interview with Lee.

18. Interview with Wyatt.

19. Video recording of session, in author's possession.

20. Harry Boyte and Blase Scarnati, "Transforming Higher Education in a Larger Context: The Civic Politics of Public Work," in *Civic Studies: Approaches to the Emerging Field,* ed. Peter Levine and Karol Edward Solan (Washington, DC: Bringing Theory to Practice, 2014).

15

Participation and Transformation in Twenty-First-Century Appalachian Scholarship

Gabriel A. Piser

Regional Scholarship in Sacrifice Zones

Across the globe, environmental changes caused by human activity are rapidly transforming the contexts in which scholarly knowledge production occurs. If recent decades are any indication, this century will see compounding crises in economic, ecological, and sociopolitical spheres. Many scholars are acutely aware of today's alarming trends, which track the unequal distribution of harm resulting from increasing economic inequality, environmental toxin exposure, atmospheric greenhouse gas concentration, the explosion of prison populations, and the mounting frequency of catastrophic technological and environmental disasters. Myriad responses to these trends, from geoengineering to free trade zones to prison employment schemes, have been proposed, but few consider the ways that these responses reflect dominant societal forces like white supremacy, sexism, and neoliberal market fundamentalism. No less dangerous is the public's withering ability either to articulate compelling alternatives to the status quo or to invent strategies to experiment with creating such alternatives. In an age of permanent and lucrative crises, the definition of problems and the articulation and implementation of solutions are deeply political struggles. At the center of these struggles are conflicting forms of knowledge, political power, and subject formation, struggles from which regional scholars cannot exempt themselves.

In this chapter, then, I suggest that today we—Appalachian and other regional scholars—need a practice of critical experimentation. To do this work, I enlist theoretical perspectives on power, feminist studies, and political ecology to identify strategies for participatory research, that is, research centered on community-led decision making and collective action, that can address the issues regional scholarship faces in the twenty-first century and the demands placed upon us. We must redouble our efforts to critically define problems and experiment with solutions. In light of these crises, we must confront the lie of impartial research. We must respond to the unequal distribution of good and bad effects. We must monitor the political forces shaping how effects are assessed and addressed. We must highlight the ways these effects are—or are not—considered worthy of intervention. We must critically assess the sorts of interventions that are pursued: we must ask why, how, to what effect, and for whom they are pursued.

These sorts of questions are not new to Appalachia's rich knowledge traditions, traditions that can provide crucial guidance in our work today. For centuries, popular and scholarly knowledge in Appalachia has described changing economic, ecological, and sociopolitical systems. Scholars have long held out hope that we could solve persistent issues by better documenting and explaining these systems. At the midpoint of the second decade of this millennium, surrounded by violent and synergistic crises, our work must go beyond the diagnostic and explanatory to seek new experimental forms of perception and action.

Violent Environments and Complex Effects

In a violent age of growing crises, we must renew our commitment to producing knowledge that serves three crucial functions. First, this violence demands work that reveals the location-specific and scale-specific effects and outcomes of various regional developmental interventions. Second, these effects indicate the need for work that imagines alternatives to current development interventions. Third, the widespread negative outcomes of traditional development suggest a need to enact and evaluate alternatives with people from the regions themselves. To that end, I offer a few theoretical and methodological tools as a friendly provocation, calling for us to better perceive how the violence of the present is unequally distributed across the globe, and to reshape our utopian political horizons by reigniting our stultified collective imagination.

Since the industrial revolution, the depth and breadth of human impacts on the planet have grown exponentially. The practices of certain humans, primarily those in the global North, threaten human flourishing generally, while many effects appear in complex and unequal ways and at specific locations and scales. I suggest that in response to these practices and their effects, we must continue to pursue regional scholarship that is fundamentally critical, participatory, and interventionary. Such work improves our understanding of the effects of human practices through deep collaboration with those affected by them. In addition, it enables experimentation with new and different economic, ecological, and sociopolitical systems, helping us to contest the existing and harmful systems of the status quo.[1]

Below I present a series of perceptive and interventionary tools, models, and intellectual communities well suited for this sort of twenty-first-century regional scholarship. I first describe critical participatory action research (CPAR) as both a methodology and an epistemological critique (relating to the nature and scope of human knowledge) that values subordinated/local knowledges and emphasizes political action. To better understand shifting social and political relationships of inclusion/exclusion, care/disregard, fear/desire that shape relations between humans and with the earth, I suggest that affect theory offers a valuable—but underutilized—theoretical resource. I then offer a brief description of the intellectual and practical communities of political ecology (PE) and feminist geography (FG) together with a summarized account of representative projects. These traditions, when inflected by theories of affect and deployed through a CPAR model, offer valuable insight into how regional scholarship in the twenty-first century can better understand the past, engage the present, and shape the future.

CPAR: For Popular Expertise

The twenty-first century's overlapping crises require us to perceive both the effects of humans on the earth generally and the capacity of an earth so transformed to reciprocally affect humans. Such a relationship demands that we cultivate our ability to more fully perceive our rapidly changing contexts and to more critically intervene in beneficial ways. Appalachia scholars have long recognized that knowledge is political and its creation and transmission are powerful tools for both good and ill. When certain forms of knowledge begin to assert their dominance, existing relations of inequality can become further entrenched. As evidenced in the regional legacy of colonialism, turning unruly land and people into well-disciplined and economically productive regions and populations requires the destruction of existing forms of knowledge and ways of life. Such destruction operates—in part—by limiting our view of these forms of knowledge and ways of life. The perceptive tools one uses always shape the scope of what one perceives. CPAR, as a methodology that can include multiple forms of perception, expands this scope. CPAR also contests the "epistemic violence" by which certain forms of perception have been systematically denied the status of "knowledge."[2]

Participatory action research (PAR) unites the political, epistemic, and activist commitments of emancipatory literacy programs from the global South with the analytical emphasis and institutional affiliations of traditional action research in the social and organizational psychology of Europe and North America. Since the early 1990s, *critical* participatory action research has emerged as the theory and practice of PAR refracted through numerous interventions from critical social theory. CPAR asserts the validity and importance of multiple forms of knowledge and collaboratively deploys them in response to important contemporary issues. In addition to educational theory, literacy studies, and organizational psychology, CPAR also draws on post-structural social theory, including continental philosophy, Marxism, feminist science studies, decolonial/postcolonial philosophy, and queer/antiracist philosophy. These traditions of thought have productively transformed the theory and practice of collaborative and interventionary research.[3]

CPAR offers three main contributions to the goals of regional scholarship proposed above. First, it requires of researchers greater scrutiny of how subjectivity impacts perception. Researchers must attend to the ways that perception is shaped both by people's multiple positions within systems of power and by their unstable identities. Second, CPAR assumes that knowledge claims and meaning making are sites of intense political struggle. By highlighting knowledge production as a highly politicized struggle, CPAR disrupts purportedly "neutral" science. For example, environmental impact statements often produce knowledge that serves to legitimate and protect existing development plans rather than to substantively assess their harm or disrupt them. And third,

CPAR assumes a direct relationship between action and knowledge, suggesting that action, as a necessary component of the practice of ethical and useful scholarship, must emerge from research to test its validity.[4]

Popular assessments of, and responses to, the effects of development interventions should be as valuable as—if not more so than—knowledge produced through a purportedly detached objectivity. To critique the notion of detached objectivity, or the idea that researchers are not influenced by their social location when collecting and analyzing research data, is not a refusal to produce meaningful quantitative and qualitative data. Rather, it shows a commitment to substantively reflect on the mode of knowledge production, to expand the scope of what can be considered "data," to query from whose "expertise" such data is drawn, and to consider to whom it is directed. The prevailing narratives of environmental crises are increasing a general reliance on a narrow concept of expertise. This trend is changing the processes by which social and environmental policy is generated, enacted, and evaluated. Around the world and throughout Appalachia, the work to produce and manage concepts like "nature" and "economies" is increasingly the domain of the "experts," and it is to this context that CPAR responds with its radical epistemological and methodological challenge. CPAR questions the problems and solutions imposed by others in favor of critical and participatory reflection by those experiencing the problems directly. I suggest that an action-focused collaborative research methodology, with attention to interventions from critical theory, provides a strong and ethical base for regional scholarship.[5]

CPAR projects strive to include mutual participation at every step, and operate as a "spiral" rather than a "cycle." Instead of thinking about the research process as cycling back to its point of origin, CPAR imagines it to be spiraling outward, perceiving and transforming the context in which the research occurs, an idea that has strong precedence in Appalachia. The Highlander Research and Education Center in East Tennessee has, since its founding in 1932, been a space for popular education that is very similar in practice to what was later called CPAR. CPAR participants collaboratively analyze a shared context, define a problem, design and execute a particular form of knowledge production, and then plan and implement actions to respond to the problem based on the knowledge created. At the start of the next iteration, the context is reanalyzed for any changes, including an assessment of the effects of any actions taken, and the process begins again. The new forms of perception and action we need today must be locally calibrated while also linked to other locations, contexts, and forms of popular and scholarly knowledge. CPAR leverages contributions from both scholarly and popular knowledge traditions to expand the participants' capacity to perceive effects and to cultivate the political capacity to oppose those effects that are harmful.[6]

In an age of overlapping crises, official "experts" respond with new projects and policy interventions. The effects of these interventions are very complex and often inadequately understood. Sometimes these interventions occur at the expense of groups that were supposed to benefit from them, and their effects often accumulate along lines of race, gender, and class. Furthermore, the experiences and knowledge these groups offer about the complex effects of a policy or project are discounted. In response, our methodological and epistemological positions must expand the participants' capacity to create—and act on—meaningful knowledge. Regional scholars must strive to create a research practice that maintains its ethical and analytical value through situated and critical cycles of collaborative perception and intervention. But what sort of perceptions and interventions are required? I argue that we must develop perceptive tools that can offer clearer understandings of how these ecological, economic, and sociopolitical systems relate to one another. From there, we can begin to ask how their interrelation can be shaped more strategically.[7]

From Meaning to Force

For at least the past two decades, scholars from a wide range of disciplines have increasingly turned their attention to questions of emotions, affects, and embodied knowledges to explain sociopolitical dynamics. Affective perception includes emotions and feelings, not as personal possessions or private experiences but as ways to think about relations between bodies. Bodies, in this view, are not simply individual physical objects or organisms but processes resulting from the interrelations among material, conceptual, and affective systems. Unlike personal and private feelings, affects suggest that bodily existence hinges on interconnection. Attending to affect means recognizing and exploring these interconnections in a mode of curious, critical, and open partiality. Thus to engage with "affect," one must engage the *perception* of being affected and the *intervention* of affective transmissions as processes or connections. The so-called affective turn as it has appeared in the humanities and social sciences contributes a powerful set of perceptive and interventionary tools to reshape our work as regional scholars in a new century. Central to this task is a willingness to be excited, confused, discomforted, and ultimately transformed or "affected" by the research encounter.

The affective turn marks a transition in emphasis from stable meanings toward an attention to the forces that shape our concepts of attachment and separation, our fears and desires, and the horizon of our imagination of the future. While the affective turn includes both psychobiological questions of cognition and cultural or philosophical questions of sense and power, for our purposes it is in the second meaning that affect is examined here. While some scholars draw a hard line between affects, feelings, and emotions, here I do not maintain such a sharp divide, nor have I the space to parse the different positions. Without exploring this perceptive capacity, we risk being unable to grasp certain relationships, resulting in severe social and political implications.[8]

All forms of ecological and economic intervention, from dams to taxes, reflect material, cognitive, and affective relationships. These relationships exhibit conditions of inclusion and exclusion, care and disregard, fear, desire, curiosity, confusion, and many other states. These conditions apply to the ecological communities we protect and the people whose well-being we prioritize. In essence, it is a question of who and what are worthy of consideration—and who and what are not. In this new century, as hydrocarbons grow scarcer and national economies stumble, Appalachia will undoubtedly see further conflicts over development, land use, and resource extraction. The outcomes of interventions like these will tend to reinforce the lines of care and disregard, revealing a need for new tools to understand and engage these affective forces that permeate and exceed ecological and economic registers and are central in shaping material and cognitive systems.[9]

The issue of pesticide drift in agricultural communities offers a clear illustration of these implications. Migrant laborers suffering from exposure to agricultural toxins often do not disclose their illnesses or seek care due to numerous barriers, and legislation to protect their health is vigorously opposed on economic grounds. On the other hand, legislation to protect the health of local citizens is more rarely opposed. These outcomes are certainly in part due to legal and linguistic factors, but the ways these strictures are understood and navigated may prove closely linked to affective states like fear and uncertainty. Through an affective lens we can also see how exchanges between citizens, firms, and regulatory apparatuses combine the material flows of agricultural production with the conceptual forces of labor and environmental law, and we can discern the affective forces by which effects seem to matter differently for different bodies. Without an ability to engage the affective dimensions of an issue, we are left with a deficient understanding of the factors shaping the kinds of action (or more often inaction) that come about.[10]

Combined with historical examinations of economic and environmental justice struggles in Appalachia, affect can help us understand why and how certain bodies become more worthy of consideration and protection than others. The group dynamics of conflict and mutual aid that accompany conditions of economic precarity, environmental degradation, and resource scarcity offer a rich source of affective content. For example, scholars of affect have traced happiness, optimism, love, fear, and hate, examining how they relate to anthropocentrism, nationalism, white supremacy, heterosexism, and, more broadly, to the growth of the practices and cultural values of neoliberal capitalism.[11]

Affect, as a force, provides a framework that offers new insight into aspects of subject formation, political expression, and the goals of "regional development." Regional scholarship in the twenty-first century must register power as a multiplicity of effects composed of material practices, cognitive models, and affective forces. By disrupting conventional distinctions between the material, semiotic, and affective registers, authors like Kathleen Stewart theorize power in ways that take seriously the interactions between these registers and so transform Appalachian scholarship for a new age.

In her 1996 book, Stewart travels through West Virginia coal country, tracing the interrelationships between bodies, landscapes, kinship structures, religion, formal and informal economies, fears, and desires. By offering narratives of the everyday material, cognitive, and affective exchanges at work in these wayside spaces, Stewart reveals how "narrative becomes a form of perception that traces lines of force with a life of their own into the space of big meanings that leave people reeling."[12] As we continue to shape the trajectory of a new generation of Appalachian scholarship, we must be prepared to adjudicate on this reshaping, on the different effects that result, and how these varied effects are experienced by people and landscapes.

Having presented CPAR as a valuable model to shape participatory and interventionary knowledge production, and having presented affect as a framework to understand lines of force by which bodies relate to one another, I now introduce two communities of thought that supply models useful for grasping how ecological and economic relationships are formed, how they change, and how their effects are distributed and understood.

Living Landscapes Entwined

Appalachia has long been a site of scholarship that investigates interactions among humans, nonhuman life, and the biogeochemical cycles of the earth. Absent from much of this early work was an attention to the interrelationship among the political, economic, and cultural forces that shape these inter-actions. In contrast, political ecology (PE) affords us ways to perceive how human land-use practices interface with material, cognitive, and affective systems and to understand why they are configured one way over another. Emerging primarily out of the disciplines of anthropology, geography, and environmental studies, PE can connect disparate forms of perception and action through its staunch resistance to both rigid disciplinarity and excessive dogmatism. PE can link spatial flows of energy, matter, nutrients, and water to global abiotic environmental forces like geological or climatic patterns. PE can also diagram flows of matter and force as they shape specific loca-tions and bodies, helping to explain highly unequal distributions of effects.

Early in their modern histories, PE's primary disciplinary antecedents were concerned with relatively distinct objects and methods but relatively similar theoretical and epistemological assumptions. Early scholars explored purportedly discrete objects like human social organizations, spatial rela-tionships, and "nature." Their research methods often sought to categorize and delineate groups and subgroups, demarcating their "proper" location. By the middle of the twentieth century, some scholars in the social and natural sciences began to respond to interventions from critical social the-ory, setting the political and epistemological stage for PE to cohere around the complex forces that determine developmental outcomes. By situating people, groups, and landscapes as entwined within the structures of power that both produce them and delimit their potential, PE enables more robust and detailed maps of material and cognitive relationships.

The current range of critical scholarship in PE is very broad, and can aid Appalachian scholars in at least three ways. Together, this work can improve our ability to (1) map some of the lines of force that shape bodies and landscapes, (2) describe some of these forces' effects, and (3) critique the changes these forces undergo through—and in spite of—shifting politi-cal and economic systems, conceptual models, and the behavior of human and nonhuman actors. In concluding this section, I review an example of PE scholarship on some ecological, economic, and affective aspects of regional development in Appalachia.[13]

In their 2001 article, J. Todd Nesbitt and Daniel Weiner produced a narrative of environmental struggle in central Appalachia. Specifically, they offer an account of the emergence of, and tensions between, conflicting environmental imaginaries. The concept of environmental imaginaries builds on prior work on spatial and social imaginaries. Social, spatial, and environmental imaginaries describe the ways that certain conceptions of society, space, and nature emerge through discourses and material practices. The objectives of their research include tracing the relationships among human and more-than-human bodies and landscapes, marking the connections between environmental histories and the effects of "development and underdevelopment" in Appalachia, linking these histories to regional environmental imaginaries, and finally showing how these local environmental imaginaries produce "local politics of nature and natural resource conflict."[14]

Nesbitt and Weiner examine how central Appalachian environmental imaginaries form through historical struggles over the capture and management of the environmental resources upon which many inhabitants depend for social reproduction, cultural identity, and pleasure. Against the so-called outsider imaginary, which idealizes a mythical untouched nature that can be commodified for recreation, the imaginary these authors document "support[s] many forms of cultural resistance and the desire to maintain some of the social values and practices of the past." They find that some "local resistance to 'development,'" contrary to common assumptions regarding the formation of resistant environmental subjects, is "being expressed through a grassroots populism which is linked to right-wing affiliation and activism." The concept of environmental imaginaries allows the authors to generate a clearer understanding of how these affiliations form, the effects they have, and the tensions that result. Against scholarship that aspires to be apolitical, the authors position local actors, landscapes, and developmental outcomes as "the result of a complex web of interacting forces."[15] They disrupt the stability of conventional causal explanations, finding them problematically reductive and unable to fully account for the inequitable distribution of developmental benefits and harm.

In place of these deficient accounts, Nesbitt and Weiner have produced a regional political ecology that disputes both the idea that environmental conflict in Appalachia stems only from coal extraction and the idea that the outcome of such struggle is always left-leaning populism. By assessing the web of multiple forces that are constitutive of environmental imaginaries, they improve our ability to grasp the "growing uneasiness in the case study area." Their research documents the "concern and anxiety" that result from a lack of self-determination regarding resource access and use. They assert that this research offers a more complete picture of the conflicting imaginaries at work in the Appalachian landscape, and that from this improved picture of conflicting imaginaries we can "better incorporate local residents' environmental knowledge and politics in our assessments of proposed and ongoing development initiatives." Too often PE is limited to the economic and ecological registers; as Nesbitt and Weiner's work shows, an increased attention to affects like "unease . . . concern and anxiety" would improve both our analyses and our interventions.[16]

The Limits of Capitalism

The overlapping crises of our age underscore the importance of tools to understand the spatial organization of life; the ways that networks of human, nonhuman, and abiotic elements are arranged; and the modes of social reproduction that are enabled or foreclosed by these arrangements. Of central importance in the twenty-first century is the work of intersectional Marxist feminist geographers Katharine Gibson and Julie Graham, whose writings and practices have sought ways to identify and cultivate new forms of economic and political subjectivity.

Writing under the name J. K. Gibson-Graham, these feminist geographers pose important questions about how people's beliefs and practices relate to the struggle against neoliberal capitalism. They explore capitalism's mode of economic subjectification and confront the problems of thinking of capitalism as a stable and pervasive totality. For them, capitalism is just one of the multiple overlapping logics ordering ecological, economic, and sociopolitical landscapes. They argue that lines of socially produced difference such as race and gender and myriad noncapitalist productive relationships must figure more centrally in how subjectivity is thought to encounter capitalism. Feminist geography (FG) has opened up new ways of imagining and enacting different conceptions of economic subjectivity by widening the horizon of economic activity to encompass multiple forms of noncapitalist production and exchange. FG offers scholars new forms of perception and action around the formation of economic subjects and the modes of social reproduction in which they engage. By mapping existing networks of noncapitalist production and exchange, FG strives to engender nonexploitative economies that are based on the already existing regional practices of solidarity, care, and mutual aid. FG collaboratively reimagines the purpose and operation of economies and asks how different forms of noncapitalist subjectification might emerge, as exemplified by the work of the Community Economies Collective (CEC).[17]

In 2002, CEC members Julie Graham, Stephen Healy, and Kenneth Byrne published an article in the *Journal of Appalachian Studies* in which they outline the Rethinking Economy Project as an "academy-community collaboration that recently completed participatory action research on the hidden and alternative economies in western Massachusetts. The goals of this project are to create an alternative knowledge of the regional economy, highlighting the prevalence and viability of non-capitalist economic activities, and to mobilize activism to support those activities and associated organizations." The authors describe a project that worked to simultaneously document and produce "hidden and alternative economies." Graham, Healy, and Byrne frame their article as an extension of Herbert Reid and Betsy Taylor's call for a new model of civic professionalism in Appalachian studies. Graham, Healy, and Byrne explicitly differentiate Reid and Taylor's concept of civic professionalism from two alternatives. The first one Reid and Taylor oppose uncritically celebrates regional differences while glossing over issues of "social, economic and environmental power and justice." The second fails to ask crucial prior questions about the hazards of constant adaptation to the economic violence of capitalist globalization.[18]

Graham, Healy, and Byrne call on regional scholars to join the "counter-discourse and counter-politics" emerging in response to the spread of corporate globalization. They suggest that such methods must include a "critical response to globalism," one that is "localist without being parochial, globalist without serving the imperatives of transnational capital, [and] activist without displacing the knowledge and experience of community partners." To that end, they echo Reid and Taylor, who urge us to continue "extending and deepening our community partnerships and participatory research." Graham, Healy, and Byrne suggest that as we do, we will find connection to others who are likewise working to document and enact principles of "social justice, democracy, environmental sustainability, and economic wellbeing at the regional and community scales."[19] It is in response to this provocation that Graham, Healy, and Byrne share how they sought to rethink and reshape the multiple economies at work in a small region of western Massachusetts in the final years of the twentieth century.

Their essay describes a five-stage project, each stage building on the previous one in a spiral of perception and transformation. During stage 1, the researchers convened focus groups drawn from inhabitants who were "key participants in the local economic development conversation." Stage 2's "community economic audit" was the product of a collaborative assessment of existing "nontraditional or undervalued economic activities."[20] Through grant funding, the researchers paid a group of nonacademic local residents, people often considered marginal to the formal economy, to work as co-researchers investigating the existing aspects of the community economy of the Pioneer Valley.

Stages 3, 4, and 5 can be usefully considered a nested cycle. In stage 3, researchers produced case studies of the region's network of alternative economic organizations to investigate and promote linkages and synergies between alternative projects in the region. In stage 4, researchers presented their findings to participants from the previous stage's interviews, focus groups, and case studies. The assembled group then assessed the findings "to think collectively about how we might enact a shared alternative vision of regional economic development." The project's fifth stage involved an "ongoing process in which working groups emerging out of the community conferences are trying to bring specific alternative institutions or practices into being."[21] At the heart of this work is the desire to create forms of research and action that can instigate new subjectivities and new forms of life that are better able to serve the needs of the region's inhabitants. While the material and cognitive aspects of such experiments are often central, scholars from the CEC have begun to discuss the role of affect in shaping the various outcomes of economic development. For them, distribution patterns of poverty, toxics exposure, or geographic amenities clearly reveal relations of care and disregard.[22]

Toward a Critical Experimental Practice

The impacts of nearly half a century of neoliberal domestic and foreign policy have resulted in declining US agricultural and manufacturing sectors, inflamed debates surrounding mountaintop removal and hydraulic fracturing, and exacerbated tensions between urban and rural residents. Today's overlapping crises demand forms of scholarship that produce knowledge as well as concrete positive changes in human-environmental relationships. In considering such transformative work, three broad concerns emerge. First, how do material, cognitive, and affective forces determine the distributions of effects that result from certain development initiatives? Second, what are the impacts of institutional power and expert knowledges in collaborative and transformative research? Finally, how do these effects impact the emergence and operation of new conceptions of development that better serve various and diverse needs? Social theory, while not the sole solution, offers insights to help us answer these important questions. The examples outlined above afford practitioners in Appalachia a capacious set of explanatory and transformative tools that can better respond to present and future challenges. They are here presented to provoke a kind of scholarship that refuses to sit quietly while harm continues to accumulate. Rather than just documenting things as they are, we ought to seek to conjure things as they might be. We must engage, critique, and extend the work of those who have come before as we collectively cultivate the emergence of new forms of life. Such cultivation will not strive to define one definite outcome in advance. Rather, through critical, participatory, and transformative practice, we can continue to experiment with new forms of knowledge and action in the ongoing struggle for a future that is profoundly enticing, sustainable, and just.

Notes

1. Paul Crutzen and Eugene Stoermer, "The 'Anthropocene,'" *Global Change: The International Geosphere-Biosphere Programme Newsletter* 41 (2000): 17–18; Crispin Tickell, "Societal Responses to the Anthropocene." *Philosophical Transactions of the Royal Society A: Mathematical, Physical and Engineering Sciences* 369, no. 1938 (2011): 926–32.

2. Amy D. Clark and Nancy M. Hayward, *Talking Appalachian: Voice, Identity, and Community* (Lexington: University Press of Kentucky, 2013); bell hooks, *Belonging: A Culture of Place* (New York: Routledge, 2009); Gayatri Chakravorty Spivak, "Can the Subaltern Speak?" in *Marxism and the Interpretation of Culture,* ed. Cary Nelson and Larry Grossberg (Chicago: University of Illinois Press, 1988), 271–313.

3. Orlando Fals Borda and Md. Anisur Rahman, *Action and Knowledge: Breaking the Monopoly with Participatory Action Research* (New York: Apex, 1991); Davydd J. Greenwood and Morten Levin, *Introduction to Action Research: Social Research for Social Change,* 2nd ed. (Thousand Oaks, CA: Sage, 2007); Jenny Cameron and Katherine Gibson, "Participatory Action Research in a Poststructuralist Vein," *Geoforum* 36, no. 3 (2005): 315–31; Maria Elena Torre, Michelle Fine, Brett Stoudt, and Madeline Fox, "Critical Participatory Action Research as Public Science," in *APA Handbook of Research Methods in Psychology,* vol. 2, ed. Harris M. Cooper (Washington, DC: American Psychological Association, 2012), 2–31; Sandra Harding, ed., *The "Racial" Economy of Science: Toward a Democratic Future* (Bloomington: Indiana University Press, 1993).

4. Torre et al., "Critical Participatory Action Research."

5. Timothy Mitchell, *Rule of Experts: Egypt, Techno-politics, Modernity* (Berkeley: University of California Press, 2002).

6. For CPAR readings, workshops, and exemplary projects, see the Public Science Project of CUNY at www.publicscienceproject.org.

7. Tania Li, *The Will to Improve: Governmentality, Development, and the Practice of Politics* (Durham, NC: Duke University Press, 2007); Karl S. Zimmerer, "Cultural Ecology: At the Interface with Political Ecology—The New Geographies of Environmental Conservation and Globalization," *Progress in Human Geography* 30, no. 1 (2006): 68–71.

8. Melissa Gregg and Gregory J. Seigworth, *The Affect Theory Reader* (Durham, NC: Duke University Press, 2010); Margaret Wetherell, *Affect and Emotion: A New Social Science Understanding* (Los Angeles: Sage, 2012).

9. John Protevi, *Political Affect: Connecting the Social and the Somatic* (Minneapolis: University of Minnesota Press, 2009); Michele Morrone and Geoffrey L. Buckley, *Mountains of Injustice: Social and Environmental Justice in Appalachia* (Athens: Ohio University Press, 2011); Stephen L. Fisher, ed., *Fighting Back in Appalachia: Traditions of Resistance and Change* (Philadelphia: Temple University Press, 1993); Shannon Elizabeth Bell, *Our Roots Run Deep as Ironweed: Appalachian Women and the Fight for Environmental Justice* (Chicago: University of Illinois Press, 2013).

10. Jill Lindsey Harrison, *Pesticide Drift and the Pursuit of Environmental Justice* (Cambridge, MA: MIT Press, 2011).

11. Eve S. Weinbaum, *To Move a Mountain: Fighting the Global Economy in Appalachia* (New York: New Press, 2004); Lauren Berlant, *Cruel Optimism* (Durham, NC: Duke University Press, 2011); Sara Ahmed, *The Cultural Politics of Emotion* (New York: Routledge, 2004); Elizabeth Povinelli, *Economies of Abandonment: Social Belonging and Endurance in Late Liberalism* (Durham, NC: Duke University Press, 2011).

12. Kathleen Stewart, *A Space on the Side of the Road: Cultural Poetics in an "Other" America* (Princeton, NJ: Princeton University Press, 1996), 168.

13. Paul Robbins, *Political Ecology: A Critical Introduction,* 2nd ed. (Malden, MA: Wiley-Blackwell, 2012).

14. J. Todd Nesbitt and Daniel Weiner, "Conflicting Environmental Imaginaries and the Politics of Nature in Central Appalachia," *Geoforum* 32, no. 3 (2001): 333–49; Richard Peet and Michael Watts, eds., *Liberation Ecologies: Environment, Development, Social Movements* (New York: Routledge, 2004).

15. Nesbitt and Weiner, "Conflicting Environmental Imaginaries," 340.

16. Ibid., 347. For more work on affect in political ecology, see Jane Bennett, *Vibrant Matter: A Political Ecology of Things* (Durham, NC: Duke University Press, 2009); Bruce Braun, "Futures: Imagining Socioecological Transformation—An Introduction," *Annals of the Association of American Geographers* 105, no. 2 (2015): 239–43; Stephen Healy, "The Biopolitics of Community Economies in the Era of the Anthropocene," *Ecology* 21 (2014): 127–221; Sarah Wright, "More-Than-Human,

Emergent Belongings a Weak Theory Approach," *Progress in Human Geography* 39, no. 4 (2015): 391–411.

17. J. K. Gibson-Graham, *The End of Capitalism (as We Knew It): A Feminist Critique of Political Economy* (Minneapolis: University of Minnesota Press, 1996); J. K. Gibson-Graham, *A Postcapitalist Politics* (Minneapolis: University of Minnesota Press, 2006). More information about the CEC can be found at www.communityeconomics.org.

18. Julie Graham, Stephen Healy, and Kenneth Byrne, "Constructing the Community Economy: Civic Professionalism and the Politics of Sustainable Regions," *Journal of Appalachian Studies* (2002): 51, 50; Herbert Reid and Betsy Taylor, "Appalachia as a Global Region: Toward Critical Regionalism and Civic Professionalism," *Journal of Appalachian Studies* (2002): 9–32.

19. Graham, Healy, and Byrne, "Constructing the Community Economy" 50–51.

20. Ibid., 52.

21. Ibid., 52–53.

22. Ethan Miller, "Community Economy: Ontology, Ethics, and Politics for Radically Democratic Economic Organizing," *Rethinking Marxism* 25, no. 4 (2013): 518–33.

(Re)introduction

The Global Neighborhoods of Appalachian Studies

Rebecca Adkins Fletcher

Downstream

I began to consider the concept of "downstream" in January 2014 as I followed the news coverage after the MCHM (4-methylcyclohexane methanol) chemical spill into the Elk River in Charleston, West Virginia.[1] The prevailing advice offered to the thousands worried about chemical exposure, the safety of their water supply, and the economic effects of this disaster was to just "wait for it to go downstream." I began to contemplate "downstream" simply, perhaps, because I lived downstream. A couple of days later, the telltale sweet (licorice) smell and oily feel of MCHM appeared in my water supply, as it had moved downstream from the Elk into the Ohio River. Sparked by this incident, the idea of "downstream" took on broader significance in my thinking about the Appalachian region, evolving into an uncomfortable awareness of my own location in the geographic and political landscape being reconstituted in the wake of the MCHM spill. While those in the center of the affected area might take some comfort from knowing that the problem would eventually dissipate, for those on the periphery (downstream) this meant that trouble was on the way. What this specific industrial, environmental, and health disaster solidified to me in the subsequent days and weeks was a concrete example of what Powell calls an "act of definition" in which regional maps are redrawn, reenvisioned, and, in essence, further complicated around an event or idea.[2] Following a critical regionalism perspective, places become understood as outcomes of relational activity, including geographic, cultural, economic, and political transformation. Mapping a region is not a neutral action; rather, it is quite purposeful, necessitating decisions of inclusion/exclusion, connectivity, and representation. Integral to this process is the situatedness of the mapmaker, as mapping outcomes reflect levels and types of knowledge (evidence based or anecdotal) and the boundary marker's relation to the region. This also conveys an understanding that actions of regional cartography include those of organizations, such as the Appalachian Regional Commission, the Centers for Disease Control and Prevention, and the Environmental Protection Agency, as well as individual acts of regional cultural boundary making, as seen in the use of stereotypes and caricatures to explain or excuse difference or the decontextualized activities of those within the boundary.

In the case of the MCHM spill, the application of critical regionalism becomes an important tool for understanding that Charleston, West Virginia, and central Appalachia did not exist as isolated spaces, geographically or culturally, and this event was neither unforeseeable nor simply an accident. Rather, this event demonstrates the inherent connections with broader cultural forces involved in disaster creation. This includes the long history of factory and chemical industries that pollute and sicken the environment and people that rely on it (and defend it) for their livelihoods, the American symbols that uphold regional stereotypes and ultimately the conventional (but changing?) acceptance that such disasters are inevitable and necessary to support the American way of life. To follow Biggers's (see also Reid) sentiment that "we all live in the coalfields now," the MCHM spill is yet another example of the interconnectedness of regions and the farcical notion that there are safe (binary) havens from environmental degradation to be had simply by distancing oneself (either geographically or theoretically) from affected areas.[3] Thus, we all live downstream. The chemical spill becomes a phenomenon through which to evaluate ideas of pollution, relative exposure, health effects, and defined space (atmospheric) outcomes of the disaster.

As the MCHM spill saw the creation of new cultural and regional boundaries, it also symbolized regional connectedness. For example, like many others, I purchased bottled water for drinking, assuming it was a safe alternative. However, in reading the water bottle labels, I realized the sources for the vast majority of bottled water on the store shelves originated in Pennsylvania, a place with concerns about water safety due to natural gas fracking pollution (see Yahn's chapter 8 in this volume) and in Cincinnati, Ohio (downstream), where municipal water sources also utilized the Ohio River. Was I paying for slightly less contaminated water from a downstream source? Was I safe?

Following Dwight Billings, the MCHM spill caused me to consider my place regarding "things from afar from where I *am* and where I am *from*."[4] The event offers new understandings of situatedness and connections, remapping relationships in terms of the flow of objects (such as MCHM), ideas, and people. All too clear was the fallacy of downstream as a place of safety or a means of solving a problem. As Wendell Berry noted, "We must quit solving our problems by 'moving on.' We must try to stay put and to learn where we are geographically, historically, and ecologically."[5] Does place matter? Indeed it does! Water flows from place to place, connecting locales and peoples as it transports hosts of material and ideological artifacts. Downstream implies a unidirectional force, a binary of here and there, giving a false impression of separation. As an alternative to the downstream narrative, I offer a view of the MCHM spill as a watershed moment that teaches a particular lesson of the connectivity of past, present, and future, of regions and peoples, and underscores the need for individuals and groups to be free from having to make false choices in the politics of either living in a healthy community or providing for one's family. Inevitably, the downstream approach delays response by hindering active resistance, questions, and accountability. It offers a false sense of safety, denying the fact that "downstream" is some real place with a problem coming its way. Hence, following Schumann's discussion of Harvey and Powell in his introduction to this book, we see how "downstream" becomes actively constructed as a space through the rhetorical tools of political difference making that are part and parcel of neoliberal economic transformation.[6] So here I ask: in what ways is "Appalachia" used as a rhetorical tool to establish identity, cultural difference, and place? What are the threads that connect and create Appalachia as a constellation of identity, environment, economic transformation, activism, and community engagement? How do these threads create webs that link past and present peoples and cultures seeking to preserve quality of life, tradition, and culture while fully engaging in a twenty-first-century global experience?

Downstream takes on special meaning when it is applied in terms of regional relations. Appalachia, as an American region, is too often dualistically associated with danger, isolation, and waste, on one hand, and with scenic playgrounds and as a reservoir of traditional American culture on the other.[7] If we follow the stream as it naturally meanders across artificial boundaries, things such as county, state, and regional divides are no longer barriers. The point here is that Appalachia is intricately and holistically linked within, not isolated from, the rest of America and the world, a concept that reflects a broader view of regional continuity and change. This metaphor reflects the view of *Appalachia Revisited,* as the chapters in this volume demonstrate the ways Appalachia continues to be remapped in the ongoing processes of place-making through a variety of theories, methods, and comparative contexts.

Revisiting the Appalachian Narrative

What do people in Papua New Guinea, India, Ghana, Haiti, and Sweden have in common with Appalachian residents? For decades, international travelers have been coming to the Appalachian Mountains to learn from people acknowledged as innovators in challenging destructive aspects of the modern global world. While environmental degradation, economic underinvestment, and inadequate access to health care are well-known regional struggles for social justice in Appalachia, these issues are well integrated within global aspects of economic transformation and activism that are increasingly, and similarly, affecting disparate peoples.

One of the inspirations for this chapter came from a photograph of Larry Gibson talking with a World Wildlife Fund–sponsored delegation from Papua New Guinea, about mountaintop removal mining surrounding his home on Kayford Mountain, West Virginia. According to the article describing their visit, the New Guineans were astounded at the extent of the destruction and left resolved not to let this type of environmental destruction happen in their country. There have been other international exchanges, of course, including an Indian/Appalachia Coal Activist Exchange on Blair Mountain in 2011. This was part of the larger March to Blair Mountain in southern West Virginia to commemorate the ninetieth anniversary of the historic 1921 labor battle. Unlikely allies, the United Mine Workers of America and environmental activists worked in common cause to save the mountain from deforestation and preserve it as a historical and cultural heritage site. The global importance of the Blair Mountain story is that it symbolizes the worst of globalization—environmental destruction, decreasing job security, declining living and health standards—in the name of progress and development. However, Blair Mountain also came to symbolize a benefit of globalization—the power of technological communication between determined community and grassroots leaders in fighting for common cause and justice.[8]

My mind (and heart) returns to Blair Mountain with each new protest somewhere in the world against destructive environmental and social practices, and I am reminded once again of the dynamic ways in which seemingly disparate regions and peoples are connected in their relation to and creation of local-global spaces. For example, in 2011 the Telengit people, who live on the border between Russia and China, joined forces with Russian environmental groups seeking to stop a joint Russian-Chinese venture to build a natural gas pipeline from Siberia to China across their culturally sacred and environmentally sensitive highlands.[9] This story bears an unfortunate resemblance to the ongoing fight against the proposed Keystone XL pipeline in the United States and Canada, a part of the larger resistance against the Canadian tar sands bitumen extraction led by indigenous (First Nations) peoples in both nations.[10] Similar energy-related protests are taking place in South America. In March 2012 several hundred indigenous people embarked on a two-week, 435-mile march across Ecuador to protest large-scale open-pit copper mining by a Chinese company.[11] In Brazil, protests continue against the building of the Belo Monte Dam, which since construction began in 2011 has resulted in a host of environmental and quality-of-life problems for nearby residents.[12] In April 2014, Achuar protesters in Peru occupied the country's largest oil field to demand the cleanup of decades of spilled crude oil linked to cadmium and lead contamination of food and water.[13] While this is not an exhaustive accounting, the similarities in the problems communities face in terms of health, environment, and economics are no mere accident of place that connects (remaps) communities across these three continents. Indeed, I was prompted by the connectivity of these issues and grassroots responses to mine a bit further within my own work in consideration of the global implications of Appalachian activism.

In my research in central Appalachia, two examples stand out as placing Appalachia on the global map in terms of activism and community building. The first is my work with a Central Labor Council and its involvement in the 2007 Kentucky gubernatorial race. Organized labor considered this an important election, as the incumbent Republican governor, Ernie Fletcher, had introduced "right to work" legislation (which was not passed), tried to repeal the prevailing wage laws, and worked to eliminate collective bargaining in Kentucky. Hence, the actions of organized labor in promoting the Democratic candidate, Steve Beshear, in this election must be understood as part of a larger state and national process by the AFL-CIO in conjunction with Kentucky labor councils to remove antiunion politicians from office and improve conditions for working families. During one Saturday morning canvassing event in October, my group was accompanied by a staff writer from a local newspaper, a freelance photographer, and a Swedish labor journalist. As I learned, Swedish labor unions have an interest in US labor union political activism, and this reporter's account of the Central Appalachian Member-to-Member walks rated his newspaper's front page. The *LO* (Swedish National Organization of Labor Unions) article, "Union Tests the Election Machinery," included photos of the Labor Council president and a member of the Steelworkers' union, dressed in yellow T-shirts reading, "Kentucky Labor 2007 . . . It's Our Time," talking to potential voters on the front porches of their homes. The article noted that the unions had given Democratic challenger Beshear their full support and had invested full resources to remove Republican Fletcher from the governorship. Indeed, the Swedish reporter found that in Kentucky labor unions and "boots on the ground" activism still hold promise, albeit limited, for political and economic change in the region, as evidenced in their role in Governor Fletcher's eventual defeat. The presence of the Swedish reporter also underscores the global importance of connecting collective resistance efforts to economic transformation and political policies that are increasingly harmful to families and communities around the world.[14]

While labor unions maintain varying levels of influence in Appalachia, activism and coalition building take many forms. Wilson in chapter 14 of this volume emphasizes the role of university-community engagements that produce meaningful relationships by focusing on local assets and challenging the status quo of Auburn University's (southern Appalachia) hidden truths and experiences of racial integration. Taking the initiatives of CPAR to the next level, Piser (chapter 15) calls for Appalachian and regional scholars to move further beyond diagnosing and explaining crises to embrace new, alternative forms of perception and action. Finally, Loeffler and King (chapter 13), investigating the work of Fahe, also make an argument for positive change that utilizes local resources in ways that promote sustainable development by building social capital and networks. Importantly, an emergent theme in these examples is the purposeful recognition of local assets to actively foster coalition building among nontraditional organizations and individuals, breaking through traditional barriers and binary modes of engagement. These authors take a new approach to answering the question "What is Appalachia?" Instead of looking for what's missing, they remind us, as researchers, activists, citizens, and Appalachians, to innovate through local assets.

The second example I offer comes from my ethnographic research with

Frontier Nursing Service (FNS). Through primary interviews with nurse-midwives and nurse practitioners, I described the complexities of gendered health care from the perspective of advanced practices nurses who worked at FNS between the 1950s and the 1970s.[15] Central to this story were the gendered and insider/outsider, class-based relationship complexities involved in health-care provision in underserved rural areas of eastern Kentucky.

Mary Breckinridge, a member of the Kentucky elite, established FNS in Leslie County, Kentucky, in 1925, with the mission to provide quality health care to women and families in underserved and rural areas. Importantly, the clinic she established was intended to serve as a model that could be implemented elsewhere across the United States. From its inception, FNS was a transnational organization. As a child, Breckinridge lived in Russia, France, Switzerland, and Britain, and she studied nursing in the United States, England, Scotland, and France. Breckinridge initially staffed her nursing service with nurse-midwives trained in Great Britain. FNS expanded, and in 1939 it became not just a health-care provider but also the nation's first school of nurse-midwifery.[16]

Eager to share her work, Breckinridge invited health-care providers from many nations to visit the service's headquarters at Hyden, Kentucky, to see firsthand her health-care delivery model. Unfortunately, as Goan describes, these efforts were hindered by Breckinridge's racial prejudices, and she was discriminatory in her hiring practices and visitor selection.[17] In the 1950s, Breckinridge reluctantly allowed visitors of color to visit and observe FNS's work, and an obstetrician from Ghana, sent by the State Department, became the first black visitor. However, in 1952, Breckinridge and the Hyden Committee refused to hire a Japanese American nurse with excellent credentials because "they assumed that if anything happened to a patient under her care, it 'would be blamed on the nurse's yellow skin.'"[18] While Mary Breckinridge is clearly a controversial and complicated figure, her innovative model of rural public health and maternal and child care has had a global reach.

In 2014, on the occasion celebrating seventy-five years since the founding of the graduate school of midwifery, the lead story on the Frontier webpage declared, "As health care reform increases the demand for medical professionals across the country, the work that Mary Breckinridge started in 1939 is becoming increasingly mainstream."[19] This statement was a full-circle moment for me, as it mirrored my own transition as a medical anthropologist: from studying the FNS nurses to my current work addressing access to health care as linked to economic transition and health policy reform (Affordable Care Act) in central Appalachia.[20] Thus, Appalachia tells the story of global health, a story that requires understanding the warp and weft threads that map the patterns of interconnection among economics, geography, biodiversity, pollution, politics, finance, tradition, identities, and activism that can be measured in health outcomes.

Certainly, the health-care service Breckinridge started in Kentucky has come of age in the modern world. To better reflect the school's status as a graduate education institution, in July 2011, the name was changed to Frontier Nursing University (FNU). As president and dean Dr. Susan Stone states: "The evolution of the name of our institution reflects both the amazing 'chronicle' of our past, as well as the incredible opportunities which lie in our future. All of these milestones are directly attributable to the far-reaching vision of Mary Breckinridge, the dedication of our faculty, staff, students and alumni and the increasing world-wide demand for trained women's and family health care professionals."[21]

As Stone indicates, the outlook and influence of FNU is now global, and the organization has come full circle to fulfill Breckinridge's vision. In the mid-1920s foreign nurse-midwives came to Kentucky to provide health care to rural and underserved women and families. FNU forged international relations: public health representatives from around the world traveled to Leslie County to learn about Breckinridge's innovative public health-care model for rural health-care provisioning. Through the Community-Based Distance Education Program, the Frontier School of Midwifery and Family Nursing welcomed nursing students from every US state and international students from Canada, Germany, Japan, and Costa Rica.[22] This program, which uses state-of-the-art Web-based distance education courses, allows students to stay in their home communities and work with clinics, hospitals, and preceptors as they pursue their advanced practice degrees, including doctorate of nursing practice and master of science in nursing, with tracks in nurse-midwifery, family nurse practitioner, and women's health-care nurse practitioner. Today FNU is ranked by *US News & World Report* for 2016 as number one on the best nursing schools for nurse midwifery list in the United States.[23] Remarkably, as part of its mission, FNU has found a way to foster and grow Breckinridge's sense of community responsibility, something she called, in her book of the same title, "wide neighborhoods." Today, advanced practice nurses trained through FNU work in diverse locations around the world. Overcoming the racial politics of the organization's founder, FNU has broadened the neighborhood by redrawing the global village maps. For example, Frontier alumna Nadine Brunk founded the Midwives for Haiti Project and recruits midwife volunteers to work and train midwives in Haiti.[24] Through FNU's influence we are reminded not only that local and community problems with accessing health care are not limited to rural Appalachia but that these issues are often rooted in the same global processes of economic transformation and development. This is best summarized by FNU's proclamation: "*Community is more than just 'where you live.'*"[25] Hence, with health care its core mission, FNU promotes broader ideals of community well-being that are based in understanding location and tradition while embracing innovation to meet the needs of yesterday and today.

We All Live Downstream

Although it is many things, globalization is ultimately about crossing borders—regional, national, and cultural. Appalachia is no longer understood as a peripheral region but as vibrantly interconnected to the United States and the world. As demonstrated in the chapters in this volume, stories of globalization and of border crossings hinge on the (re)drawing of geographical and cultural maps that simultaneously and symbolically ally some regions and groups together while hiding connections to others. Unfortunately, however, the popular assumption and stereotyping of Appalachia as a land and people separated from modernity remains too prevalent in the popular imagination.[26] As the chapters by Ooten and Sawyer (10), Kant-Byers (9), Puckett (11), and Blackburn (6) indicate, the links between identity, place, and economics are constructed by groups in ways with measurable economic and political outcomes. Over the years, many well-intentioned efforts to eradicate poverty have followed the assumption that poverty results from being left behind, from failing to progress, from failed cultural scripts. In actuality, poverty in the modern world often results from the uneven investment and extraction of resources (including human capital) and the ironic conflation of development and destruction (see Ooten and Sawyer; Yahn). The cases presented in this chapter and volume (Loeffler and King; Ezzelle [chapter 12]; Piser; Puckett) demonstrate that Appalachian innovation and activism might well be viewed as a type of "global commodity." We see in Appalachia models for applying place-based knowledge in effective and just ways. As Herbert Reid and Betsy Taylor argue, understanding and sharing place-based knowledge is crucial in struggles for global social justice.[27] While many of the most grievous injustices challenging people the world over today result from the worst of global processes, we also see the best of globalization in the utilization of technology as a means of sharing place-based knowledge between peoples from one place to another.

Revisiting Appalachia . . .

As *Appalachia Revisited* represents a current view of the theoretical, methodological, and contextual work in, of, and about the region, it also represents an acknowledgment of the remapping of Appalachian studies. Hence, in partial response to Reid and Taylor's challenge that "work in Appalachian studies needs rethinking in terms of global regional studies," *Appalachia Revisited* invites you to revisit place-making through multiple global twenty-first-century Appalachian contexts.[28]

Situated throughout this volume are new maps of critical engagement in scholarship, community activism, and work to promote sustainable lives. It is in the unraveling of binary identities that we see the expansion of community, the widening of neighborhoods, and the increased potential for research, advocacy, and citizenship participation that will enable regaining the commons. Appalachia is not, nor has it ever simply been, about "insiders" versus "outsiders." What we see represented in *Appalachia Revisited* are effective ways to conceive and link local and place-based problems, research, advocacy, and solutions in ways that demonstrate that place matters because it is a point of thought, a point of action or inaction, and an evolutionary point from which to reach out and connect the dots in the webs of global interconnection. We also see how place matters in the interdisciplinary perspectives offered here within these chapters. For researchers, teachers, students, advocates, and citizens, place matters in terms of perspective in education, theory and methodology, and as a starting place.

People are reorganizing the interconnections among places and peoples in efforts to establish systems of sustainable living, a redoing of place. I offer that place becomes an active ideology rather than a static space. Sustainable, community-based development and PAR have become staples in the local-regional fight against the onslaught of consumerist capitalism and its debasing of rights and dignity. For example, Ezzell describes a framework for reevaluating our understandings of communities through an inclusive, mixed-methods model viable on a regional level, and Puckett examines the construction of a civic commons through local music festivals. It is within the redoing of place that we see newly reorganized ways of thinking of identities, particularly the deconstruction of binary categories, including academic/ activist, researcher/participant, local/global, Appalachian/non-Appalachian.

Critically important in this volume is the prevalence of feminist theory within many chapters, highlighting the inclusion of feminist theoretical perspectives to evaluate identity formations in complicated ways. Duvall, Dorgan, and Hutson (chapter 1) deconstruct the identity boundaries between researcher, participant, and Appalachian. Central to their effort is the application of intersectional feminist theory, allowing for the recognition of multiple identities and reducing the fallacy of exclusive binary identity (insider/ outsider; researcher/participant; Appalachian/non-Appalachian). Similarly, Zeddy (chapter 3) uses a case study of gender and political engagement to evaluate the constructed identity of Louise Broyhill. Terman (chapter 4) follows feminist intersectionality theory to investigate regional and urban/ rural identity formations. Piser draws upon feminist geography to inform his argument for the need for critical engagement and reciprocity in knowledge production that is beyond neoliberal cooptation. Together, these contributions showcase theoretical and methodological means to expand upon the heterogeneity of people and place and evaluate identity construction in relation to multiple categories of belonging and exclusion. These examples help to move the needle forward and, in keeping with Reid and Taylor, demonstrate a "rethinking of prevailing notions of professional authority, regional identity and representation, place, 'development,' 'environment,' and so on" and represent models for creating place-based "democratic public spheres" that resist being place-bound.[29]

Appalachian scholars and activists have argued for some time against notions of Appalachian land, people, and culture as static or lost in time. Indeed, from an anthropological perspective, culture is necessarily dynamic and fluid, and static depictions serve political functions of upholding social hierarchies of rights and exclusion. Hazen et al. (chapter 7) remind us with concrete examples of the importance of language and dialect in this process. As one means of establishing and upholding stereotypes and hierarchies, dialects come to symbolize geographic and social place. Their chapter demonstrates the importance of *doing* place to reveal complex social realities. As dialects must be studied in locally defined places, it is the carefully measured patterns of continuity and change as established through the study of sounds that reveal regional cultural transitions over time, class differences among residents within regional communities, and interconnections among communities and regions. We understand the importance of local dialects: they simultaneously serve as a means to recognize one's traditional place in society and as a way to guard one's current position in reference to speech patterns of the present/future society. Additionally, the contribution of students as researchers and writers in this chapter is an important example of the voice and competence of Appalachian youth and the necessity of mentorship as we imagine and create a just and equitable future in Appalachia. In Taylor's chapter 5 also we find opportunity to rethink *doing place,* here in terms of how rhetoric shapes the lives of urban Appalachian identity and the need for models of respectful, ethically oriented engagement of marginalized groups.

It is through storytelling, poetry, art, and music that we learn those first lessons of love of home (place). Through such artistry we share and create identities and make livelihoods from reinterpreting images of place. Not only do we learn of the actions of important people, these stories *take place* in spaces that are as integral to the telling as the characters themselves. For example, Appalachia becomes more than mere subject matter in artistic renderings of mountain scenery; it becomes a symbolic character that tells a particular story of nostalgia and connection (Kant-Byers). Music allows us to transform and transport ourselves, altering identity and reshaping (remapping) ideas of belonging. In this way music allows for the reinterpretation of ethnic identity through performance, rhythm, and rhyme. As Barbour-Payne describes in chapter 2, the sounds of the Carolina Chocolate Drops are not limited to the binaries of black and white. Indeed, music and performance transcend racial-cultural barriers, becoming a focal point for global discourse regarding Affrilachian and Appalachian identities.

Ultimately, with its numerous examples of regional connectivity and identity formations, *Appalachia Revisited* offers examples of how many of the poverty-related problems in Appalachia and in communities around the world are directly related to inequitable capitalist interventions, especially as related to energy extraction industries. Citing Helen Lewis's *Colonialism* as an example, Gaventa argues, "Appalachian studies has long borrowed models and paradigms for understanding inequality from other parts of the world to understand our own development."[30] As I related in the examples of the Swedish reporter and FNU, Appalachia exists as a *place of knowledge,* offering models of engagement recognizable in other global places. *Appalachia Revisited* represents the changing theoretical, methodological, and contextual models of knowledge, experience, and activism within the region, offering opportunities for learning and the exchange of ideas on a global scale. Indeed, following Gaventa, our contributors have discovered how to make themselves both Appalachian and global citizens.[31] In so doing, they demonstrate the deconstruction of identity binaries, avoiding the limitations and ethical dilemmas of insider/outsider politics, a necessary step in expanding the global community, widening the neighborhood, and looking upstream.[32] It is in these ways that Appalachian studies writ large and *Appalachia Revisited* specifically address Appalachia as a place that is a product of human-environmental developments that offer strategies not only for creating knowledge about the region but also for the sharing of knowledge and advocacy paradigms with other marginalized groups enmeshed in similar global processes of change. Here the importance of critical regionalism and interdisciplinary collaboration is apparent, especially in models of civic professionalism that redefine the commons in understanding that place is relational and rooted in the production of knowledges about peoples and the places they inhabit. It is in the remapping (destabilizing) of the local/global binary that we see the political-economic spectrum of place as an indicator of economic and ecological health and community well-being.[33]

Ultimately, *Appalachia Revisited* argues not only that *place matters* but *how we do place* also matters. Just as the MCHM spill flowed downstream, carrying with it fear, mistrust, and health concerns, it flowed from place to place. As one more example of twenty-first-century corporate-based inequality in Appalachia, this event is also directly related to the overall energy extraction industry, which has left trails of environmental pollution and cultural degradation in places the world over. Indeed, we all live downstream, and it is localized examples of inequality and resistance that show us, in the bigger picture, how places matter. As John Stephenson remarks about Appalachian studies, "Our stuff is seeping out from under the woodwork and beginning to make a noticeable mess on the floor."[34] As Appalachian studies and activist engagement flow downstream, Appalachia is becoming mainstream. The *place* lessons from Appalachia *matter*.

Notes

1. For introductory information regarding the health and environmental effects of the MCHM spill, see Marin Cogan, "Is the Water Safe Yet?" *Atlantic*, March 28, 2014, http://www.theatlantic.com/health/archive/2014/03/is-the-water-safe-yet/359781/

(accessed March 31, 2014); Mark Drajem, "West Virginia Chemical Spill Spurs Study of Health Effects," *Businessweek*, February 13, 2014, http://www.businessweek.com/printer/articles/680043?type=bloomberg (accessed February 17, 2014); Pamela Pritt, "Safety Board: PPH, MCHM Should Not Be in Drinking Water at Any Level," *Register-Herald*, January 25, 2014, http://www.register-herald.com/news/safety-board-pph-mchm-should-not-be-in-drinking-water/article_38db3b4f-cf6a-5f07-a276-1ca8c92f4ba9.html (accessed January 29, 2014).

2. Douglas Reichert Powell, *Critical Regionalism: Connecting Politics and Culture in the American Landscape* (Chapel Hill: University of North Carolina Press, 2007), 5.

3. Jeff Biggers, *Reckoning on Eagle Creek: The Secret Legacy of Coal in the Heartland* (New York: Nation Books, 2010); Herbert Reid, "We All Live in the Coalfields Now," *North of Center*, April 17, 2010, http://noclexington.com/?p=513 (accessed December 28, 2014). Tom Cormons expresses a similar idea regarding the MCHM spill: "Coal-Related Spills Connect Us All," *Appalachian Voices*, February 19, 2014, http://appvoices.org/2014/02/19/coal-related-spills-connect-us-all/ (accessed December 28, 2014).

4. Dwight B. Billings, "Response #3: Place Matters," in "Future of Appalachian Studies: A Roundtable," ed. Ted Olson, *Journal of Appalachian Studies* 17, nos. 1–2 (2011): 188–213.

5. Wendell Berry, "The Future of Food Is Not Distinguishable from the Future of the Land," *Washington Post*, May 10, 2011, http://www.washingtonpost.com/lifestyle/food/the-future-of-food-is-not-distinguishable-from-the-future-of-the-land/2011/05/05/AFhvN2iG_story.html (accessed June 20, 2014).

6. David Harvey, *Spaces of Capital: Towards a Critical Geography* (New York: Routledge, 2001); Powell, *Critical Regionalism*.

7. Dwight B. Billings, Gurney Norman, and Katherine Ledford, eds., *Confronting Appalachian Stereotypes: Back Talk from an American Region* (Lexington: University Press of Kentucky, 1999).

8. Janet Fout, "Just Say *No* to Mountaintop Removal / Valley Fills in Papua, New Guinea," *Winds of Change: The Newsletter of Ohio Valley Environmental Coalition (OVEC)*, December 2003, http://www.ohvec.org/newsletters/woc_2003_12/article_21.html (accessed February 1, 2012). I came to this article through its use in the introductory chapter of Herbert Reid and Betsy Taylor, *Recovering the Commons: Democracy, Place, and Global Justice* (Urbana: University of Illinois Press, 2010), 1. Matt Wasson, "Labor and Environment—A Match Made in 'Almost Heaven,'" *Appalachian Voices*, June 10, 2011, http://appvoices.org/2011/06/10/labor-and-environment-a-match-made-in-almost-heaven/ (accessed February 1, 2012); Nicole Ghio, "Coal Country: From India to the Heart of Appalachia, Day Three," *Compass*, September 29, 2011, http://blogs.sierra-club.org/compass/2011/09/coal-india-appalachia.html (accessed December 28, 2014).

9. "Russia/China: Pipeline Threatens Sacred Highlands," *Cultural Survival*, August 4, 2011, http://www.culturalsurvival.org/take-action/russiachina-pipeline-threatens-sacred-highlands/russiachina-pipeline-threatens-sacred (accessed February 1, 2012).

10. Natalie Hand and Kent Lebsock, "Lakota Allies Gather to Stand Their Sacred Ground," Indigenous Environmental Network, March 15, 2014, http://www.ienearth .org/lakota-allies-gather-to-stand-their-sacred-ground/ (accessed November 6, 2014); Daniel Schwartz and Mark Gollom, "N.B. Fracking Protests and the Fight for Aboriginal Rights," *CBC News Canada*, October 9, 2013, http://www.cbc.ca/news/canada/n-b-fracking-protests-and-the-fight-for-aboriginal-rights-1.2126515 (accessed November 6, 2014); Aldo Seoane and Wica Agli, "House Vote in Favor of the Keystone XL Pipeline an Act of War," *Lakota Voice Rez News*, November 14, 2014, http://lakotavoice .com/2014/11/15/house-vote-in-favor-of-the-keystone-xl-pipeline-an-act-of-war/ (accessed December 28, 2014).

11. "Indigenous Peoples March against Open-Pit Copper Mining," *Cultural Survival*, March 9, 2012, http://www.culturalsurvival.org/news/indigenous-people-march-against-mining-ecuador (accessed December 28, 2014).

12. "Brazil's Belo Monte Dam Sacrificing the Amazon and Its Peoples for Dirty Energy," *Amazon Watch*, http://amazonwatch.org/work/belo-monte-dam (accessed November 6, 2014).

13. Dan Collins, "Indigenous Protesters Occupy Peru's Biggest Amazon Oil Field," *Guardian*, April 25, 2014, http://www.theguardian.com/environment/2014/apr/25/ indigenous-protesters-occupy-perus-biggest-amazon-oilfield (accessed November 6, 2014).

14. Rebecca Adkins Fletcher, "'Money Gets Things Done, but Legwork Does Too': Labor's (Re)claiming of Community Space in a Privatized Public," *Journal of Appalachian Studies* 21, no. 2 (2015): 189–206; Anders Eld, "Rökstopp på fängelse kan leda till ökat våld," *LO Tidningen*, November 2, 2007. Thank you to N. Thomas Hakansson of the University of Kentucky for translating this article.

15. Rebecca Adkins Fletcher, "An Investigation of Women's Health Care and Childbirth Practices in Twentieth Century Eastern Kentucky" (MA thesis, University of Kentucky, 2003).

16. Mary Breckinridge, *Wide Neighborhoods: A Story of the Frontier Nursing Service* (Lexington: University Press of Kentucky, 1981).

17. Melanie Beals Goan, *Mary Breckinridge: The Frontier Nursing Service & Rural Health in Appalachia* (Chapel Hill: University of North Carolina Press, 2008), 236–37.

18. Ibid., 238.

19. Brittney Edwards, "The Frontier Nursing Story, 1939 to 2014: Celebrating 75 Years of Blazing New Frontiers as Pioneers for Healthcare," n.d., Frontier Nursing University, http://www.frontier.edu/news/frontier-nursing-story (accessed October 1, 2014).

20. Rebecca Adkins Fletcher, "Keeping Up with the Cadillacs: What Health Insurance Disparities, Moral Hazard, and the Cadillac Tax Mean to the Patient Protection and Affordable Care Act," *Medical Anthropology Quarterly* (2014): 1-19, http://onlinelibrary .wiley.com/doi/10.1111/maq.12120/full (accessed January 12, 2016).

21. Susan E. Stone, "Frontier School of Midwifery and Family Nursing Officially

Became Frontier Nursing University on July 1, 2011," n.d., Frontier Nursing University, http://www.frontier.edu/namechangefaqs (accessed October 1, 2014).

22. "Frequently Asked Questions: Distance Education," n.d., Frontier Nursing University, http://www.frontier.edu/faqs#d1 (accessed October 1, 2014).

23. "Nurse Midwifery," *US News and World Report*, n.d., http://grad-schools.usnews.rankingsandreviews.com/best-graduate-schools/top-nursing-schools/midwife-rankings (accessed January 18, 2016).

24. Midwives for Haiti, "Our Story," n.d., https://www.midwivesforhaiti.org/contact-us/our-story.html (accessed January 2, 2015).

25. Frontier Nursing University, "Distance Learning," n.d., http://www.frontier.edu/distance-education (accessed October 1, 2014).

26. Emily Satterwhite, *Dear Appalachia: Readers, Identity, and Popular Fiction since 1978* (Lexington: University Press of Kentucky, 2011).

27. Reid and Taylor, *Recovering the Commons.*

28. Herbert Reid and Betsy Taylor, "Appalachia as a Global Region: Toward Critical Regionalism and Civic Professionalism," *Journal of Appalachian Studies* 8, no. 1 (2002): 23.

29. Ibid., 21–22.

30. John Gaventa, "Appalachian Studies in Global Context: Reflections on the Beginnings—Challenges for the Future," *Journal of Appalachian Studies* 8, no. 1 (2002): 84.

31. Ibid., 88.

32. Reid and Taylor, "Appalachia as a Global Region."

33. Powell, *Critical Regionalism;* Arlif Dirlik, "Civic Scholarship: Comments on 'Appalachia as a Global Region: Toward Regionalism and Civic Professionalism,'" *Journal of Appalachian Studies* 8, no. 1 (2002): 39.

34. Jean Haskell, "Response #6: Planting by Signs," in "Future of Appalachian Studies: A Roundtable," ed. Ted Olson, *Journal of Appalachian Studies* 17, nos. 1–2 (2011): 205.

Appendix

Teaching Exercises

Chapter 1: Duvall, Dorgan, and Hutson

BRACKETING INTERVIEW EXERCISE

Brackcting interviews allow investigators to engage in self-reflection and recognize biases about the proposed project or target population before beginning data collection. Bracketing emphasizes acknowledging beliefs, knowledge, values, and experiences about a topic or target population because these preconceptions can have a profound impact on data collection, analysis, and presentation.

For this activity, students should divide into pairs and agree upon an interview topic. Each student prepares interview questions to guide the discussion. Students will conduct audio-recorded interviews with one another for fifteen to twenty minutes. Each student will transcribe the interview for which he or she was the interviewer. Finally, the student will reflect on his or her experiences as both interviewer and interviewee and discuss these with his or her partner in a debriefing.

In a short reflective paper, students will describe their experiences in each role. What did it feel like to be the investigator? What assumptions did you have about the topic before the interview? What did it feel like to be the interviewee? Did you think the investigator had assumptions about the topic? What new insight do you have on the data collection process? If you had to do the activity over again, how might the questions be adapted?

Chapter 2: Barbour-Payne

MUSIC AND IDENTITY

Use musical performance to promote critical thinking and discussion of identity, culture, and sense of place.

1. Attend a local music festival. Write ethnographic field notes and describe the performances, audience, and local culture. Code the data either individually or in small groups and analyze for patterns in thematic subjects. Try to answer the following questions: What cultural and music genre(s) are represented, and how are these reflected in the performers' bodies, music, and performances? In what ways do (or do not) the performers create a sense of shared identity with the audience? How do the performers uphold or reject stereotypes through vocal and visual performance? Do you see evidence of "local" culture in any of the performances? Do you see evidence of the commercialization of the "local" culture in the performances?

2. Evaluate your personal music collection. What musical genres are present? Describe how you relate to each genre or to particular artists. Do you share an assumed sense of cultural, ethnic, or gender identity with the music and/or artists? Which music do you like, want to like, or dislike because it represents an identity that is similar to or different than your own?

3. As a group, identify a song that is "controversial" (explain why). Watch a performance of the song on YouTube. Write individual five-minute essays describing your reaction to the performance and share these in class. Do the performances enhance or reduce the controversial elements of the music (lyrics)?

Chapter 3: Zeddy

IDENTIFY SCHEMAS OF THE AMERICAN DREAM

Have each student write down an identity schema for a hypothetical person that includes race, gender, class, regional identity, sexuality, education level, age, familial relationships, religious identity, able-bodied status, and citizenship identity. Next break the students into groups of three or four to discuss and think reflectively on how likely (or unlikely) their hypothetical person is to achieve, or desire achieving, the elusive "American Dream," given the subject's intersecting and multiple identity schema. Have someone in each group write down the thoughts, findings, and conclusions of the participants. After at least twenty to thirty minutes of small-group discussion, have the students "report back" to the entire class.

The following Web resources should help facilitate the group discussions as well as explain further the concept of the American Dream.

http://www.pewstates.org/news-room/press-releases/50th-
anniversary-of-the-war-on-poverty-85899525820
http://www.pewstates.org/research/data-visualizations/
faces-of-economic-mobility-85899503593
http://www.pewstates.org/research/reports/
moving-on-up-85899518104

Chapter 4: Terman

THINKING ABOUT IDENTITY

The first activity involves critical thinking. Individually or in a group, take two minutes to generate a list of words that you think define "Appalachian." Next, take five minutes to circle any words that might imply a certain gender, race, sexuality, class, age, or other identity. Using the concept of intersectionality, take ten minutes to write about or discuss the ways in which these words and your generated definition of "Appalachian" might be expanded or changed. Keeping in mind this intersectional version of "Appalachian," what are the boundaries of Appalachian identity? Can anyone be an Appalachian? Why or why not?

The second exercise is used to practice intersectional analysis and method. Individually or in a group, identify an issue or topic in Appalachia or your community specifically that you think is important (improving education, clean water, access to health care, resources for artists, and so on). Summarize the issue and discuss who is affected by it and who can influence it. How might identity categories like gender, race, sexuality, and class be relevant to this issue? How might these identities come together to create various social barriers and opportunities regarding this issue? How could you find the answer to the previous question if you are unsure?

Chapter 5: Taylor

COMMUNITY-BASED RESEARCH

The following exercise encourages students to develop ideas for community-based research projects, especially with identity-based groups.

Step 1: Take five to ten minutes to write reflectively about a local neighborhood or community that is disrespected or stereotyped by the wider region. What struggles do you imagine residents in that community face?

Step 2: Conduct online research to identify a nonprofit organization or community group that works to improve the lives of residents in the community you identified. Gather information about the organization or group: What is its mission? What services does it provide to the community? How does it impact the lives of community residents? Write a paragraph that addresses these questions.

Step 3: Imagine that you will conduct a community-based research study with the organization or group you identified in step 2. Sketch a plan for your research study: What research questions will you ask? Who will you need to speak with at the organization and in the community? In other words, who will be your research participants? What do you anticipate learning from this research experience?

Finally, share the results of your exercise with other members of your class. Discuss the potential benefits and challenges of community-based research. Reflect on the resources you would need to make your research really happen.

Chapter 6: Blackburn

DIGITAL RHETORICS OF APPALACHIA

Select any two websites that turn up on a search for "Appalachia .com" (not "Appalachia.com"—be sure to leave a space between the words to reach commercial sites with *Appalachia* as a keyword). Write a short summary of the online rhetorics of each website, that is, uses of language, images, audio and video content, color, font, links, and other formatting elements. Compare the summaries of each site to analyze how each is rhetorically situated as "Appalachian." Based on your own experience in Appalachia, conclude your study by analyzing how each site either builds on or rejects regional stereotypes through rhetorical strategies.

Chapter 7: Hazen, Lovejoy, Daugherty, and Vandevender

LINGUISTIC EXERCISE

These examples illustrate how some consonants changed through time. Old English, usually dated between 450 and 1066, was the first period of English as it transitioned from three different German dialects into a separate language.

Old to modern: Transitions in English

	Old English	Modern English
H words	hraven hnutu hlavord heofan	raven nut lord heaven
WH words	hwelc hwonne hwæl hwettan	which when whale whet
W words	wicca wendan waille (Middle English) wæt	witch wend wail wet

Try to pronounce the words in the Old English column as they are spelled. How do they differ from your pronunciations of the words in the modern English column? If you consider just the spelled letters, in what environment is the letter *h* lost between Old English and modern English? What kinds of sounds come after the lost letter *h*?

A sound like the vowel in *nod* is voiced because your vocal folds are vibrating when you say it out loud. If you whisper, all the sounds are voiceless because the vocal folds are not vibrating. For words like *when, what, why, whale,* and *wheat,* is your *w* voiceless or fully voiced?

Do you have a difference in how *long* your *h* sounds are in some words? Pronounce the following pairs of words out loud and see if the *h* in the first word is shorter than the one in the second:

- huge; help
- human; hope
- Houston; Hartford

Some speakers in the United States have a shorter *h* in the first words, if they have any at all. This shortening probably happens because of the next sound in those words, represented by linguists as [j]: this is the first sound in the words *yellow* and *yes.*

Consonant variation has happened in several places among English speakers, but we often keep our spelling stable rather than change it to reflect changes in pronunciation. Consider the word *knight*. Both the *k* and the *gh* used to be pronounced, but through regular variation, both were lost. Do you think we should reform our spelling to reflect modern pronunciations? If so, whose dialect should we use as the foundation for the new pronunciations?

Chapter 8: Yahn

RECIPROCAL TEACHING

History is controversial, a point that we often overlook. This chapter considers the implications of fracking in northern Appalachia within the larger context of American history, giving specific attention to the nation's economic transitions. Ask students to identify a historical argument made in the chapter that they (1) have further evidence to support, (2) would like to challenge, and (3) wish to expound upon.

Each student should prepare a short and well-articulated argument to present in two to three minutes during a small-group (three to four students) discussion. After each discussant's presentation, peers in the group should respond, during which time the discussant should listen but not reply. The round of discussion ends with the discussant providing closing remarks to clarify, refute, or expound upon peer responses.

Chapter 9: Kant-Byers

FINDING PATTERNS OF REPRESENTATION IN APPALACHIAN IMAGES

Content analysis allows researchers to identify patterns in cultural behaviors and artifacts, including images of Appalachia.

Select about twenty images of Appalachia and organize them as slides in a presentation or word-processing software program. These could be paintings, commercial art, graphic design, or webpages, but it is a good idea to select the same type of image (for example, paintings only) so that students have a single medium for analysis.

Each slide should be viewed for about ten seconds. Ask students to record the main subject, theme, or trait of each image—these subjects become *codes* from which patterns of icons emerge. Remind them that what they record may or may not be the first thing that catches their eye, but it is *that object or theme that other elements in the image support or lead them to see and focus on for a while.*

Ask the students to group the subjects (codes) into three to five groups (categories of code types), and count the frequency, or number of times each group of subjects was observed.

Ask students to report on the image patterns they observed. Draw attention to differences between students' analyses. Invite students to share any assumptions they may have made regarding each of the categories and, if time permits, each of their codes. Discuss how individuals' cultural assumptions and beliefs shape the interpretation of meaning in Appalachian images.

End the exercise by pointing out that this method is useful for understanding patterns in representations of Appalachia. Doing so further shows students how knowledge of such patterns is produced by researchers.

Chapter 10: Ooten and Sawyer

USING DATA TO UNDERSTAND THE GROWTH OF PRISONS

Utilize information from the Bureau of Justice Statistics' national prisoner statistics to chart increasing prison populations from 1978 to the present. Visit the Corrections Statistical Analysis Tool (CSAT)—Prisoners at http://www.bjs.gov/index.cfm?ty=nps to create customized tables and graphs to chart trends over time.

Go to the VERA Institute of Justice website to find out how much your state spends on prisons each year. Then research welfare and/or higher education spending in your state. Compare expenditures and whether spending in each area has been increasing or decreasing over time.

For example, Virginia's prison fact sheet (2012) can be found here: http://www.vera.org/files/price-of-prisons-virginia-fact-sheet.pdf.

Chapter 11: Puckett

COMMUNITY ASSETS AND THE COMMONS

One problem of neoliberalism is an overemphasis on exploiting the financial value of local resources. However, a community's development assets span much more (and may not even include direct financial assets!): human skills and training (that is, human capital), social networks of action (social capital), and environmental resources (natural capital). Have students work in small groups to identify lists of human, social, and natural capital in communities near your college or university. Next, have them sort the lists into two groups: assets *currently* utilized and assets *potentially* utilized. Based on the chapter discussion of neoliberal development ideologies, ask students to discuss (1) why those assets that are only of *potential* use are not better utilized, and (2) what strategies might be helpful in shifting resource use to sustainable strategies for revitalizing a sense of the commons in Appalachian communities.

Chapter 12: Ezzell

BUILDING COMMUNITY ENGAGEMENT

Students can identify potential partnerships between universities and community groups through a short interview exercise.

Have students freewrite ten questions intended to gather data about the activities, needs, and assets of a community organization in your area. Place the students into small groups to present their questions to each other. Each group then pares down the individual questions into a master set of ten to twelve questions in a well-ordered sequence. The questions should cover all areas of inquiry necessary to determine the profile of a community organization and reflect the least-biased ways of asking questions on specific subjects (for example, "Do you believe there is bias in research?" is a better question than "Can you tell me about bias in research?"). Each group should then present its master set to another group and repeat the process of selecting the best-written and best-ordered interview list. Repeat this process until the class has decided on one master interview list everyone will use.

Each student must then select a community organization to interview. Results will be presented in class.

Based on the interview data, use additional class time to promote a discussion among students about the capacity of individual community organizations to work in partnerships for applied student learning in the future.

Ask the students to identify which campus offices, programs and departments, student clubs, or other groups might be a good fit to work with each community organization interviewed. Then ask students to report their interview data to those campus entities to encourage collaboration and partnerships.

Chapter 13: Loeffler and King

IDENTIFYING SOCIAL CAPITAL

"Social capital" is defined as the cultural norms and social networks that facilitate collective action in a community. For this exercise, have students generate a list of traits or characteristics that reflect social capital networks in communities, then ask them to answer the following questions:

1. What types of institutions, groups, and individuals are linked through social capital networks?

2. To what extent do individual networks of social capital overlap or conflict (for example, religious belief networks, political networks, school/education networks, youth networks)?

3. What are some sources of potential conflict and collaboration across networks and groups?

4. How might the combined social capital of network stakeholders in your home community be utilized to address a local problem or issue?

Students can share their responses in class to facilitate discussion about developing leadership skills in students.

Chapter 14: Wilson

CONDUCTING DEEP HISTORY ON RACE

A big part of the success of the student-led research described in chapter 14 was based on a deep historical understanding of local and university histories of race in Appalachian Alabama. What is your own college or university's history of race relations and collaboration with communities of color? Invite a range of stakeholders to class to encourage a discussion about these issues with your students. Campus stakeholders might include university historians/archivists, the equity office, representatives of multicultural student organizations, and admissions officers. Community stakeholders might include community groups, religious leaders, government officials, and historical societies. Have each student write a short analysis of how your college or university might better engage with diversity issues based on the class discussion.

Chapter 15: Piser

FINDING INTERCONNECTIONS AT HOME

In this activity you will learn to see interconnections in the world around you by identifying multiple forces that shape landscapes and human lives: ecological, economic, and sociopolitical.

Begin by dividing the class into groups that are small enough that everyone can participate. Each group should agree on one major transformation that is currently at work in the region where you live. This might be a prominent local issue, a contentious debate, or a persistent tension between groups with different ideas about what the future should look like. Each group should answer the following questions:

Ecological: What ecological relationships are involved in the issue? Make an exhaustive list, including animal and plant communities, physical landscapes as they are shaped by humans, and geological and climatological systems.

Economic: How do people (including you) make a living in your region and how does your issue impact employment and economics? Does it affect each economic group or industry equally? (Why or why not?) How do you, and those around you, respond to economic difficulties? What practices of mutual support, sharing, and cooperation can you think of? Who is involved in these practices?

Sociopolitical: What organizations or associations are you a part of? How do you describe the makeup of your organization or association, including factors such as class, race, ethnicity, gender, sexuality, religious belief, or disability? What types of power or influence does your organization or association have to address your group's issue in comparison to other organizations or associations in your region? In what ways do these entities' values, beliefs, or worldviews differ or overlap?

Each group should informally present its findings to the class. The entire class should identify similarities and differences between the ecological, economic, and sociopolitical forces presented by each group. Finally, the class can begin to explore how these forces affect one another. For example: What sociopolitical changes are resulting from recent economic shifts? How are environmental changes affecting the economic forces in the region? How are these relationships changing the distribution of benefits and harmful outcomes in your region?

Contributors

Yunina Barbour-Payne is a literature instructor at Yes Prep Public Schools in Houston, Texas, and has over a decade of stage experience in Appalachian Kentucky, Virginia, and Ohio.

Jessica Blackburn is associate professor of English at Appalachian State University.

Jaclyn Daugherty is a graduate of West Virginia University and North Carolina State University. Previously a researcher at the West Virginia Dialect Project, she is currently an editor in the Philadelphia area.

Kelly A. Dorgan is associate professor of communication studies at East Tennessee State University.

Kathryn L. Duvall is assistant director for TRIO-Student Support Services at East Tennessee State University.

Tim Ezzell is a research scientist and lecturer in the political science department at the University of Tennessee, Knoxville.

Rebecca Adkins Fletcher is a lecturer at University of North Carolina, Wilmington, Department of Anthropology.

Kirk Hazen is professor of linguistics in the Department of English at West Virginia University and director of the West Virginia Dialect Project.

Sadie P. Hutson is associate professor and coordinator of the Nursing Honors Program at the University of Tennessee College of Nursing.

Kristin Kant-Byers is an adjunct faculty member in anthropology at the

Rochester Institute of Technology, where she teaches courses in cultural anthropology, qualitative research methods, and tourism.

Jim King is president of Fahe, a regional nonprofit financial intermediary based in Berea, Kentucky, that provides collective voice and access to capital for the creation of housing and promotion of community development in central Appalachia.

Diane N. Loeffler is senior lecturer at the University of Kentucky College of Social Work.

Jordan Lovejoy, formerly a researcher at the West Virginia Dialect Project, is a doctoral student in English at Ohio State University.

Melissa Ooten is associate director of the Women Involved in Living and Learning (WILL) Program and teaches courses in women's, gender, and sexuality studies at the University of Richmond.

Gabriel A. Piser is a doctoral candidate in the Department of Comparative Studies at Ohio State University with a specialization in human geography and political ecology. He combines his expertise in environmental studies, critical theory, and collaborative research with over a decade of work advising and collaborating with activist groups throughout Appalachia.

Anita Puckett is associate professor in the Department of Religion and Culture at Virginia Tech. She directs the Appalachian Studies Program and is president of the Appalachian Studies Association in 2015–2016.

Jason Sawyer is assistant professor at Norfolk State University's Ethelyn R. Strong School of Social Work, where he teaches social policy and community practice.

William Schumann is associate professor of Appalachian studies and director of the Center for Appalachian Studies at Appalachian State University.

Kathryn Trauth Taylor is CEO of Taylor Technical Consulting, a writing consultancy specializing in public rhetoric and community engagement.

Anna Rachel Terman is assistant professor of sociology at Ohio University.

Madeline Vandevender worked on the West Virginia Dialect Project while a student at West Virginia University and is now a quality control analyst at Johnson Matthey Catalysts in Smithfield, Pennsylvania.

Mark Wilson is director of civic learning initiatives at the College of Liberal Arts at Auburn University and an Appalachian teaching fellow with the Appalachian Regional Commission.

Jacqueline Yahn is a native of northern Appalachia and focuses much of her research on the impacts the natural gas rush has on schools and communities in the region. The middle childhood education coordinator/lecturer for Ohio University's Eastern campus, she is currently a doctoral student in Ohio University's educational administration program.

Amanda Zeddy, doctoral candidate in political science at the University of California, Santa Barbara, is coauthor of *Democracy and Domination: Technologies of Integration and the Rise of Collective Power* (2009).

Index

activism, 17, 25, 46, 49, 50, 56, 85, 103, 268, 270, 277–80, 282–84, 287; Appalachian activism, 56, 76; online activism, 44; virtual activism, 56, 76

advocacy, 50, 91–92, 94–95, 284

Affrilachia, 43–57, 75, 91, 286; Frank X Walker, 45, 75

African American, 8, 44, 46–47, 49, 51–53, 55, 77, 79–82, 100, 102, 121, 125, 174, 192–93, 200–203, 247–48, 255–57

age, 77, 83, 121, 125, 129, 143, 193–94, 259–60, 264, 266, 269, 282

Alabama, 2–3, 20, 246–48, 250, 254, 257; Auburn, 247–48, 250–51; Auburn University: 246–48, 253, 255–57, 280; Mason County, 246–51, 255, 257; Tuskegee, 246–54, 257

ancestry, 50–52, 54, 66, 162

Anglo-Saxon, 162

Appalachia, 1–21, 29–32, 34, 36–38, 59, 61, 63–64, 66–67, 69, 108, 114, 119–20, 124–25, 133–34, 140–42, 144–51, 155–61, 166–68, 171–76, 178, 180–81; Appalachian culture, 80, 96, 98, 117, 155, 157–61, 163, 166–68, 213; as a construct, 167; cyber Appalachia, 105, 107, 109–11, 116–17; as an internal colony, 12–13, 172,

180, 262; representations of, 1–2, 7–8, 15, 161–63, 166, 277; urban Appalachia, 91–94, 96–103, 286

Appalachian Landownership Taskforce, 215

Appalachian Regional Commission (ARC), 3–5, 13, 17, 20, 109, 111, 214–15, 217–19, 224–26, 246, 276

Appalachian studies, 10, 12, 16–19, 23, 59, 73–76, 82–85, 91, 94, 105–7, 117, 155, 246, 270, 284, 286–87

Appalachian Teaching Project, 24, 248, 253, 257

Appalasians, 75

art, 11, 16, 92, 102, 155–56, 159–61, 163, 166–67, 192, 194, 202–4, 205, 286; artistic rhetorics, 92, 94, 102, 103; artists, 44, 56, 75–76, 82, 91, 155–61, 163–68, 257

Berry, Wendell, 146, 277

Billings, Dwight, 277

Blair Mountain, 278

bluegrass music. *See* music

Broyhill, Louise, 19, 59–61, 64, 66, 69–70, 285

cancer, 6, 18, 29–38

capital, social, 219, 229–39, 241–42

capitalism, 5, 10, 12, 16–17, 139, 143, 168, 174, 181, 185, 266, 269, 284; capitalist exploitation, 12, 17, 174,

Place Matters: New Directions in Appalachian Studies

Series Editor: Dwight B. Billings

This series explores the history, social life, and cultures of Appalachia from multidisciplinary, comparative, and global perspectives. Topics include geography, the environment, public policy, political economy, critical regional studies, diversity, social inequality, social movements and activism, migration and immigration, efforts to confront regional stereotypes, literature and the arts, and the ongoing social construction and reimagination of Appalachia. Key goals of the series are to place Appalachian dynamics in the context of global change and to demonstrate that place-based and regional studies still matter.

Appalachia Revisited: New Perspectives on Place, Tradition, and Progress
Edited by William Schumann and Rebecca Adkins Fletcher

The Arthurdale Community School: Education and Reform in Depression Era Appalachia
Sam F. Stack Jr.

Sacred Mountains: A Christian Ethical Approach to Mountaintop Removal
Andrew R. H. Thompson

Rereading Appalachia: Literacy, Place, and Cultural Resistance
Edited by Sara Webb-Sunderhaus and Kim Donehower

CPSIA information can be obtained
at www.ICGtesting.com
Printed in the USA
LVOW03s0039241117
557330LV00004B/865/P

9 780813 174419